The
Reference Shelf®

Embracing New Paradigms in Education

The Reference Shelf
Volume 86 • Number 4
H. W. Wilson
A Division of EBSCO Information Services
Ipswich, Massachusetts
2014

GREY HOUSE PUBLISHING

The Reference Shelf

The books in this series contain reprints of articles, excerpts from books, addresses on current issues, and studies of social trends in the United States and other countries. There are six separately bound numbers in each volume, all of which are usually published in the same calendar year. Numbers one through five are each devoted to a single subject, providing background information and discussion from various points of view and concluding with an index and comprehensive bibliography that lists books, pamphlets, and articles on the subject. The final number of each volume is a collection of recent speeches. Books in the series may be purchased individually or on subscription.

Library of Congress Cataloging-in-Publication Data

Embracing new paradigms in education / [compiled by H. W. Wilson]. -- [First edition].
    pages : illustrations ; cm. -- (The reference shelf ; volume 86, number 4)
  Edition statement supplied by publisher.
  Includes bibliographical references.
  ISBN: 978-1-61925-435-0 (v. 86, no. 4)
  ISBN: 978-1-61925-261-5 (volume set)
  1. Education--United States. 2. Education--Standards--United States. 3. Education--United States--Finance. 4. Computer-assisted instruction--United States. 5. Teacher effectiveness--United States. I. H.W. Wilson Company. II. Series: Reference shelf ; v. 86, no. 4.
LA209.2 .E43 2014
370.973

Cover: © Universal Images Group/Getty Images

The Reference Shelf, 2014, published by Grey House Publishing, Inc., Amenia, NY, under exclusive license from EBSCO Information Services, Inc.

Printed in the United States of America

Contents

2

Public and Private: The Class Gap

3

Affordable Education: Majoring in Debt

4

E-Learning: Are We Learning Better?

5

Politics of the Good Teacher

Preface

Embracing New Paradigms in Education

For each generation of Americans, one of the most important issues is the perennial struggle to improve the American education system and to develop new educational theories, paradigms, and strategies that will enable American students to survive and thrive in a rapidly changing global culture.

The twenty-first-century debate over the future of education involves a number of complex issues, including the degree to which federal intervention is needed or desired in primary and secondary education. Initiatives like No Child Left Behind and the Common Core programs have been among the most controversial facets of this ongoing debate. Other major issues include the rising cost of education, the growing economic disparities in both primary and secondary education, and the ongoing debate over the best ways for both teachers and students to embrace and utilize technology. Beyond specific debates, the goal of educators and legislators remains the same today as it was a century ago: to bring education to the greatest number of people and to foster knowledge in the American public that will enable Americans to compete in the global sphere.

Quality in Teaching and Learning

The No Child Left Behind (NCLB) Act of 2001 and the Common Core State Standards Initiative of 2009–2014 are the two most important American education initiatives of the twenty-first century thus far. Both programs represent an unprecedented move toward direct federal intervention and involvement in state educational systems, by linking the dispensation of federal funding to the performance of students and schools as measured by standardized testing and adherence to national standards of knowledge.

NCLB was a bipartisan piece of legislation passed during President George W. Bush's first term in office. Since the 2002 implementation of NCLB, national estimates indicate overall improvements in English and mathematics scores on standardized tests given across the nation. Supporters of the program have used these statistics as evidence of the law's success. Supporters have also pointed out that testing reveals a narrowing gap between white and minority students since the beginning of the program.

A state-level initiative sponsored by the National Governors Association and the Council of Chief State School Officers, the Common Core State Standards are a set of guidelines establishing basic knowledge and skills that American K–12 students should have at the completion of each grade. As of 2014, forty-four states and the District of Columbia had adopted the standards, which were initially presented as an improvement on the standards-based assessment of the NCLB program. The Common Core standards were implicitly endorsed by the federal government when the administration of President Barack Obama used adherence to the standards as one of the criteria for awarding federal money to states under the Race to the Top education funding program. Announced in 2009, Race to the Top offered schools the opportunity to compete for more than $4 billion in funding for educational innovation and reform, based in part on the success of their students in standardized tests. By the end of 2013, all program funds had been disbursed to eighteen states and the District of Columbia.

Although recognized as landmarks of education reform, NCLB and the Common Core standards have also been highly controversial. For one, the focus on standardized testing has been blamed for creating an environment in which teachers focus only on facts that will appear on the tests, rather than presenting a more comprehensive and balanced education. Further, independent psychological studies indicate that standardized tests are often biased toward individuals from certain cultural, economic, and racial backgrounds, thus fostering a widening achievement gap among American students.

While the goal of these programs is to create fair national standards of knowledge that will help to make student assessment more accurate, many educators argue that standardized tests are not the best method available. Some schools utilize an alternative, performance-based evaluation method in which student knowledge is assessed based on the student's ability to apply their knowledge to problem solving in real-world situations. In some cases, public high schools utilizing the performance-based system reported lower dropout rates and higher graduation rates.

The debate over standards for measuring student success can be extended to the ongoing debate over how best to measure the effectiveness of teachers. Controversial state and federal proposals for standardized teacher assessment have raised the question of whether it is possible to evaluate all or most teachers based on a core set of standards. Teacher evaluations, in which students rate their experiences with teachers, have long been conducted for the use of teachers and administrators, but some schools are currently debating whether these results should be made available to the public and to parents guiding their children's education.

Class and Cost in Education

Another major issue affecting families and students is the rising cost of education and the growing class gap between public and private options both for K–12 students and in higher education. The cost of private education has risen steadily in the twenty-first century; a 2012 article in the *New York Times* reported that the cost of private schooling for first-grade students in New York rose 48 percent between 2002 and 2012. In some cases, the cost of a single year in a private preparatory high school may exceed the cost of a year in one of America's top colleges.

The tuition paid to private schools results in a number of key benefits, including more advanced technology available to both teachers and students, smaller classrooms where teachers can dedicate more time to each student, and peripheral staff that can provide individualized tutoring and assistance. Collectively, private school students may enjoy an advantage in terms of preparation for both higher education and employment, and yet the rising cost of private education places a financial strain on families struggling to afford the best education for their children.

The debate over the advantages and disadvantages of private versus public education extend also to the hundreds of for-profit educational institutions in the United States, attempting to fill an educational niche through a business-oriented model of operation. These controversial organizations have been accused of sacrificing educational quality to enhance profit.

Another issue in the economics of education concerns the rising cost of public and private college tuition. A 2014 article in the *Economist* noted that American students carried more than $1.1 trillion in debt, which is more than the debt owed to American credit card companies. The issue of college debt and costs is considered by many to be a national crisis, and President Obama mentioned the issue in his State of the Union address every year from 2009 to 2014.

Studies have further shown that tuitions continue to rise and that the return on this investment varies greatly between students. While broad analyses indicate that individuals with a college education enjoy vastly superior earning potential, this estimate is skewed by the fact that different degrees pay different returns. Since the beginning of the 2008 economic recession, for instance, students obtaining degrees that once translated into high employability have been faced with a lack of jobs and difficulty in repaying their student loans. Nationwide in 2010, nearly 15 percent of students defaulted on their loans within three years of leaving college due to inability to obtain work sufficient to meet their financial needs.

The depth of the cost and debt problem has, in some cases, stimulated proposals to combat the issue with innovative solutions. A pilot program in Oregon called the Pay It Forward, Pay It Back program, for instance, involves providing undergraduate education at no upfront tuition cost to students, and then having them pay a percentage of their income back to the state over the next twenty years after graduation. While solutions like this may not be feasible on a nationwide scale, the complexity of the debt issue may mean that trying such innovative strategies is the only way to address this issue effectively.

While the financial implications of college debt are in many cases immediately apparent, educational analysts also warn about the unintended consequences of this phenomenon for the future of American society as a whole. If students increasingly focus on career paths with immediate rewards, this might reduce involvement in disciplines that provide fewer opportunities for immediate lucrative employment. On the whole, this pattern discourages students from engaging in the arts, philosophy, history, and the basic sciences, as careers in these fields are marked by lower income at entry levels. The threat of debt and the increasing severity of this problem may therefore threaten the diversity, creativity, and innovation of American culture, leading to a generation pursuing conservative educational goals out of a desire to minimize debt, rather than pursuing their passions and interests, which is often the path to creative innovation.

Technology and Education

The evolution of technology is one of the characteristic features of the modern era in human culture. Social media, wireless connectivity, and an increasingly global network of communication and interaction are defining features of the twenty-first century. The benefits of global connectivity are widely acknowledged but are not equally shared, and the issue of how to integrate technology into education and thus extend the benefits of technology to a greater portion of society has become one of the most pressing issues facing American schools.

While students in America's top schools often enjoy access to the latest in modern technology and the resources to learn how to communicate and conduct research online, these resources are often reduced or lacking in America's most impoverished school systems. For instance, a 2012 article from the *Huffington Post* reported on a school in urban Chicago where nearly one thousand students share access to just twenty-four computers through the school's homework lab. By contrast, students at some of the nation's most affluent schools may be provided with individual laptops and even tablet devices.

Educators argue that familiarity with technology and online communication is rapidly becoming an educational necessity rather than simply a benefit or advantage. As online and computing technology have gradually been integrated into fields ranging from art history to automotive repair, legislators and school administrators must struggle with how to provide technology and teach technological competence as part of a basic education.

In addition to access to technology, educators are also increasingly experimenting with providing education online, through video lectures or video conferencing, allowing students to learn from home rather than having to meet in a classroom. Flipped classrooms (where students watch lectures at home and do what used to be homework in the classroom) and online degree programs are just two ways teachers have experimented with enhancing educational opportunities for students. While the benefits and detriments of online education are a matter of debate, the increasing familiarity of young students with online communication means that online learning may become an increasingly effective way for students and teachers to communicate. Cloud sharing and connectivity now enable online students to work together on the creation of documents or other projects and to collaborate in ways previously only possible in a shared physical space.

In many ways, the evolution of technology and communication has outpaced the capability of the educational system to adjust, and many educators have fallen behind their students in terms of technological competence. This represents a third facet of the debate over technology and education: the need to educate teachers as well as students on the newest technological trends and to help educators learn how to better utilize information technology in their classrooms.

Many of the issues in American education, including the ongoing effort to measure student and teacher success and the complex issues surrounding class and income gaps in educational achievement, have been perennial issues in the education debate for more than a century. Issues surrounding the integration of advanced technology into education are more recent but no less important in a society rapidly evolving through the information age. While the problems facing the education system may at times appear insurmountable, difficult problems can also bring out the best and most innovative solutions. Around the nation and around the world, there are many passionate educators, administrators, and politicians searching for ways to enhance and extend the benefits of education in the twenty-first century.

—Micah Issitt

Bibliography

Anderson, Jenny, and Rachel Ohm. "Bracing for $40,000 at New York City Private Schools." *New York Times*. New York Times, 27 Jan. 2012. Web. 4 June 2014.

Bauman, Kurt J., and Nikki L. Graf. "Educational Attainment: 2000." *US Census Bureau*. US Census, Aug. 2003. Web. 4 June 2014.

"Fast Facts: Educational Attainment." *National Center for Education Statistics*. US Dept. of Educ., 2013. Web. 4 June 2014.

Flamm, Michael. "Facing the New Millennium." *Gilder Lehrman Institute of American History*. Gilder Lehrman Inst. of Amer. History, n.d. Web. 4 June 2014.

Kim, Susanna. "Oregon Lawmakers Pioneer Tuition-Free 'Pay It Forward, Pay It Back' College Plan." *ABC News*. ABC News Internet Ventures, 5 July 2013. Web. 4 June 2014.

Spring, Joel H. H. *Political Agendas for Education: From Race to the Top to Saving the Planet*. 5th ed. New York: Routledge, 2014. Print.

"Student Loan Debt Statistics." *American Student Assistance*. Amer. Student Assistance, 2014. Web. 4 June 2014.

Weis, Lois, Kristin Cipollone, and Heather Jenkins, *Class Warfare: Class, Race, and College Admission in Top-Tier Secondary Schools*. Chicago: U of Chicago P, 2013. Print.

1

Report Card:
Common Core Standards

Dr. Lynn House, interim superintendent of the Mississippi Department of Education, brought her message for the new Common Core standards being put in place in school districts across Mississippi and most of the nation. The new standards in math and language arts are to be in place in kindergarten through 12th grade by fall 2014.

The Common Core Controversy

About the Common Core

Despite its vociferous supporters and detractors, the Common Core academic standards seem misunderstood by both sides. Prior to 2010, every state in the United States adopted its own set of standards, which identified the skills students were expected to master upon completion of each grade level. But while state-specific standards allowed greater autonomy over curriculum development, students graduated from high schools across the country with inconsistent skill sets, and many were underprepared for the academic rigors of college.

Additionally, according to the 2000 US Census, nearly 18 percent of children and their families had moved during the prior year. Students relocating to new towns or states while still in school, especially during the academic year, may find the transition complicated by the different expectations of their new schools. Some students might be significantly ahead of their new peers and lose educational ground, while others might be significantly behind and struggle to catch up.

To address the problems caused by this patchwork of academic standards, the Common Core State Standards Organization (CCSSO) and the National Governor's Association for Best Practices (also known as the NGA Center) coordinated a state-led effort to develop the Common Core standards in 2009. The purpose of the Common Core is to standardize the skills taught in public schools across the United States so that all students, regardless of state or school district, are taught the same language and math skills at the same grade levels. As of 2014, forty-four states and the District of Columbia have adopted the standards and are implementing them in the classroom.

What Is the Common Core?

Conflicting commentary demonstrates much confusion among politicians, educators, parents of school-age children, and the general public as to what the Common Core entails. It is not a predefined national curriculum, but instead defines a list of skills that students are expected to master by the end of each grade level. Each state then determines how to implement the standards within its curriculum.

For example, the standards for English Language Arts include "determine an author's point of view or purpose," "determine the meaning of general academic and domain-specific words," and "trace and evaluate the argument and specific claims in a text." The Common Core emphasizes informational texts because, while school reading traditionally focuses on fiction, most college-level and daily-life reading is nonfictional material such as historical, scientific, and technical texts. To address this discrepancy, the Common Core prescribes a more even split of fiction and nonfiction materials, and teachers instruct students to dig deep into each text—not just give a cursory glance and apply it anecdotally to their own lives—and to use context to interpret unfamiliar vocabulary.

One common misconception is that the Common Core contains a large amount of required nonfiction reading and abolishes the study of literary works. In reality, the Common Core documentation provides suggested texts for teaching each required skill, but few specific materials are actually required under the standards. When required texts do appear (in late high school), they include documents of historical and literary significance, such as the US Constitution.

Mixed Reviews from Educators

Several national teacher associations, including the National Education Association and American Federation of Teachers, support the Common Core standards. These organizations appreciate the consistency provided by nationally adopted standards, and recognize the importance of ensuring that students across the country possess the same literacy and critical thinking skills upon high school graduation, regardless of where those students live.

However, as a practical matter, many individual teachers are unhappy with the nationwide rollout of the new standards. Some support the idea of basic skill standardization by grade level, but they are displeased about not being consulted during the development process, and believe that the decision-makers—often politicians or higher-level administrators such as school district superintendents—lack a realistic understanding of students' capabilities. As of March 2014, surveys suggested that about 70 percent of teachers felt that the transition to the Common Core curriculum was not working, and about 66 percent said that they were not given any input into how the new curriculum should be implemented at their schools. Both parents and educators voice concerns that the required analytical and critical thinking skills are not developmentally appropriate for the age level to which they are assigned, thus setting children up for frustration and disappointment rather than a higher level of achievement.

Educational historian and New York University professor Diane Ravitch notes that, while the Common Core standards sound reasonable in theory, they were not field tested prior to nationwide rollout. As a result, nearly every state is struggling to understand and implement the new standards. Many issues remain, including how to address widespread skill deficiencies, especially in higher grades where students' progress may lag significantly behind the new standards. In the meantime, school districts are instituting new standardized testing procedures to monitor students' progress on the standards, and sometimes tying teacher compensation and job security to student performance.

Student Assessment and Standardized Testing

Assessment of student performance under the new Common Core standards is at the heart of many teachers' concerns. Educators and policy-makers often debate the effectiveness and consequences of standardized testing: some believe it ensures that schools meet minimum standards, while others believe it reduces teacher autonomy. Critics assert that, rather than motivating teachers to improve their curricula, it instead pressures teachers to narrowly focus on test preparation rather than teaching broader skills and concepts to their students.

This debate looms large as school districts try to improve performance by tying teacher compensation and tenure to students' test results, and the debate moved to the forefront when trial administrations of the new Common Core tests in New York showed significant drops in student scores compared to prior assessments. It also revealed discrepancies based on socioeconomic status, race, and ethnicity. Overall, 34 percent of students obtained a score that was up to the new standards, but only 20 percent of students with a lower socioeconomic status, 16 percent of Hispanic or Latino students, and 12 percent of black students passed. As a result, teachers and their representative unions fear accountability for poorly understood test results, while other Common Core states approach the new assessments with greater caution. Teachers worry about lacking the time within a single school year to bring students up to the newly raised standards while also covering the new required material. They argue that full implementation of the new standards across all grade levels must be a multiyear process, and that they are receiving insufficient support from their administrators—many of whom barely understand the new standards themselves—to attain these lofty goals.

As a practical matter, administering and scoring statewide standardized tests is expensive. According to the Partnership for Assessment of Readiness for College and Careers (PARCC), it would cost about $29.50 per student for the company to administer and score a Common Core–aligned math and reading test—nearly twice as much as some school districts currently spend on student testing. Educational testing companies stand to make significant amounts of money from the changing assessments, leading some critics to suspect that the purpose of the Common Core is more about corporate profit than improved education.

Additionally, many parents who exercise their right to opt their children out of standardized testing meet severe resistance from the school district. School districts' performance metrics, as well as their eligibility under 2009's Race to the Top education funding initiative, are tied not only to student performance, but also to the percentage of students who actually take the tests. When students opt out of testing, the reduction in district testing numbers can reduce the amount of state and federal funding the district receives.

Political Pressure and Negative Publicity

As of 2014, some of the first states to adopt the Common Core during its 2010 rollout were reconsidering. In April 2014, Indiana voted to drop the Common Core and replace it with state-developed standards. Legislators touted this as a step forward, claiming the change allowed them to enact their own "uncommonly high" standards instead. However, education expert Sandra Stotsky reviewed a draft of Illinois's new standards and concluded that much of this draft was simply copied from the Common Core standards; the English language arts standards for grades 6–12 were particularly similar, with Stotsky estimating that over 90 percent were unchanged from Common Core. In June 2014, South Carolina became the second state to drop the Common Core standards, planning to adopt a new set of standards in time for the 2015–2016 school year.

Ultimately, the debate over the Common Core is also political. The Republican Party is split, with Tea Party and libertarian-leaning Republicans worried about government control over school curricula and big-business Republicans embracing the standards because of financial opportunities. The Democratic Party is also split between those who believe a national standard helps ensure that all students receive an adequate education and those who worry it will leave students in already-underperforming school districts even further behind.

Indeed, education policy analysts suggest that the "one size fits all" approach to national standardization undermines teachers' autonomy in their classrooms and prevents teachers from adapting their curricula to meet the specific needs of their students. Stan Karp of New Jersey's Education Law Center and the liberal reform group Rethinking Schools notes that the Common Core "does not reflect the experience of many groups of students served by public education" and "does not reflect the concerns that many parents have for what they want to see in their education." This may be true especially in underperforming school districts, where life skills might trump college preparation. Karp also notes that the approach "doubles down" on what he describes as a "testing-and-punish" approach to public education that has proven ineffective for many years.

No Clear Consensus or Solution

In general, the fight against the Common Core has been a bipartisan effort. However, this may be a response to public outcry for repeal of the standards rather than careful consideration about the validity and helpfulness of the standards themselves. Ultimately, parents, teachers, administrators, and politicians agree that the United States must find a way to prepare its students better for higher education and competition in the global job market. However, disagreement abounds on whether the Common Core is the best solution to this dilemma and whether it will deliver on its promises of raising all US school districts to a uniformly high standard of education or simply generate more standardized testing and label more school districts as underperforming.

—Tracey M. DiLascio

Bibliography

Associated Press. "Indiana: Common Core Replaced with State Standards." *New York Times*. New York Times, 28 Apr. 2014. Web. 5 June 2014.

Common Core State Standards Organization. "About the Standards." *Common Core State Standards Initiative*. Common Core State Standards Initiative, 2014. Web. 5 June 2014.

Greene, Kim. "Common Core: Fact vs. Fiction." *Scholastic*. Scholastic, 2014. Web. 5 June 2014.

NPR Staff. "Q&A: A Crash Course on Common Core." *NPR*. NPR, 18 Mar 2014. Web. 5 June 2014.

Sawchuk, Stephen. "Concern Abounds over Teachers' Preparedness for Standards." *Education Week*. Editorial Projects in Education, 27 May 2014. Web. 5 June 2014.

Strauss, Valerie. "New Common Core Tests: Worth the Price?" *Washington Post*. Washington Post, 24 July 2013. Web. 5 June 2014.

Ujifusa, Andrew. "Common Core Supporters Firing Back." *Education Week*. Editorial Projects in Education, 14 May 2013. Web. 5 June 2014.

Ujifusa, Andrew. "Indiana Finally OKs Standards to Replace Common-Core Adoption." *Education Week*. Editorial Projects in Education, 28 Apr. 2014. Web. 5 June 2014.

Westervelt, Eric. "Political Rivals Find Common Ground Over Common Core." *NPR*. NPR, 28 Jan. 2014. Web. 5 June 2014.

Open Letter on Transition to Common Core

By Cheryl S. Williams
Education Digest, September 2013

Fifteen members of the Learning First Alliance, a partnership of national education organizations representing more than 10 million parents, educators, and policymakers, have agreed on the following statement:

The Learning First Alliance believes that the Common Core State Standards have the potential to transform teaching and learning and provide all children with knowledge and skills necessary for success in the global community.

To meet this potential, teachers, administrators, parents, and communities are working together to align the standards with curriculum, instruction and assessment. Their work—which includes providing the pre-service and professional learning opportunities educators need to effectively teach the standards, making necessary adaptations to implementation plans as work progresses and field-testing efforts to ensure proper alignment—will take time.

Rushing to make high-stakes decisions such as student advancement or graduation, teacher evaluation, school performance designation, or state funding awards based on assessments of the Common Core Standards before the standards have been fully and properly implemented is unwise. We suggest a transition period of at least one year after the original deadline in which results from assessments of these standards are used only to guide instruction and attention to curriculum development, technology infrastructure, professional learning, and other resources needed to ensure that schools have the supports needed to help all students achieve under the Common Core. Removing high-stakes consequences for a short time will ensure that educators have adequate time to adjust their instruction, students' focus on learning, and parents' and communities' focus on supporting children.

During this time, we urge a continued commitment to accountability. We recommend that states and districts continue to hold educators and schools to a high standard as determined by the components of their accountability systems that are not solely based on standardized tests, including other evidence of student learning, peer evaluations, school climate data, and more.

We have seen growing opposition to the Common Core as officials move too quickly to use assessments of the Common Core State Standards in high-stakes accountability decisions. Such actions have the potential to undermine the Common Core—and thus our opportunity to improve education for all students. We must take the necessary time to ensure we succeed in this endeavor.

On Behalf Of:

American Association of Colleges of Teacher Education (AACTE)

American Association of School Administrators (AASA)

American Association of School Personnel Administrators (AASPA)

American Federation of Teachers (AFT)

American School Counselor Association (ASCA)

Association for Middle Level Education (AMLE)

International Society for Technology in Education (ISTE)

Learning Forward (formerly National Staff Development Council)

National Association of Elementary School Principals (NAESP)

National Association of Secondary School Principals (NASSP)

National Education Association (NEA)

National Parent Teacher Association (PTA)

National School Boards Association (NSBA)

National School Public Relations Association (NSPRA)

Phi Delta Kappa International (PDK)

Make Room for the Common Core in Every Classroom

By Martin Chaffee and Kristine Gullen
Principal Leadership, October 2013

Forty-five states have adopted the Common Core State Standards. Two consortiums are creating and piloting assessments. The first year of the test is 2014–15.

Are you ready to lead the change?

At a district professional development session in October 2012, 80 secondary school educators were asked, "What do you know about the Common Core State Standards?" as an opening connector to their afternoon professional development session. After the initial flurry of dialogue lulled, they shared their current thinking about the Common Core:

- It's about just English language arts and math
- It requires higher-order thinking
- It leaves out art and electives
- We just have to tweak our content a little
- The Common Core starts in 2015
- Kids will take it on the computer
- It has nothing to do with social studies and science
- It's one more thing that we have to do.

Many math and English language arts teachers have been busy studying the Common Core, aligning curricula, creating units of study, and piloting assessments. Those actions may have unwittingly sent the message that the Common Core excludes other disciplines and minimizes the need for leadership. Yet when unpacking the Common Core pilot assessments, it becomes apparent that learning from all disciplines is essential for student success. Leadership is needed to facilitate, coordinate, enact, engage, and guide all teachers in the implementation of the Common Core.

Building Ownership

Common Core test items and performance tasks that provide valuable insights into the upcoming assessments are being piloted and released. To build a connection with the Common Core, "begin with the end in mind" (Covey, 1989, p. 97). The following five-step guide for educators explains how to anchor assessments to quality instruction, find shifts and gaps in current instructional and assessment practices, connect new expectations to every classroom, and create scaffolds to prepare students for success.

Provide Quality Instruction

Educators possess a wealth of experience. To capitalize on their knowledge, ask teachers to write down a list of elements that describe quality instruction. Group the teachers in small teams of four to six of their colleagues to discuss their lists and expand and deepen their initial thinking. Each team should draft a definition of quality instruction and share it with the whole group. Next, teachers identify examples of quality instruction that was present in their classrooms during the past week. Through a paired conversation, educators share and listen to those real-life examples and report exemplary instructional practices they have heard.

Elevating examples of quality instructional practices honors the good work already happening and creates a positive tone to anchor the upcoming dialogue.

Examine Performance Assessments

Understanding the pivotal role that assessment plays in demarcating content, Bambrick-Santoyo (2012) said, "Standards are meaningless until you define how to assess them. Assessments, therefore, are the roadmap to rigor" (p. 28). In the next step, teams of educators receive six Common Core performance assessments (two elementary, two middle, and two high school items). Each participant chooses one task to examine and answers each of the following questions:

- What are your first impressions?
- What skills and thinking are required?
- What elements of quality instruction are included?
- What are the instructional and assessment shifts?
- What is needed to support student success on this performance task?

The questions are designed to help educators manage personal transitions (Waters & Cameron, 2006). Connecting their individual values and beliefs (i.e., their personal definitions of quality instruction) to the expectations found in the Common Core helps teachers make shifts in their thinking and practice.

There is a perception that implementing the Common Core will change everything. Managing their personal transitions allows educators to articulate, "This is the quality work we do now" and to implement the Common Core, "Here's what we need to do next."

Share Impressions and Align Perspectives

Educators can use a jigsaw strategy (Wormeli, 2004) to further explore the elements required in performance assessments. Participants form triads with colleagues from other teams who explored the same performance task in the previous exercise. The participants in the second, "expert" groups share their discoveries of the skills and thinking required in the performance assessments, the elements of quality instruction they found, and the ways they can support students' success. After a few minutes, educators move back to their original groups.

Beginning with the tasks for the primary grades, educators explore the alignment of content as it progresses through elementary to middle school and then to high school. Ask teachers to think about the tasks' level of cognitive demand, how the skills and thinking develop, and what is required for student success.

When discussing the details of a fourth-grade performance task, a teacher who is also a parent of an elementary student asked, "Do you think it is developmentally appropriate for a fourth grader to provide evidence in their essay from an introductory classroom activity?" (That is an expectation in one of the primary tasks.) As the teacher's group examined the middle school and then the high school items, the teachers began to uncover a sequence. Identifying a resource for evidence in the elementary task was foundational because in middle school, students are expected to reference several different media resources when writing an argumentative article. And at the high school level, students are expected to evaluate the credibility of and summarize six sources to create a report addressing arguments and counterarguments.

The jigsaw exercise helps practitioners gain a perspective about how the Common Core will look across grade levels in a way that honors current practices and incorporates instructional and assessment shifts. Examining a sample of items from each level clarifies student expectations and emphasizes the knowledge and skills they will need in future grades.

Teachers have said that exploring performance tasks "makes the upcoming Common Core real," rather than "something that is coming a few years down the road." It can provide insight into instructional shifts that need to occur.

Articulate Shifts

Give educators a stack of sticky notes to respond to the following prompt, What are the instructional and assessment shifts in the Common Core? Ask them to write a different idea on each note. After three or four minutes, teachers share their ideas and cluster similar concepts on a piece of chart paper, articulating an overarching idea for each grouping. The small groups then take turns sharing the big ideas with the whole group until all ideas are represented.

The articulated shifts were a surprise to many in the room who have had little contact with the Common Core. The media specialist expressed excitement at the importance that finding, citing, and examining sources for credibility has in the standards. When staff members articulated shifts, it became apparent that the technology literacy skills that some students received in an elective class could be connected to content that was essential for all. That was just one of the many connections staff members made.

Allowing educators to personalize the assessment expectations of the Common Core and find gaps in their current practice creates "a sense of urgency" (Kotter, 1996, 2008), an essential step when leading change.

Close Gaps

Analyzing the collection of responses, educators reflect and identify a shift or gap between current instructional practices and expectations on the upcoming assessments using the questions, How do you support student success on the performance tasks? and, What can you do to move your teaching and your students' learning closer to those expectations?

A pair of high school teachers from different departments answered those questions by reflecting on an 11th-grade performance task from the Smarter Balanced Assessment Consortium. In the assessment, students take the role of a congresswoman's chief of staff. The students must prepare a report about the pros and cons of a proposed nuclear power plant. This task requires Internet research, an evaluation of resources for credibility, data analysis, a summary of arguments and counterarguments, and a report of their findings and recommendations. To accomplish this assignment, students use the knowledge and skills they gained in science, social studies, math, English, technology, debate, and possibly other classes.

To prepare students for cross-content assessments, the teachers designed a performance task linking knowledge from each of their classes. After completing their successful collaboration, the two teachers planned future iterations that would expand their work into three content areas, then four, thus scaffolding the complexity of the project and their lesson design, while moving their teaching and student learning closer to the multidisciplinary expectations in the Common Core.

Another group of educators wanted to focus on technology literacy. A science teacher, a social studies teacher, and a media specialist created mutual expectations for the number, type, and quality of resources for research projects. Students received instruction on conducting Internet research, such as how to link keywords, the functions of symbols, and the ways to expand and narrow a search. Additional lessons supported the verification of credible sources and defined such terminology as *plagiarism, copyright, bias, fiction,* and *nonfiction.* Students also learned to create citations for books, Internet sites, videos, and blogs.

That unit gave students the skills and knowledge they needed to examine, critique, and cite more evidence-based sources. Deepening their skills and ability to speak from fact rather than opinion resulted in projects, papers, and classroom discussions having a higher level of rigor and credibility. The unit moved teaching and learning closer to the technology-literacy expectations embedded in the Common Core.

Conclusion

Building ownership for the implementation of the Common Core in every subject takes leadership. Exploring primary source assessments can reveal possible gaps between current practices and upcoming expectations. Such reflection is fundamental to creating urgency. As City, Elmore, Fiarman, and Teitel (2009) said, "We learn the work by doing the work" (p. 33).

But acknowledging instructional and assessment shifts is just the beginning. Identifying and enacting strategies in every classroom to ensure that each student meets the new expectations are the goals. As one teacher commented, "Common Core honors the complexity of real-life by requiring the integration of knowledge, experiences and skills. Students have to bring all their learning with them—from all their classes—in order to solve these tasks."

Are you ready to lead the change?

Bibliography

Bambrick-Santoyo, P. (2012). *Leverage leadership: A practical guide to building exceptional schools.* San Francisco, CA: Jossey-Bass.

City, E. A., Elmore, R. E, Fiarman, S. E., & Teitel, L. (2009). *Instructional rounds in education: A network approach to improving teaching and learning.* Cambridge, MA: Harvard Education Press.

Covey, S. R. (1989). *The 7 habits of highly effective people: Powerful lessons in personal change.* New York, NY: Simon & Schuster.

Kotter, J. P. (1996). *Leading change.* Boston, MA: Harvard Business Review Press.

Kotter, J. P. (2008). *A Sense of Urgency.* Boston, MA: Harvard Business School Publishing.

Waters, T & Cameron, G. (2006). *The balanced leadership framework: Connecting vision with action.* Denver, CO: Mid-continent Research for Education and Learning.

Wormeli, R. (2004). *Summarization in any subject: 50 techniques to improve student learning.* Alexandria, VA: ASCD.

Q & A: A Crash Course on Common Core

By *NPR*, March 18, 2014

Confused about the Common Core State Standards? Join the club. That's not to say the new benchmarks in reading and math are good or bad, working smoothly or kicking up sparks as the wheels come off. It is simply an acknowledgement that, when the vast majority of U.S. states adopt a single set of educational standards all at roughly the same time, a little confusion is inevitable.

Below is a handy FAQ about Common Core.

What Are the Common Core State Standards?

With the Core, it's best to begin at the beginning. They are benchmarks in English language arts and math that clarify the skills each child should have at each grade level. From the Common Core's own website: "The standards were created to ensure that all students graduate from high school with the skills and knowledge necessary to succeed in college, career, and life, regardless of where they live." If you have a few hours you're looking to fill, you can tuck into the standards one by one.

The standards have been adopted in 45 states and the District of Columbia. One good way to understand what they are is to know what they're replacing. States control their learning standards, and Common Core doesn't change that. But before the Core, state standards varied widely across the country and, in many cases, were weak and outdated. The Core standards are widely considered an upgrade.

The other problem the standards are meant to address is student mobility. Kids move around a lot. The 2000 census found that 18 percent of kids had moved in the last year. And, when they moved from school to school or state to state, many found themselves struggling to cope with very different standards.

Opponents of the Common Core Argue That the Standards Tell Teachers What Texts They Should Teach. Do They?

Not really. The only required reading from Common Core comes in the 11th and 12th grades, when kids will be expected to read and understand foundational documents of historical and literary significance: the Declaration of Independence, the Preamble to the Constitution, the Bill of Rights and Lincoln's second inaugural address.

Much of the confusion comes from the Core's Appendix B. It includes dozens of titles that the Core's writers consider "text exemplars"—in other words, suggestions for teachers looking for age-appropriate reading material that will help their students reach Core benchmarks. They include everything from *Green Eggs and Ham* to Shakespeare's Sonnet 73. But these texts are recommended, not required. The standards also call for a balance of informational texts and literature but, again, do not require specific books or reading materials.

Will the Core Come with New Standardized Tests?

Yes. The states that have adopted the Core have divided into two consortia, and each will soon field-test new, Common-Core-aligned assessments. Beginning next week, some 4 million students (in grades three to 11) will take these new tests in math and language arts for the first time. This early testing will help test makers figure out what test items truly gauge "proficiency" (or grade-level skills) and what the cutoff scores should be. These tests are expected to be tougher for many of the children who take them. New York, an early adopter of the Core, has already administered Core-aligned tests and seen significant drops in student scores.

How Do Teachers Unions Feel about the Common Core?

That's tricky. Both the National Education Association and American Federation of Teachers support the standards, but their rank-and-file are uncomfortable and increasingly unhappy with the standards' implementation. Seven out of 10 teachers say the transition to a curriculum tied to Common Core isn't working. Two-thirds of teachers say they were not asked for input on how to develop the implementation plan. Teachers also say they need time to make sure they understand the standards and are able to talk to parents about them. In the meantime, the unions are calling for a delay not in implementation of the new standards but in holding teachers accountable for test results. In California, Governor Jerry Brown has already said teachers there won't be judged this year on student performance as the state transitions from old standards to new.

Common Core: Fact vs. Fiction

By Kim Greene
Instructor, Fall 2012

Think informational text = boring? Reinvent your reading lessons with dinosaurs, artists, and geologists!

Second-grade teacher Erin Klein says her students gravitate toward informational text. "They are naturally curious," says Klein, who teaches in Bloomfield Hills, Michigan. "Nonfiction helps quench their thirst for answers."

Despite students' interest in informational text, it has played second fiddle in literacy instruction for years. In 2000, Nell Duke's groundbreaking study "3.6 Minutes per Day: The Scarcity of Informational Texts in First Grade" found that primary teachers dedicated the vast majority of instructional time to fiction.

Now, though, nonfiction is getting its turn in the spotlight. The Common Core State Standards require that students become thoughtful consumers of complex, informative texts—taking them beyond the realm of dry textbooks and self-selected reading. "We live in an exciting time where our information isn't solely from thick textbooks but rather from websites, blogs, and magazines," says Klein. "By introducing students to print-rich materials and digital media, we are shaping an authentic experience for the way they take in information."

Why Now?

What has triggered the push for more informational text? For one, the goal of Common Core is to prepare students for college and career, both of which require a reservoir of knowledge about the natural, physical, and social world around them. And that's exactly what informational texts provide them.

"About 90 percent of what most adults read is informational text," says Laura Candler, a retired teacher of grades 4 through 6 from North Carolina. "Yet in school, it seems we've spent far more time reading fiction."

Another rationale can be summed up in one word: *assessment*. The developers of the standards sought to align the instructional balance of literary and informational text with that of the National Assessment of Educational Progress, or NAEP—tests administered across the country at grades 4, 8, and 12. According to this model, fourth-grade students should receive a 50–50 balance between the two types of texts across the school day.

Informational Text 101

Ready to master the basics of informational text and Common Core? What follows are answers to some commonly asked questions.

What Is Informational Text?

Common Core uses "informational text" as another term for "nonfiction text."

This category includes historical, scientific, and technical texts that provide students with factual information about the world. Typically, they employ structures such as cause and effect, compare and contrast, and problem and solution. They also contain text features like headlines and boldface vocabulary words.

Because of their narrative structures, biographies and autobiographies do not look like other nonfiction texts. In fact, they are often classified as literary nonfiction. But the Common Core considers them to be informational text as well.

Another category of informational texts includes directions, forms, and information contained in charts, graphs, maps, and digital resources. Simply put, if students are reading it for the information it contains, it's informational text.

Who Is Expected to Teach It?

Just about everyone. In grades K to 5, teachers are expected to use informational texts throughout the school day. "I've always included a fair amount of informational text in my instruction," says Klein. "However, the way I teach it has evolved. I now integrate my content areas in a manner that allows for cross-curricular themes, rather than teaching concepts or themes in isolation. The connections between literacy and social studies and science engage students at a much higher level."

In grades 6 to 12, one strand of informational text standards falls to English teachers. A separate strand includes literacy in history and social studies, as well as literacy in science and technical subjects. That means that social studies and science teachers will also be expected to teach vital literacy skills in their relevant content areas.

What Do the Standards Call For?

Common Core calls for close readings of meaty, high-quality texts. The focus is placed squarely on the text—not on making connections to outside experiences or dwelling on prior knowledge. Students should get their hands dirty by digging into the text to uncover the evidence that supports their answers.

In each grade, the 10 reading informational text standards build upon the ones taught in previous grades, from kindergarten all the way through high school. "Most are the same as my current standards, but some are more in depth," says Jenaya Shaw, a first-grade teacher in Georgia. "Common Core gives us more direction and specific areas to work on."

What's the Difference between Academic and Domain-Specific Vocabulary?

Across all grades, informational text standard 4 calls for students to determine the meaning of unfamiliar vocabulary. The phrase "academic and domain-specific vocabulary," which appears several times, refers to words readers often encounter in textbooks across all subject areas. Among such words are *analyze*, which might be unfamiliar to a second-grade student, and *discourse*, which could be a new vocabulary word for a seventh grader.

Domain-specific vocabulary words, on the other hand, are likely to be encountered only in a particular content area. For example, a word such as *photosynthesis* falls within the realm of biology.

Putting It into Practice

With an understanding of what the standards are calling for, it's time to start thinking about what instruction in informational text could look like in your classroom. Here are a few ideas.

Grades K–2

LESSON: Text Features in the News
GRADES: 1–2
STANDARD: 5 (Know and use various text features.)
THE GIST: Laura Candler, the retired teacher from North Carolina, suggests using *Scholastic News Weekly Reader* to identify text features. Students can complete a three-column chart to extend their understanding.

ARTICLE	TEXT FEATURE	PURPOSE

LESSON: Author Study Preview
GRADE: K
STANDARD: 5 (Name the author and illustrator and define the role of each.)
THE GIST: Kick off an author study unit by displaying several of the author's books. Have students identify the author's and illustrator's names on the cover of each book (sometimes they are one and the same). Discuss the contributions made by each. Then have students team up in author-illustrator duos to create their own books.

Grades 3–5

LESSON: Word Detectives
GRADES: 4–5
STANDARD: 4 (Determine the meaning of general academic and domain-specific words.)
THE GIST: Prompt students to identify "suspect" words that may be hindering their understanding of a text. They can flag the suspects with sticky notes or write them on a separate sheet of paper. Have them find contextual clues to determine their meaning. Such clues usually come in the form of outright definitions, neighboring synonyms or antonyms, or other information that can yield useful inferences.

LESSON: Pinterest Pictures
GRADE: 3
STANDARD: 3 (Describe events, ideas, or concepts using language that pertains to time, sequence, and cause and effect.)
THE GIST: "For many students, there is a learning curve to understand the vocabulary of informational text," says third-grade teacher Suzy Brooks of Massachusetts. She uses images from a Pinterest board to introduce these concepts. To teach sequencing, for example, Brooks shows a photo of a dog chasing a ball and asks students what likely happened both before and after the photo was taken.

Grades 6–8

LESSON: Slice of the Pie
GRADES: 6–8
STANDARD: 6 (Determine an author's point of view or purpose.)
THE GIST: Draw a pizza P.I.E. ("persuade, inform, entertain") organizer on the board and discuss what is meant by "author's purpose." Talk about several informational texts and classify the purpose or purposes of each by writing the title in the appropriate slices of the pie. (Yes, an informational text can be intended to persuade *and* entertain!)

LESSON: State Your Case
GRADES: 6–8
STANDARD: 8 (Trace and evaluate the argument and specific claims in a text.)
THE GIST: After they've read an informational text with a central argument, have students pretend that they are lawyers in a courtroom. Ask them to state the author's main claim, and provide ample evidence from the text to back it up. The goal is to convince the classroom jury to agree with the author's argument.

Cut to the Core: Distinguishing Common Core Myth from Reality

By Margaux DelGuidice and Rose Luna
Publishers Weekly, September 9, 2013

In PW's inaugural Common Core column, we look at the controversy swirling around the new standards, and the opportunities that they create.

The Common Core State Standards have been adopted by 46 states in hopes of better preparing students for college and their careers. Broadly speaking, there is a lot to like about the Common Core—especially the focus on literacy and critical thinking. But a number of citizens, educators, and lawmakers are wary about the standards. And, as with many education initiatives, testing has been one of the main sources of controversy around Common Core.

One prominent critic, Diane Ravitch, an educational historian and N.Y.U. professor, questions whether the standards will actually work. Once agnostic toward Common Core, Ravitch, in February of [2013], publicly came out in opposition. In a blog post entitled "Why I Cannot Support the Common Core Standards," she cited concern over the lack of field testing.

"Maybe the standards will be great. Maybe they will be a disaster. Maybe they will improve achievement. Maybe they will widen the achievement gaps between haves and have-nots. Maybe they will cause the children who now struggle to give up altogether," Ravitch wrote in the post. "Would the Federal Drug Administration approve the use of a drug with no trials, no concern for possible harm or unintended consequences?" she asked, concluding that the Common Core adoption has made us "a nation of guinea pigs, almost all trying an unknown new program at the same time."

Meanwhile, parents and educators are rising in opposition to the plethora of new exams that will be used to assess student learning under the Common Core standards. This opposition has culminated in the formation of a national "opt out" campaign from a nonprofit group: The United Opt Out National offers state-by-state guidelines on its Web site that parents can use to affirm their right to opt their children out of state tests. The Web site also features a toolkit of sample letters and other resources for parents and concerned citizens to share at PTA and school board meetings, and with the general community.

Fanning the flames, last month, the state of New York released new standardized test results. As expected, the scores were not good. Just 31% of students grades

3–8 across the state met or exceeded the English Language Arts (ELA) proficiency standard, and just 31% met or exceeded the math proficiency standard. And the scores of minorities reflected the concerns Ravitch expressed about achievement gaps: only 16% of African-American students and 17% of Hispanic students met or exceeded the ELA proficiency standards. Just 3% of English Language Learners exceeded the standard. As expected, the drop in student scores has fueled resistance to the standards among educators and parents.

In July 2013, meanwhile, politicians in Georgia and Oklahoma decided not to adopt the standardized tests created to measure student outcomes in relation to the Common Core standards. The reason cited for the defection: cost. Lawmakers in a number of other states are also seeking to withdraw from the testing consortium, and legislators in Maine are considering a total repeal of the standards.

Cost is a legitimate concern. In July, the *Washington Post* published a piece that focused on the costs of administering the Common Core tests—as much as $29.50 annually per student for the math and reading tests. There are also costs associated with training teachers and purchasing new materials to support the new curriculum. Opponents fear that school administrators may be unable to locate the additional funding needed for the Common Core changes without dipping into programs such as the arts, music, and library media services.

But here is another point of concern: two-thirds of respondents to an annual PDK/Gallup Poll admitted they don't even know what the Common Core standards are. Furthermore, many educators responsible for teaching and implementing the new standards don't fully understand them, as a dearth of resources has led to a lack of training for teachers and administrators.

In response to the opposition, supporters of Common Core remain steadfast in their efforts to uphold the standards and dispel the myths that they feel surround them.

What Is Common Core? Untangling the Standards, Testing & Teacher Evaluations

By Erin Barrett
Ithaca Times, March 8, 2014

The Common Core State Standards are a fact of life nearly nation-wide, with 45 states and several territories adopting them as their standard for K–12 education. The standards were developed as part of a state-based initiative, led by the Council of Chief State School Officers and the National Governors Association, to create a research-based, rigorous, and internationally benchmarked set of standards. The English language arts (ELA) and math standards were released in June of 2010 and established what material students should know at the end of each grade level and what graduating seniors need to know to be college and career ready.

New York State rolled out the new standards and rewrote state tests to align them with Common Core at the same time as the new Annual Professional Performance Reviews (APPR), which in part rely on student performance on the new standardized tests, were implemented. This has led to confusion and frustration among educators, parents and legislators, and a plethora of sensational headlines declaring Common Core to be a failed experiment. Ithaca City School District (ICSD) Master Educators Liddy Coyle and Lily Talcott, and Evaluation Officer Lynn VanDeWeert, explain the differences among the often-conflated terms of the debate and why the Common Core standards are an important breakthrough in education.

APPR and State-Mandated Testing

APPR is a state mandate that went into effect in the 2012–13 school year. The timing—implementing APPR at the same time as the Common Core standards—explains why the two separate initiatives have been confused in public opinion. According to VanDeWeert, APPR would be a fact of life for NYS teachers even if Common Core standards had not been adopted. In order to receive "Race to the Top" funding from the federal government, the states had to implement an APPR plan that incorporated measures of student learning.

"Last year was the first year that districts were required to come up with a numerical rating for teachers," said VanDeWeert. "Teachers have always been evaluated. In Ithaca we've always had a program of evaluation in which teachers are observed by their supervisors—either building principals or department leaders—and given feedback based on those observations. These observations are now 60 percent of the APPR. The difference is that now there's a score associated with these evaluations."

The other 40 percent of teacher evaluations comes from two separate measures of student learning. "That's the piece of APPR that raises the most angst and concern among teachers and administrators," VanDeWeert said, "because it's really difficult to show correlation. Good teaching is critical to student learning, but to make the leap that a student's performance on one measure or one test is directly related to teacher performance is a big leap to make. There are so many extenuating circumstances. Teaching is a really messy, complex process, as is learning, so that piece feels threatening, I think."

The two achievement measures split evenly between a "growth component," which measures student performance at two points in time looking for an increase in student learning, and an "achievement measure" that looks at the results of an end of year exam or assessment.

The achievement measure is often referred to as the "local component" because school districts are empowered to decide whether or not to track the measure individually or as a shared measure. "For our local component," said VanDeWeert, "every teacher in Ithaca will have the same score because we're looking at how teachers and teams vertically and horizontally collaborate to improve student achievement district-wide."

If a teacher or principal receives an overall composite rating of "developing" or "ineffective," the school district is required to develop a teacher or principal "improvement plan" that must be implemented within the first ten days of the next school year.

"An improvement plan defines specific standards-based goals," explained VanDeWeert, "that a teacher or principal must make progress toward attaining within a specific period of time, and includes areas that need improvement, a timeline for achieving improvement, the manner in which improvement will be assessed, and, where appropriate, differentiated activities to support improvement in these areas."

Tenured teachers and principals with a pattern of ineffective teaching or performance—defined by law as two consecutive annual "ineffective" ratings—may be charged with incompetence and considered for termination through an expedited hearing process.

Another misconception surrounding the Common Core is that suddenly students are spending a lot more time in state-mandated testing. "The state has not added any testing for the Common Core or for the modules. However, the content of pre-existing tests has shifted to align with Common Core standards," said VanDeWeert.

Coyle addressed poor results from last year's Common-Core-aligned exams and the criticism that state exams push teachers to teach to a test: "I think if teachers were clear on the material kids are going to be tested on," she said, "they would do a better job of teaching to those standards. There are some people who think it's terrible to teach to a test, but if the test is good and is truly measuring a standard, then it's good to teach to the test.

"Are the tests well made? I think the jury is still out on that," she admitted. "[That] there were some questions that were impossible for a kid to answer, compounded with very little time to know exactly what the state was asking for . . . resulted in unsatisfying scores."

Some parents are concerned that the transition period to Common Core standards in testing will negatively impact their child's academic career. "Kids don't automatically get any sort of remediation based on their test scores," Coyle explained. "Even before Common Core the state said that academic intervention services should be decided by the school, taking into account the state test and everything else we know about the student."

"Education Commissioner [John] King was really clear last spring," the master educator went on, "when he said these scores are going to be lower because they pushed this forward really fast, not because kids can't do well on them. The fact that he said that should make every concerned parent understand that this is not his or her kid; this is a transition period."

Common Core Standards

The Common Core standards for math and ELA, adopted by New York State in 2010, contain both "content standards"—specific information students should know to be at grade-level—and "process standards," which focus on how students learn and transfer information into knowledge and understanding.

According to Antonia Valentine, spokesperson for the New York State Education Department (SED), "The Common Core standards are the first learning standards to be back-mapped from the skills and knowledge students need to succeed in college and careers. The standards detail what students should know and be able to do at each grade level, from kindergarten on."

The new standards make at least four significant interventions. They call for (1) a more rigorous, interdisciplinary approach to learning; (2) pedagogical shifts that focus on the process and assessment of learning; (3) establishing clear, grade-specific standards that build on each other from kindergarten through grade 12; and (4) creating collective standards that enable educators nation-wide to engage in the same conversation.

"The standards aren't that different. They're more specific, and they're now grade by grade," said Coyle. "In past iterations from the state, they've had grade level bands, and it's been frustrating as a teacher because bands, such as K–2[nd grade], require a lot of decoding and figuring out what is more appropriate for first grade or more appropriate for second grade."

According to Talcott, the new, grade-specific standards create a continuum of learning within and between grades. "You'll see a lot of connections among the standards within a grade, and among the grades as you continue on. We're pushing kids to know a lot more about how to do stuff, be it math or reading or writing or speaking, within the context of something they're going to need to know or be able to do later on."

Part of implementing the more rigorous educational standards is a shift in the theory behind teaching and learning. "Within both the ELA and math standards—pre-K through 12—there are specific pedagogical shifts that New York State highlights, which is a really helpful place to start," said Talcott. "There's information that kids have to know, like vowel sounds and how to decode, and things like that, and there are standards for that in the ELA. But you also need to synthesize and interpret information visually, orally, and quantitatively.

"We see this really explicitly in the standards for mathematical practice," Talcott continued, "which get at the heart of critical thinking in mathematics and why we even use math. The standards ask students to make sense of problems and persevere in solving them, use appropriate tools strategically, and look for and make use of structure. These are the same standards for pre-K through 12.

"So yes, you still need to know how to divide," she said, "but knowing why you divide and finding that structure in division and the relationship to addition and subtraction and multiplication, is so much more important."

In first grade, for example, the standard for "the equal sign" requires that the student understand the meaning of the symbol and be able to determine whether equations involving addition or subtraction are true or false. "This is a much deeper standard than simply: know what the equal sign is," said Talcott. "As a teacher, in order to assess this standard, kids are going to need to explain that to me and to each other. You can't just say true or false. Embedded within the content standards we find these process standards."

Talcott will be the first to say that the new standards require active and ongoing work on the part of educators and administrators to not only make sense of what the state wants students to know, but to figure out how to teach them. "These are just the standards," she said. "The preparation and the way we put these into practice as educators can vary a lot. The standards require us as teachers to be cognizant of critical thinking skills and engage our students in learning them. They're the foundation for the structure that can be as cool and interesting and awesome as you want to make it as a teacher. Sure the standards are better, but what we do with them will be what gets kids college and career ready."

"I think the fact that these standards are nation-wide," the master educator said, "opens up our professional learning community so much more. Instead of just working with teachers in my school, my district, or even my state, I can work with teachers across the country around, for instance, the informational reading standards for third graders. We can talk about what our students are doing and share ideas and resources to help each other learn and grow and ultimately impact our kids in better, more efficient, more exciting and more effective ways."

EngageNY Curriculum

Media coverage of the Common Core issue has frequently ignored the differences between the standards themselves and the curriculum made available by the state. In New York State no school district or teacher is required by the state to adopt any particular curriculum. Teachers can continue teaching what they've been teaching all along, if they prepare students for Common Core standards.

As part of the rollout of the standards the SED paid for the development of curriculum modules, available for free on the SED's EngageNY website (www.engageny.org). Some districts have made the modules mandatory; others have chosen to purchase commercially available modules. Characteristically, ICSD has chosen to carve its own path through teacher-driven collaboration, asking teachers to workshop modules together, try one module in their classroom and provide feedback.

The specificity and scripted quality of the state modules have led many educators to criticize them as eliminating teacher creativity and innovation, and containing an overwhelming amount of information. "The modules give a lot of background. They tell you what your guiding questions are going to be, what your assessments are going to be, and the central texts," said Coyle. "And then each lesson has targets, supporting targets, and the observations that are going to happen. There are a lot of supporting documents. They give an agenda, teaching notes, and things you need to do in advance, and then they give a suggested class opening.

"Last year," Coyle continued, "we got in touch with the lead writer from Expeditionary Learning (one of the companies responsible for the EngageNY modules) and hired her to come and talk to our K–5th grade teachers. She made it clear that they don't expect teachers to read the lessons word for word to the students or even to do everything in them. She described them as professional development for teachers. The lessons are everything the writers could think of that the teacher might want to do. She acknowledged that it could be completely overwhelming, but she made it clear to our teachers that they wanted to include as much as possible because this way of teaching is very new to a lot of teachers."

There are three units in every module. In each unit there are two assessments and a final performance task at the end of the third unit. "The assessment does not look like an assessment to kids," said Coyle. "It's not an 'everyone-put-away-your-books-and-do-this-test' evaluation. Some of it is paper and pencil, but it really is performance of understanding.

"For example," the master educator said, "it could be: write a script of what you think these two people would say in colonial times after you've learned that one of them is the candle-maker and the other is the farrier. What do you think they would say on the street, and what would they need from each other? So it's really a deep thinking sample of how the kids have processed all the things they've learned."

Some educators have criticized EngageNY modules for containing inappropriate content for a particular grade level or being hurriedly put together and released at the last minute. "We haven't found anything inappropriate or slapped together," said Coyle. "We have prefaced it to our teachers by saying we know the people who wrote this are looking for feedback, so I think our teachers were not expecting a perfectly polished piece.

"We have over 80 teachers who have been a part of this process of looking at the standards," Coyle said, "asking what they mean and how they fit together. There are protocols of what to do with kids that can be a lot to learn. So not only is it new content and new lessons, but a lot of it is new approaches too."

Coyle said the state could have improved the Common Core rollout by financially supporting district professional development efforts, allowing teachers to spend time working together to understand the standards and the modules, which, she said, is critical to teacher and student success. "I think it's a hard transition to all the standards," said the master educator, "and it's a hard transition to this deep interdisciplinary thinking, but we're going to come out with kids thinking a lot more deeply and empowered to be life-long thinkers."

Talcott had one final piece of advice for folks grappling with the headlines, the abysmal state testing results, and wondering why the state adopted Common Core in the first place. "Just read the standards," she suggested. "If there are specific ones you don't like, let's talk about why. Let's be critical thinkers about why and what we should do next."

When Will We Ever Learn: Dissecting the Common Core State Standards with Dr. Louisa Moats

By Mark Bertin, M.D.
The Huffington Post, January 22, 2014

Dr. Louisa Moats, the nationally-renowned teacher, psychologist, researcher and author, was one of the contributing writers of the Common Core State Standards (CCSS). The CCSS initiative is an attempt to deal with inconsistent academic expectations from state to state and an increasing number of inadequately prepared high school graduates by setting high, consistent standards for grades K–12 in English language arts and math. To date, 45 states have adopted the standards. I recently had the opportunity to discuss the implementation of the CCSS with Dr. Moats.

Dr. Bertin: *What was your involvement in the development of the Common Core state standards (CCSS)?*

Dr. Moats: Marilyn Adams and I were the team of writers, recruited in 2009 by David Coleman and Sue Pimentel, who drafted the Foundational Reading Skills section of the CCSS and closely reviewed the whole ELA section for K–5. We drafted sections on Language and Writing Foundations that were not incorporated into the document as originally drafted. I am the author of the Reading Foundational Skills section of Appendix A.

Dr. Bertin: *What did you see as potential benefits of establishing the CCSS when you first became involved?*

Dr. Moats: I saw the confusing inconsistencies among states' standards, the lowering of standards overall, and the poor results for our high school kids in international comparisons. I also believed that the solid consensus in reading intervention research could be reflected in standards and that we could use the CCSS to promote better instruction for kids at risk.

Dr. Bertin: *What has actually happened in its implementation?*

Dr. Moats: I never imagined when we were drafting standards in 2010 that major financial support would be funneled immediately into the development of standards-related tests. How naïve I was. The CCSS represent lofty aspirational goals for students aiming for four-year, highly selective colleges. Realistically, at least half, if not the majority, of students are not going to meet those standards as written, although the students deserve to be well prepared for career and work through meaningful and rigorous education.

Our lofty standards are appropriate for the most academically able, but what are we going to do for the huge numbers of kids that are going to "fail" the PARCC (Partnership for Assessment of Readiness for College and Careers) test? We need to create a wide range of educational choices and pathways to high school graduation, employment and citizenship. The Europeans got this right a long time ago.

If I could take all the money going to the testing companies and reinvest it, I'd focus on the teaching profession—recruitment, pay, work conditions, rigorous and ongoing training. Many of our teachers are not qualified or prepared to teach the standards we have written. It doesn't make sense to ask kids to achieve standards that their teachers have not achieved!

Dr. Bertin: *What differences might there be for younger students versus older students encountering it for the first time?*

Dr. Moats: What is good for older students (e.g., the emphasis on text complexity, comprehension of difficult text, written composition, use of Internet resources) is not necessarily good for younger students who need to acquire the basic skills of reading, writing, listening and speaking. Novice readers (typically through grade three) need a stronger emphasis on the foundational skills of reading, language, and writing than on the "higher level" academic activities that depend on those foundations, until they are fluent readers.

Our CCSS guidelines, conferences, publishers' materials and books have turned away from critical, research-based methodologies on how to develop the basic underlying skills of literacy. Systematic, cumulative skill development and code-emphasis instruction is getting short shrift all around, even though we have consensus reports from the 1920s onward that show it is more effective than comprehension-focused instruction.

I'm listening, but I don't hear the words "research based" as often as I did a decade ago—and when CCSS proponents use the words, they're usually referring to the research showing that high school kids who can't read complex text don't do as well in college. Basic findings of reading and literacy research, information about individual differences in reading and language ability, and explicit teaching procedures are really being lost in this shuffle.

Dr. Bertin: *What benefits have you seen or heard about so far as the CCSS has been put in place, and what difficulties?*

Dr. Moats: The standards may drive the adoption or use of more challenging and complex texts for kids to read and a wider sampling of genres. If handled right, there could be a resurgence of meaty curriculum of the "core knowledge" variety. There may be more emphasis on purposeful, teacher-directed writing. But we were making great inroads into beginning reading assessment and instruction practices between 2000–2008 that now are being cast aside in favor of "reading aloud from complex text"—which is not the same as teaching kids how to read on their own, accurately and fluently.

Dr. Bertin: *What has the impact been on classroom teachers?*

Dr. Moats: Classroom teachers are confused, lacking in training and skills to implement the standards, overstressed and the victims of misinformed directives from administrators who are not well grounded in reading research. I'm beginning to get messages from very frustrated educators who threw out what was working in favor of a new "CCSS aligned" program, and now find that they don't have the tools to teach kids how to read and write. Teachers are told to use "grade level" texts, for example; if half the kids are below grade level by definition, what does the teacher do? She has to decide whether to teach "the standard" or teach the kids.

Dr. Bertin: *You've raised concerns elsewhere that CCSS represents a compromise that does not emphasize educational research. How do the CCSS reflect, or fail to reflect, research in reading instruction?*

Dr. Moats: The standards obscure the critical causal relationships among components, chiefly the foundational skills and the higher level skills of comprehension that depend on fluent, accurate reading. Foundations should be first! The categories of the standards obscure the interdependence of decoding, spelling, and knowledge of language. The standards contain no explicit information about foundational writing skills, which are hidden in sections other than "writing" but which are critical for competence in composition.

The standards treat the foundational language, reading and writing skills as if they should take minimal time to teach and as if they are relatively easy to teach and to learn. They are not. The standards call for raising the difficulty of text, but many students cannot read at or above grade level and therefore may not receive enough practice at levels that will build their fluency gradually over time.

Dr. Bertin: *How about recommendations for writing?*

Dr. Moats: We need a foundational writing skills section in the CCSS, with a much more detailed progression. We should not be requiring third graders to compose on the computer. Writing in response to reading is a valuable activity, but teachers need a lot of assistance knowing what to assign, how to support writing and how to give corrective feedback that is constructive. Very few know how to teach kids to write a sentence, for example.

Dr. Bertin: *In an article for the International Dyslexia Association, you said "raising standards and expectations, without sufficient attention to known cause and remedies for reading and academic failure, and without a substantial influx of new resources to educate and support teachers, is not likely to benefit students with mild, moderate, or* *severe learning difficulties." You also mention that 34 percent of the population as a whole is behind academically in fourth grade, and in high poverty areas 70–80 percent of students are at risk for reading failure.*

How does the CCSS impact children who turn out to need additional academic supports for learning disabilities, ADHD or other educational concerns?

Dr. Moats: I have not yet seen a well-informed policy directive that addresses the needs of these populations. There are absurd directives about "universal design for learning" and endless accommodations, like reading a test aloud, to kids with learning disabilities. Why would we want to do that? The test itself is inappropriate for many kids.

Dr. Bertin: *How does it relate to concerns you have about teacher training in general?*

Dr. Moats: What little time there is for professional development is being taken up by poorly designed workshops on teaching comprehension of difficult text or getting kids to compose arguments and essays. This will not be good for the kids who need a systematic, explicit form of instruction to reach basic levels of academic competence.

I've been around a long time, and this feels like 1987 all over again, with different words attached to the same problems. When will we ever learn?

Common Core: A Puzzle to Public

By Lesli A. Maxwell
Education Week, August 28, 2013

In a pair of new national polls aiming to capture the American public's view of the state of K–12 education, one finding is clear: Most of those surveyed are clueless about the Common Core State Standards.

Sixty-two percent of all respondents in a poll from Phi Delta Kappa and Gallup had never heard of the Common Core, and awareness among public school parents was not much better, at 55 percent. In a separate survey from the Associated Press and the NORC Center for Public Affairs Research, which polled parents of K–12 students, 52 percent said they knew little or nothing about the Common Core, even though educators have begun putting the more rigorous standards in English/language arts and math into practice in classrooms in the vast majority of states and school districts.

But in trying to glean what the public and parents think about another marquee issue in public schooling—standardized testing—the polls paint a much murkier picture. Depending on how the question is worded, respondents are either fed up with testing, as found in the PDK/Gallup survey, or believe it's essential for knowing how well students are stacking up, as found in the AP survey.

"People's views are just much more complex than an answer to a single question," said Jean Johnson, a senior fellow at Public Agenda, a New York City-based opinion-research organization that studies a range of public policy issues including education. "Having these polls out together actually provides a lot of information, and in some ways, suggests issues that need some attention. Clearly, Common Core is one of those."

Skeptics Abound

In trying to better understand what those who had heard of the Common Core know and think about the standards—adopted in nearly every state—the surveys had somewhat similar results.

The PDK/Gallup survey found that just 41 percent of respondents who had heard of the standards believe they will make the United States more competitive in the world. Forty-seven percent of respondents in the Associated Press poll said they believe the standards will improve the quality of education.

Of those in the PDK/Gallup poll who had heard of the Common Core, many were confused by, or misunderstood, the standards and their genesis. At the same time, 95 percent of poll respondents said they think schools should teach critical-thinking skills, one of the main goals of the Common standards.

In a third, wide-ranging national poll also published last week, this one by the journal *Education Next*, 65 percent of respondents said they support to some degree states' adoption of the Common standards, up slightly from the journal's 2012 survey. But the new survey of 1,138 adults also found a near doubling of opposition to the standards' adoption from last year, with 13 percent now saying they were opposed.

"Whether you are a supporter or an opponent of the Common Core, you'll find things that support your point of view in all of these polls," said Michael Brickman, the director of national policy for the Thomas B. Fordham Institute, which is one of *Education Next*'s sponsoring institutions. "The standards will remain an unsettled issue until we start to see the actual widespread practice of using them and testing for them at the school and classroom level."

Turbulent Time

The PDK/Gallup poll—the 45th annual survey on public attitudes toward public schools from the professional educators' group and the giant polling organization—was conducted by telephone in May. The national survey of 1,001 respondents 18 and older has a margin of error of 3.8 percentage points.

The poll also found strong support for charter schools and opposition to tuition vouchers, broad confidence in the safety of schools, and mixed opinions on hiring armed guards for schools. (*Education Week* partners with Gallup on a separate survey project, known as the Gallup-*Education Week* Superintendents Panel.)

Such findings come at a particularly turbulent time in public education, as the new standards and the tests being designed to measure how well students are mastering them have become the latest focus of battles over the future direction of U.S. schooling.

Forty-six states and the District of Columbia have adopted the standards, which were developed through an initiative led by the Council of Chief State School Officers and the National Governors Association. (One of the 46, Minnesota, has adopted the English standards only.)

Almost as many states have signed on for the common tests being devised to replace their old assessments. Already, educators are warning that those tests—expected to be much harder—will cause student scores to drop initially.

Nearly 40 states are also working on redesigning teacher and principal evaluations to include student test scores.

Reacting to the low level of public awareness shown in the polling, Pedro Noguera, an education professor at New York University who favors the Common Core, said: "This underscores the real challenge we are likely going to see, which is major pushback from the public and parents because they don't fully understand what the standards are, and they are going to be very upset about their kids' lower scores on the new tests."

Deborah A. Gist, the commissioner of education in Rhode Island, said her biggest worry is the abundance of misinformation about the standards. Many of the

PDK/Gallup respondents who had heard of the Common Core said, erroneously, that the federal government had forced states to adopt the standards, that the standards would cover all academic-content areas, and that they were an amalgamation of existing state standards.

"That's what we particularly need to address," Ms. Gist said. "There is so much misinformation out there that it could be problematic for us to carry this through. I think these results are a message to us that we need to engage our families much more in this transition," she said.

Views on Testing

The PDK/Gallup findings on standardized testing—that fewer than one in four of those responding believe that more student testing has led to better public schools—stand in sharp contrast to the results in the Associated Press poll. But the questions posed in the two surveys were quite different.

The PDK/Gallup poll prefaced its question by saying there had been "a significant increase in testing," before asking those being surveyed whether they thought more testing had helped, hurt, or made no difference in the performance of public schools. Forty-one percent said that more testing had made no difference, 36 percent said it had hurt, and 22 percent said it had helped.

The AP survey—which polled 1,025 parents and guardians with children in grades K–12—posed a different question. It asked parents how important it is for schools to regularly assess students, and found that 74 percent said it was either extremely or very important to use tests to gauge how their children are doing.

In the same poll, 61 percent of parents said their own children are given about the right number of standardized tests; 26 percent said their children are overtested. Sixty percent also said students' scores on state tests should be included in teacher evaluations.

The *Education Next* poll, meanwhile, found that just about half of all respondents favored, to some extent, linking teachers' salaries in part to how well students perform on state tests.

The PDK/Gallup survey found that 58 percent of respondents oppose requiring that teacher evaluations include student scores from standardized tests. That's a big jump in negative opinion from last year, when 47 percent of PDK/Gallup respondents opposed using test scores in evaluations.

Terry Holliday, the commissioner of education in Kentucky, said that the PDK/Gallup poll's one-year change in the public's view in using scores in job evaluations is an important data point to weigh.

"For Kentucky, where we have been slow and deliberate about how we are doing our evaluations, this tells me that we need to be even more cautious," he said.

William J. Bushaw, the executive director of Phi Delta Kappa International and co-director of the poll, said the public and parents are likely being influenced by the teachers and principals in their local schools, for whom they have high regard.

"I think parents are listening to their children's teachers and are hearing their concerns about these new evaluation systems that are untested and deciding that maybe it's not fair," Mr. Bushaw said.

As has been true for decades, confidence in teachers who work in local schools is high. In the new PDK/Gallup survey, 70 percent of respondents said they have trust and confidence in those who teach in public schools, while 65 percent said the same of principals.

Range of Issues

Besides the Common Core, testing, and teacher and principal quality, the PDK/ Gallup survey delves into the public's views on school safety, school choice, home schooling, funding, and overall school quality.

Most public school parents surveyed—88 percent—said they do not worry about their children's physical safety at school. Eighty percent said they are more concerned about the actions of other students, rather than the threat of outside intruders in the school.

While 59 percent of respondents favor increasing mental-health services as the best approach to promoting school safety, 33 percent of those polled said hiring more security officers would be the most effective tactic. On the question of a need to hire armed security guards, especially in elementary schools, those polled were split, while a clear majority rejected the idea of arming teachers and administrators.

On school choice issues, respondents to the PDK/Gallup poll continued to hold charter schools in high regard, with 68 percent saying they support those independent public schools and 67 percent reporting they would support the opening of new charter schools in their communities. Fifty-two percent also said that they think students receive a better education at public charter schools than at traditional public schools.

But there was also a sharp rise in opposition to using public money to pay for private school expenses. Seventy percent said they oppose allowing families to attend a private school at public expense, compared with 55 percent last year.

Communication Dilemma

The major takeaway from this year's survey, said Mr. Bushaw of PDK, is that educators have their work cut out for them to mount an effective communications campaign about the common-core standards.

"The best ambassadors to tell the public about what is happening with the standards and the new assessments as well are teachers and principals," he said. "But I think because some of these same people have very real concerns about how the results will be used, that may be causing them to hold back."

Public Sounds Off on Common Core Standards

By Laura Leslie and Mark Binker
WRAL.com, March 20, 2014

Members of the public and representatives of think tanks, nonprofits and industry groups sounded off Thursday on North Carolina's adoption of Common Core standards, academic goals the state has adopted for its public school students.

The standards are not a curriculum. Rather, they lay out what students need to know and be able to do. School districts and classroom teachers still decide how that material is taught. Although the state Department of Public Instruction has adopted the standards, lawmakers are considering reining in their implementation, paying particular attention to costs associated with testing.

Nationally, the standards have become a point of political controversy. Although some high profile conservatives, such as former Florida Governor Jeb Bush, support Common Core, other conservative groups and lawmakers have questioned why the new standards are needed.

The standards were developed by state and nonprofit leaders, and they have been embraced by President Barack Obama's Education Department.

"First and foremost, it violates our U.S. Constitution," said Lynn Taylor, who identified herself as a private educator who has done research on Common Core standards.

Taylor expressed a common criticism of the standards, which is that they cede control of education to national and international groups.

"It replaces fact-based learning with feelings. . . . For every second we allow these standards to survive, we chip away at students' love of learning," she said.

Parents of schoolchildren, especially those in primary grades, said the Common Core standards are unreasonably demanding.

Johnston County mother Leslie Mills said she came to speak because she's worried about her children, especially her kindergartner, Elijah.

"I've looked in depth at the Common Core standards specifically for my children and they are just not developmentally appropriate at all," Mills said.

"Children and parents across our state are crying," said concerned mother Kellie Crump. "They are frustrated, they're anxious and they're giving up."

Backers of the standards say they ensure students can move from school district to school district and prepare themselves for college and careers.

Mooresville High English teacher Nancy Gardner says education must evolve with technology. She says students these days have facts at their fingertips. "But if they don't know how to critically look at what they're seeing on the Internet, think about what that means, problem solve, then learn to write about that, communicate that, we're not setting them up for success."

"Higher standards are crucial to achieving the most competent, competitive workforce in the region, the nation and the world," said Gary Salamido, vice president of government affairs at the North Carolina Chamber. "It is critical that we move forward with and build upon these higher standards."

Many business groups back the standards because they say it will equip students with better reasoning skills and the ability to work cooperatively. However, that backing from industry raises suspicions among some opponents.

Some critics suggested that Common Core is a government conspiracy involving the United Nations and the Gates Foundation, which helped to fund the initial development of the standards.

"This thing is about control," said Raynor James with the Coastal Carolina Taxpayers' Association, a Tea Party group. "...control of our children's education, control of their attitudes, control of our country at a later time."

"Common Core fits a corporate agenda to teach our children to be slaves of corporations," said Scot Rapp, who identified himself as a teacher, "and when the interest of corporations takes precedence, that's fascism."

Rapp said that Common Core language standards shifted away from well-known novels to graphic novels, instruction manuals and "government propaganda on sustainability, which we know is a lie."

Other critics suggested that the standards are immoral and negate parents' right to control what their children learn.

Ramona Timm with the Stokes County Tea Party said she covered illustrations in her daughter's health textbook because they would have offended lawmakers. Holding it up, she said, "If you could see this, you'd know this book from age 10 years old is pornographic."

Alan Hoyle, a self-described preacher, held up a Bible. "I am holding in my hand the textbook that has made America great," he said. Common Core "is pushing on our students sodomy, abortion, and feminism."

Other teachers said the standards were good and encountered problems due to a quick roll-out.

"The fast implementation has created some of the negative groundswell that you've heard," said Mark Jewell, vice president of North Carolina Association of Educators. "It's not the standards—it's the over-assessment and the time taken away from teaching."

Patrick Abele, an employee with Iredell-Statesville Schools and a parent, said Common Core helps students understand a subject beyond rote memorization.

"The standards help us go deeper with learning rather than skimming the surface of a topic or unit," Abele said. "The standards do not tell teachers how to teach.

They simply specify to teachers what knowledge and skills their students should have."

Those who spoke against the standards returned to common themes. One parent said Common Core would require students to read books that may be inappropriate for their age. Others decried that the standards de-emphasized memorization of facts, and many said the standards would translate into a "one-size-fits-all" curriculum, often citing the experience of their own children.

"Common Core standards also violate a fundamental principle of our constitution: federalism," said Bob Luebke, with the Civitas Institute.

States, not the federal government or a national nonprofit group, should determine standards for students, Luebke said.

"Common Core centralizes control of educational policy making," he said.

Teachers such as Karen Collie Dickerson, a Guilford County English teacher and 2013 Teacher of the Year, said Common Core allowed her to dive more deeply into topics with her students, even those who had previously struggled in language arts classes.

"They also promote what I like to call the new three Rs in education: rigor, readiness and relevance," Dickerson said. "This notion of increased rigor does not mean we are dumbing down."

Opponents often say the standards are eliminating material or reducing expectations, but Dickerson said the standards make sure all students understand a certain pool of common material, which they can then build upon.

"We are simply raising the floor or baseline for what they must achieve, so the ceiling can reach limitless heights," Dickerson said.

The New Smart Set

By Amanda Ripley
Time, September 30, 2013

What happens when millions of kids are asked to master fewer things more deeply?

Andrew Brennen had lived in five states before he could drive, making him an expert in everything that's wrong with American schooling. "In Georgia, I was definitely among the top students in my grade," he says. Then he moved to Maryland, and everything changed. "The level of content was definitely harder. I did not do very well." In Maryland, Brennen had to learn grammar that everyone else already seemed to know. He did so poorly in Spanish that he ended up repeating the class the next year.

In eighth grade, Brennen moved to Lexington, Ky., spinning the education roulette wheel one more time. When he got there, he did fine in science but lagged behind his friends in math. Brennen was basically the same wherever he went: a slim African-American boy with a wide smile and big plans. But "smart," he'd learned, was a relative term. This year, Brennen is a high school senior in Kentucky, applying to colleges in at least five different states—prepared to play catch-up yet again, wherever he may end up.

American education has always been run at the state and local level. Even as Washington has pushed states to try out this or that policy in exchange for federal funding, states have always chosen their own tests and learning goals. Historically this has meant that most states and districts have set the bar lower than colleges and many workplaces would like—or buried their teachers in so many competing demands that they are left to pick and choose what to teach in isolation.

All of that is about to end. This fall, for the first time, a majority of American public-school children are working to master the same set of more rigorous skills in math and English. These new targets, known as the Common Core State Standards, have been adopted by 46 states in an almost inexplicably speedy wave of reform. With only Alaska, Nebraska, Texas and Virginia abstaining, the Common Core movement represents the biggest shift in the content of American education in a century.

As such, hostilities have erupted on all sides. Tea Party groups refer to the standards as Obamacore, despite the fact that the federal government had nothing to do with their creation. The Republican National Committee condemned the standards in a resolution, calling them a "nationwide straitjacket." Under political pressure, lawmakers in a handful of states, including Indiana and Michigan, are debating whether to halt the rollout of the new standards.

Meanwhile, leftist critics have attacked the standards as "corporate" reforms, despite the fact that they were developed by teachers and researchers at the behest of a bipartisan group of governors and state education leaders. And some union leaders have called for more money and time to prepare teachers and students for tests associated with the new targets, most of which have yet to be completed.

One state bypassed all this tumult, however. It barreled headlong into the future three years ago and embraced the new targets before any other state, holding its children and teachers to a higher bar. That state, long renowned for its bourbon and racehorses, will not immediately come to mind as an educational powerhouse. But Kentucky is the undisputed leader in this historic American journey, and the parents, children and teachers who live there have much to tell the rest of us about what to expect next.

The Birth of the Core

In 1893, 10 men met in a secret session at Columbia University in New York City until midnight, debating what American high schools should teach. In the final report, the Committee of Ten concluded that students deserved a strong liberal arts education—in which "every subject [is] taught in the same way and to the same extent to every pupil so long as he pursues it, no matter what the probable destination of the pupil may be."

Ever since, generations have argued about whether these and subsequent standards are too hard or too easy for American kids and never reached a lasting consensus.

All the while, too many American students have found themselves unprepared for college or a decent job. One in five high school graduates who go to a four-year college (and half of those who go to community college) gets placed in remedial courses, stuck paying for college without getting college credit. In some states, like Hawaii, 38% of high school grads who try to enlist fail the Army's academic aptitude test; in Indiana, which has a higher child-poverty rate, only 13% fail, according to a 2010 report by the Education Trust. An American high school diploma means something radically different from state to state and from school to school, and many kids don't find out the real street value of their education until it's too late.

In 2009, hoping to disrupt this cycle of despair, the Kentucky state legislature passed a bill to throw out the state's standardized test and require higher education standards, benchmarked to international norms. "It was driven by Republicans from a conservative perspective—demanding higher standards for our kids," says Stu Silberman, executive director of the Prichard Committee for Academic Excellence, an influential education-reform organization in Kentucky.

At the same time, the National Governors Association, along with the Council of Chief State School Officers, was working on a similar blueprint. From the beginning, the Common Core standards were explicitly linked with what colleges and employers wanted young people to know. This way, students and their families could find out if they were off track much sooner—say in the third grade, when they still had time to do better, instead of in high school.

To design new standards for kindergarten through high school, a group of researchers collaborated with educators around the country. Experts in Massachusetts, which has long had among the most rigorous standards in the country, helped shape the literacy and math standards. Teachers in Georgia went to work on technical literacy, because the state had an exceptional track record in that field. Teachers from all over the country, meanwhile, pushed to keep the list of standards short and manageable.

The new standards were designed to be "fewer, clearer and higher," says David Coleman, co-founder of Student Achievement Partners, the nonprofit that helped develop the new standards, and they are precisely that, generally speaking. (You can read them at corestandards.org.) For example, on average, states used to require first-graders to learn 13 different math skills, according to veteran education researcher William Schmidt, which meant teachers did not have time to go into all of them in depth (and sometimes skipped some altogether). The Common Core requires that first-graders learn just eight skills. At the same time, the new standards are higher—more rigorous, according to a 2010 study by the Thomas B. Fordham Institute—than the existing state standards in 39 states and about the same as those in the remaining states.

They are also as high as any found in the top education systems in the world, from Finland to Japan. The ratcheting up of math expectations is vital, given that Americans rank 26th in the world on a math test given to representative samples of 15-year-olds in 70 countries (a far worse ranking than in reading). Even the country's richest teenagers perform 18th in the world in math compared with their privileged peers worldwide.

In English class, instead of writing about how a story made them feel, high school students will analyze whether an author's evidence and reasoning make the text more convincing. In addition to literature, they will also grapple with more nonfiction texts, since that is an area of weakness for American students compared with their international peers.

But writing lofty standards is much easier than making them work. To make the standards matter, teachers need time and high-quality training, two of the scarcest resources in American schools.

How Kentucky Responded

In August 2010, Kentucky schools rolled out the Common Core standards in math and English. "It was pretty much a nightmare," says Peggy Preston, a veteran math teacher in Louisville. Overnight, the Pythagorean theorem went from a 10th-grade lesson to an eighth-grade lesson. Instead of just identifying the first-person point of view, middle-school students suddenly had to be able to explain why an author chose to use it and how that decision influenced the text. "We were overwhelmed and frustrated," says Kate Grindon, an English teacher at Meyzeek Middle School.

Many teachers were also afraid the new standards were too high. "There were a lot of people in the room who said, 'Our kids can't do this.'"

What happened next depended in large part on the principal and superintendent of a given school. In the places with the strongest leaders, teachers got time to study and discuss the new standards with one another, brainstorming how they could reinvent their lessons for the higher expectations. Kentucky's education commissioner, Terry Holliday, enlisted teachers to help at every step in the process, explaining the new standards to parents and designing test questions—a model he advises other state chiefs to follow. "Teachers are your best voice in the community," Holliday says.

The following spring, the students took the first set of tests synched to the new standards. Everyone knew it would be a humbling exercise: if you raise the bar, fewer will reach it—at least for a while. So state officials warned parents, teachers, students and the media to expect lower scores and interpret them as a sign of progress rather than failure. Every teacher had flyers to give out at parent-teacher conferences explaining that the new test was different from the old one. The Jefferson County PTA held briefings to explain the Common Core to some 8,000 people across Louisville.

When the new results came out, only half of Kentucky elementary students were found to be proficient or better in reading—compared with three-quarters of kids the year before under the old standards. But citing the public outreach, Holliday says, "We had zero complaints from parents."

This school year, their third with the new targets, some Kentucky teachers seem to be thriving with the infusion of clarity, focus and autonomy they attribute to the Common Core standards. Many post specific targets on the classroom wall for all the students to see, rotating each one out every few weeks. De'Vonta Moffitt, a student at Doss High School in Louisville, explains the difference between his freshman and senior year this way: "Before, we read and then worked, read and then worked. It was easy. Basically they gave us tests from the book," he says. "Now, every three weeks we have to know a different standard. I have to actually take notes. I have to think sometimes, take my time."

Even standardized tests can be less grueling when tied to more intelligent goals. Each spring, Sydnea Johnson, a student at Fern Creek Traditional High School in Louisville, used to get migraines from all the cramming teachers asked her to do before the test—trying to cover more standards less deeply. "Now it's a lot less stressful," Johnson says, "because I can take in the information all year long, and it's just a review before the test."

This past spring, Kentucky achieved an 86% high school graduation rate—up from 80% in 2010 and above that of most other states. Test scores for the last school year, only the second with the new Common Core test, show a slight uptick of 2 percentage points. The portion of students considered college- or career-ready is up 20 percentage points to 54% since 2010, according to a battery of assessments given to seniors.

The Backlash

It's only in the past couple of months that Holliday has started to hear local opposition to the Common Core. Kentucky Senator Rand Paul, gearing up for a presidential run, has come out against the new standards, citing a "loss of local control of curriculum and instruction." One Kentucky education leader said he has stopped using the words Common Core altogether. "We call them Kentucky Core Standards or something," he said, searching for the proper euphemism. "We are even trying not to use 'rigorous.' We are trying to say, 'college- and career-ready standards.'"

If the word *rigorous* is politically incorrect in America, the Common Core is way ahead of its time. The destiny of the new standards may depend on competing bogeymen. Which is scarier, international competition for skilled workers or the loss of some local authority?

Historically, the answer isn't encouraging. Some states may step back from the standards altogether, while others will likely do what they did under No Child Left Behind and select dumbed-down tests that do not require kids to think for themselves. A few states will stand firm, continuing to work on smarter tests and better teacher training. I suspect Kentucky may be one of them.

Earlier this year, a coalition of 26 states proposed new standards—for science this time. Like those for math and reading, these new targets allow teachers to go deeper on fewer topics and focus on applying knowledge to solve real-world problems. Already the standards on climate change and evolution have unleashed a backlash, which will likely grow.

So far, just six states have adopted the standards: California, Kansas, Maryland, Rhode Island, Vermont—and Kentucky.

The Beginning of Common Core's Trouble

By Jamie Gass and Jim Stergios
The Weekly Standard, May 29, 2013

When President Obama unveiled his Race to the Top initiative in 2009, the idea was to award $4.35 billion in federal grant money to states to replicate policies that boosted student achievement. That quickly changed and the federal money was instead used to persuade states to adopt administration-backed nationalized K–12 English and math standards and tests. By last year, most states had adopted the standards, known as Common Core, and it seemed a foregone conclusion that the United States would join countries like France in having a uniform curriculum.

But what a difference a year makes. Today, a full-blown epidemic of buyer's remorse has taken hold. Popular resistance is rampant and bills to pull out of Common Core are making their way through multiple state legislatures.

Had the Obama administration been interested in policies with a proven record of improving students' academic performance, it would have looked to Massachusetts. In the early 1990s, Massachusetts was an above average but unremarkable performer on the National Assessment of Educational Progress (NAEP) and SATs. After enactment of the Bay State's landmark 1993 education reform law, SAT scores rose for 13 consecutive years. In 2005, Massachusetts became the first state ever to score best in the nation in all four categories on the NAEP's fourth and eighth grade reading and math assessments. The next three times the tests were administered—in 2007, 2009, and 2010—this feat was repeated.

While American students as a whole lag their international peers, the 2007 "Trends in International Math and Science Study" showed Massachusetts students to be competitive with top-performing nations like Japan, Korea, and Singapore. With the Bay State's eighth graders tying for first in the world in science, it could truly be said to be one of the few states to have answered the alarm bell of the Reagan administration's 1983 "A Nation at Risk" report, which declared that, "the educational foundations of our society are presently being eroded by a rising tide of mediocrity that threatens our very future."

Other states, such as Florida, claim to have developed reform models that work. But while they have shown good (though inconsistent) improvement, their performance remains below average on national tests and downright dismal on international assessments.

Given this record, you might expect strong commonality between what Massachusetts did and what the U.S. Department of Education was trying to advance.

But it would be hard to imagine an approach that has less in common with the Bay State's than the one promoted by Race to the Top.

The most obvious difference is that Massachusetts's success was built upon a relentless focus on academics, specifically on literacy, math, and the liberal arts. Common Core emphasizes experiential, skills-based learning while reducing the amount of classic literature, poetry, and drama taught in English classes. Its more vocational bent includes far greater emphasis on jargon-laden "informational text" extracts, and it supports analyzing texts shorn of historical context and background knowledge.

The impact on English classrooms in Massachusetts, which adopted Common Core in 2010, has been to reduce the amount of classical literature studied by more than half. Goodbye Charles Dickens, Edith Wharton, Arthur Conan Doyle, and Mark Twain's *Huckleberry Finn*.

In math, consider the view of Stanford University emeritus professor of mathematics James Milgram, the only academic mathematician on Common Core's validation committee. (He refused to sign off on the final draft of the national standards.) He describes the standards as having "extremely serious failings," reflecting "very low expectations," and ultimately leaving American students one year behind their international peers by fifth grade and two years behind by seventh grade.

One major practical effect is that American students will not get to algebra I in eighth grade, which is critical if our students are to be college-ready in mathematics.

Rather than learn from leading states like Massachusetts, Common Core draws from the so-called "21st century skills" movement, which elevates soft skills like global awareness, media literacy, cross-cultural flexibility and adaptability, and creativity to equal footing with academic content. This less academic approach has, in fact, been road tested in places like Connecticut and West Virginia. Predictably, the results have been dismal.

Back in 1998, Connecticut had higher reading scores than Massachusetts. But just as the Bay State was adopting clearly articulated academic goals, Connecticut opted for a "hands-on," skills-based approach. By 2005, Massachusetts's scores had jumped dramatically, and Connecticut was one of seven states experiencing outsized drops in reading scores.

West Virginia's was perhaps the most enthusiastic embrace of 21st century skills. As Matthew Ladner, a research scholar at the Foundation for Excellence in Education, has demonstrated, its impact on poor students is deeply troubling. West Virginia is the only state whose NAEP reading and math scores for students eligible for free or reduced-price lunch fell between 2003 and 2009. The major D.C.-based drivers of Common Core and national tests like the Council of Chief State School Officers, the National Governors Association, Achieve, Inc., and the Obama administration all enthusiastically support 21st century skills.

Common Core's problems, however, extend beyond academic deficiencies. No estimate was ever performed to determine what it would cost to implement the new standards. In 2011, Pioneer Institute commissioned the first independent, comprehensive cost study, which showed that transitioning states to the new standards will be $16.7 billion, more than triple the amount of the federal Race to the Top inducements. Massive technology upgrades, training and support, together with the purchase of new textbooks and instructional materials, and professional development account for most of the expense.

Most disturbing are serious questions about Common Core's legality. Three federal laws explicitly prohibit the U.S. Department of Education from directing, supervising, or controlling any nationalized standards, testing, or curriculum.

And yet Race to the Top favored a state's grant application if it adopted Common Core. The U.S. Department of Education subsequently awarded $362 million to directly fund two national testing consortia to develop common nationalized assessments. The consortia funding application clearly state that they will use federal funds to develop curriculum materials and to create a "model curriculum" and instructional materials "aligned with" Common Core. Secretary of Education Arne Duncan himself noted that the consortia would develop "curriculum frameworks" and "instructional modules."

The Department of Education then made adopting Common Core a condition for waivers from the No Child Left Behind Act's accountability provisions, even though the national standards have never been approved by Congress and are, in fact, expressly prohibited by the 1965 Elementary and Secondary Education Act (ESEA), which defined the federal government's role in K–12 education, the 1970 General Education Provisions Act, and the 1979 law establishing the U.S. Department of Education.

It is worth reminding our friends who call it a conservative policy that Common Core would have been a bridge too far even for President Johnson, who signed the ESEA, and President Carter, who signed the law creating the federal Department of Education. As syndicated columnist George Will wrote last year about the push for Common Core, "Here again laws are cobwebs. As government becomes bigger, it becomes more lawless."

The problems with what is now federal policy are not lost on state and local leaders. In just the past few weeks, Indiana lawmakers agreed to pause implementation of Common Core. Ditto in Pennsylvania. Michigan's House of Representatives voted to defund the effort. And the national standards are under fire in Alabama, Florida, Georgia, Ohio, Missouri, Oklahoma, and Utah.

Nationally, the Republican National Committee recently adopted an anti-Common Core resolution, but opposition is bipartisan. Many Democrats are troubled that Common Core is not based on research and ignores too much of what we know about how students learn. American Federation of Teachers president Randi Weingarten recently told the *Washington Post*, "Common Core is in trouble. . . . There is a serious backlash in lots of different ways, on the right and on the left."

The backlash is richly deserved. The Common Core standards are academically inferior to the standards they replaced in high performing states; and they ignore empirical lessons of how states like Massachusetts achieved historic successes. Neither local leaders nor their constituents like having policies force fed by Washington, especially when the new requirements amount to a massive, and possibly illegal, unfunded mandate. Common Core's troubles are just beginning.

Many Teachers Not Ready for the Common Core

By Stephen Sawchuk
Education Week, April 25, 2012

To ensure that students master the new standards, educators will have to change the way they teach.

A quiet, sub-rosa fear is brewing among supporters of the Common Core State Standards Initiative: that the standards will die the slow death of poor implementation in K–12 classrooms.

"I predict the Common-Core standards will fail, unless we can do massive professional development for teachers," said Hung-Hsi Wu, a professor emeritus of mathematics at the University of California, Berkeley, who has written extensively about the Common-Core math standards. "There's no fast track to this."

It's a Herculean task, given the size of the public school teaching force and the difficulty educators face in creating the sustained, intensive training that research indicates is necessary to change teachers' practices.

"It is a capacity-building process, without question," said Jim Rollins, the superintendent of the Springdale, Ark., school district. "We're not at square one, but we're not at the end of the path, either. And we don't want to just bring superficial understanding of these standards, but to deepen the understanding, so we have an opportunity to deliver instruction in a way we haven't before."

In Springdale, which is fully implementing the literacy and math standards for grades K–2 this year, kindergartners in the 20,000-student district are studying fairy tales and learning about those stories' countries of origin. Their teachers have scrambled to find nonfiction texts that introduce students to the scientific method. They've discarded some of their old teaching practices, like focusing on the calendar to build initial numeracy skills.

The Durand, Mich., district is another early adopter. Gretchen Highfield, a third grade teacher, has knit together core aspects of the standards—less rote learning, more vocabulary-building—to create an experience that continually builds pupils' knowledge. A story on pigs becomes an opportunity, later in the day, to introduce the vocabulary word "corral," which becomes an opportunity, still later in the day, for students to work on a math problem involving four corrals of five pigs.

"I'm always thinking about how what we talked about in social studies can be emphasized in reading," Ms. Highfield said. "And it's like that throughout the week. I'm looking across the board where I can tie in this, and this, and this."

Such pioneers of the standards can probably be found the country over. But data show that there is still much more work to be done, especially in those districts that have yet to tackle the professional-development challenge. A nationally representative survey of school districts issued last fall by the Washington-based Center on Education Policy found that fewer than half of districts had planned professional development aligned to the standards this school year.

Cognitive Demand

By any accounting, the challenge of getting the nation's 3.2 million K–12 public school teachers ready to teach to the standards is enormous.

With new assessments aligned to the standards rapidly coming online by 2014–15, the implementation timeline is compressed. Teachers are wrestling with an absence of truly aligned curricula and lessons. Added to those factors are concerns that the standards are pitched at a level that may require teachers themselves to function on a higher cognitive plane.

When standards are more challenging for the students, "then you also raise the possibility that the content is more challenging for the teacher," said Daniel T. Willingham, a professor of psychology at the University of Virginia, in Charlottesville. "Of course, it's going to interact with what support teachers receive."

Anecdotal evidence from a Bill & Melinda Gates Foundation study suggests that teachers already struggle to help students engage in the higher-order, cognitively demanding tasks emphasized by the standards, such as the ability to synthesize, analyze, and apply information. (The Gates Foundation also provides support for coverage of K–12 business and innovation in *Education Week*.)

As part of the foundation's Measures of Effective Teaching project, trained observers scored lessons taught by some 3,000 teachers against a variety of teaching frameworks. No matter which framework was used, teachers received relatively low scores on their ability to engage students in "analysis and problem-solving," to use "investigation/problem-based approaches," to create "relevance to history, current events," or to foster "student participation in making meaning and reasoning," according to a report from the foundation.

Supporters of the common standards say the standards encourage a focus on only the most important topics at each grade level and subject, thus allowing teachers to build those skills.

"It could make things simpler and allow teachers and schools to focus on teaching fewer, coherent things very well. That's the best hope for teachers to build in-depth content knowledge," said David Coleman, one of the writers of the English/language arts standards and a founder of the New York City-based Student Achievement Partners, a nonprofit working to support implementation of the standards.

"That said, the standards are necessary but not sufficient for improving professional development," he added.

Each of the two content areas in the standards poses a unique set of challenges for teacher training.

Mr. Wu, the UC-Berkeley professor, contends that current math teachers and curricula focus almost exclusively on procedures and algorithms, an approach he refers to as "textbook mathematics."

But the Common Core emphasizes understanding of the logical, structural concepts underpinning mathematics—the idea being that understanding how and why algorithms work is as important as crunching numbers.

Many teachers, Mr. Wu contends, will themselves need more mathematics-content preparation. But training focused at least initially on content could be especially difficult for classroom veterans to accept, he concedes.

"After 26 years of doing things only one way, the Common Core comes along and says, 'Let's try to do a little bit better at this,'" Mr. Wu said. "Well, suppose you've been smoking for that long, and someone says, 'Just stop raising a cigarette to your mouth.' It's difficult—it's 26 years of habit."

Some teacher educators believe that conversation will need to begin at the preservice level, especially for elementary teachers, who tend to enter with a weaker initial grasp of mathematics, said Jonathan N. Thomas, an assistant professor of mathematics education at Northern Kentucky University, in Highland Heights, Ky.

"It's a great opportunity to say, 'Let's just take some time to think about the mathematics and set the teaching strategies aside for a moment,'" Mr. Thomas said. "It's imperative we don't send people out the door with just strategies, tips, and tricks to teach fractions. We have to make sure they understand fractions deeply."

Teacher Gaps

Meanwhile, the English/language arts standards demand a focus on the "close reading" of texts, a literary-analysis skill that has been thus far mainly reserved for college English classes. And they call for expansion of nonfiction materials into even the earliest grades.

"We haven't worked deeply or strategically with informational text, and as the teachers are learning about the standards, they are finding their own instructional gaps there," said Sydnee Dixon, the director of teaching and learning for Utah's state office of education. "That's a huge area for us."

In the Springdale, Ark., district, instructional coach Kaci L. Phipps said those changes are also requiring teachers to pay more attention to teaching the varied purposes behind writing—something not as emphasized when most reading materials are fictional and students are asked merely for their responses.

"We keep having to say to these kids, 'Remember, it's not what you think, it's what's in the text,'" she said. "'What is the author doing? What is his or her purpose in writing? How can you support that conclusion with details from the text?'"

Pedagogical Shifts

Pedagogical challenges lurk, too, because teachers need updated skills to teach in ways that emphasize the standards' focus on problem-solving, according to professional-development scholars.

"Teachers will teach as they were taught, and if they are going to incorporate these ideas in their teaching, they need to experience them as students," said Thomas R. Guskey, a professor of educational psychology at the University of Kentucky's college of education, in Lexington. "The PD will have to model very clearly the kinds of activities we want teachers to carry forward and use in their classrooms."

Moreover, Mr. Guskey warned, many teachers won't be inclined to actually change what they are doing until they become familiar with the assessments aligned to the new standards.

Some districts don't want to wait that long, and have found other ways to help teachers begin working with the practices outlined in the standards. In the 1,700-student Durand district, Superintendent Cindy Weber has used a state-required overhaul of teacher evaluations as a springboard.

The Michigan district's new professional growth and evaluation system, which is being implemented this spring, draws key indicators of teacher practice directly from the Common Core—in essence closing the often-wide gap between expectations for student and teachers.

Principals observing teachers are trained to look, for example, at whether a teacher "uses multiple sources of information" when teaching new content, and "challenges students to present and defend ideas" in the strand on applying learning.

To gauge changes in student growth across the year, as part of the new evaluation system, the district has settled on growth in academic vocabulary as an indicator. In every grade and content area, teams of teachers have come up with those words and related concepts all students must master by the end of the year.

Ms. Weber's reasoning is that teachers will feel new standards really matter if instructing to them is part of their professional expectations.

"You look back over the course of education, and there are so many things tried, yet somehow many classrooms still look the same across the country," Ms. Weber said. "I felt that with our evaluation process, we needed to look at teacher commitment to this model and type of delivery—or teachers may give us lip service and go back to doing what they've done in the past."

State Role

States, the first stop on the professional-development train, are themselves having to change their delivery systems in preparation for the standards.

"Many states are moving away from the 'train the trainer' model and trying to have more direct communications with teachers, because the message either gets diluted or changed otherwise," said Carrie Heath Phillips, the program director for the Council of Chief State School Officers' common-standards efforts.

Delaware has reached every teacher in the state directly through online lessons that lay out the core shifts in the standards from the state's previous content expectations—a process it tracked through its education data system.

Now, state officials are hard at work building an infrastructure for deeper, more intensive work.

The state has organized two separate "cadres" of specialists, one in reading and one in math, who are fleshing out the core expectations at each grade level, outlining how each standard is "vertically linked" to what will be taught in the next grade, and crafting model lessons in those subjects. They're also each constructing five professional-development "modules" for high-demand topics, such as text complexity.

"We've had other standards, but different interpretations of what they meant," said Marian Wolak, the director of curriculum, instruction, and professional development for the state. "We want this to be very clear and distinct about how the standard applies at that grade level and what the expectations are for that standard."

Based on the cadres' work, every district will have a clearinghouse of resources for professional development and be able to tap a local specialist for additional training, Ms. Wolak said.

Utah doesn't have the benefits of Delaware's limited geography. Its strategy has been building the capacity of a critical mass of trained educators in each district, and then gradually shifting professional-development responsibilities to the local level.

In summer 2011, the state trained about 120 facilitators—teachers nominated from the field with a track record of high student achievement in their subject—in pedagogical content knowledge and adult-learning theory. Then, those teachers facilitated "academies" in ELA and in 6th and 9th grade math for their colleagues, which were given at 14 locations in the state, according to Ms. Dixon, the state's director of teaching and learning.

All teachers attending the sessions come voluntarily and are expected to have read the standards beforehand. Afterwards, "the expectation is that both the facilitators and the attendees are back in their classrooms, using the standards, working with the standards, sharing student work, and studying it in [staff meetings], so their colleagues are getting second-hand experience," Ms. Dixon said.

Additional academies are now being set up; the state estimates about 20 percent of its teachers have attended one so far.

District Pioneers

For districts, the professional-development challenge is in finding the place to begin. Those districts apparently the furthest along in the process are integrating the training with successful efforts already in place.

In Springdale, the district has focused on providing teachers with enough time to sort through the standards and observe some of them in practice. It's given teachers up to four days off to develop units aligned to the Common Core and encouraged teams to discuss student work samples, or "anchors," to help inform their understanding of expectations aligned to the standards.

This year, the district is working to train teachers in grades 3–8 in math. It has spent five years using a problem-solving approach to mathematics known as Cognitively Guided Instruction that district officials say aligns well with the common standards' math expectations. With a handful of teachers now well-versed in the curriculum, it's creating opportunities for teachers new to the district to observe those "demonstration classrooms" at work.

The Durand district's new teacher-evaluation system has helped to make the common standards real, said Ms. Highfield. And while teachers are understandably a bit nervous about the system, it's also causing them to rethink long-standing practices.

"How do I show [an evaluator] that students are thinking and analyzing without a project or experiment? It's a big challenge, and I think it will take a little time to get there," she said. "Before, with the rote learning, you could create a handout, put it in your file and just use it again next year. You can't do that when you're looking at students to apply these skills."

Nevertheless, Ms. Highfield said, she's starting to see the benefits for her students.

"Durand is a fairly poor district; a lot of students don't have a lot of experiences," she said. "We ask them, 'What do you want to do in your life, with your learning? Can you imagine it? How would you get there?'

"I've seen a change in my students, and I think that is a good thing."

The Dangers & Opportunities of the Common Core

By Jacqueline Grennon Brooks and Mary E. Dietz
Educational Leadership, December 2012/January 2013

Can public education emerge from the Common Core initiative with a renewed focus on student learning?

In the early 1980s, the two of us were young teachers in a school district led by a distinguished superintendent, Richard Doremus. After visiting many exemplary schools and programs, Dr. Doremus compiled his observations into a monograph that he titled "The Yellow School Bus." The yellow school bus, he said, reminded him of education's Common Core mission—to light up children's worlds with opportunities for learning. Emerging from fog on mountain roads, turning street corners in busy cities, or rolling along endless stretches of open prairie, the yellow school bus was a consistent symbol of schooling that united diverse education systems across the United States. That diversity of systems and structures, unified by a common mission, was good.

Dr. Doremus did not believe in a standardized curriculum. His idea of a good curriculum was to hire the most intelligent, spirited teachers you can find and then support them in their quests to build strong classrooms centered on studying what students care about. Some present-day classroom examples illustrate what he meant.

At Chadwick School in Palos Verdes, California, teacher Cris Lozon's kindergartners found a hole in the ground during recess one day that intrigued them. "Teacher, please come here," a student said. "There's a deep hole in the ground, and we don't know what it is! It wasn't there yesterday, but it's there now" (Lozon, 2012, p. 2). Earlier in the year, the students had experienced holes in the ground, as places in which they planted seeds. Now, as they speculated about what caused the hole, how deep it was, and whether it could be the entrance to an underground cave like those they had discussed in class, this simple hole became a place to select tools for measurement, hypothesize about causes, and collaborate on problem solving.

At a summer program at the Long Island Eastern Enrichment School in New York, middle school teacher Lyndsay McCabe led her students in a lively discussion of book banning. The inquiry began because Ms. McCabe had recommended Suzanne Collins's *The Hunger Games* (Scholastic, 2008), a book the students said they were not allowed to read at their home schools. In talking about the reasons books are often banned, Ms. McCabe reported, "The students assumed that banned books would have 'bad words' and violence; they were surprised that books that dealt with racism were sometimes banned, since they saw racism as a real part of history that was not to be covered up" (personal communication, July 2012). They were also surprised that censorship for racial content was more frequent in the North; they had assumed that this would be a more sensitive issue in the South. Students later consulted the librarian and multiple sources and pored over maps and statistics to find data that would answer their questions and confirm or refute patterns they had observed.

These teachers were certainly addressing rigorous curriculum standards for higher-order thinking and 21st century learning. But do such efforts fit into the standardized model that is in danger of becoming more common across the United States today?

So much has changed in the last 30 years. Diversity is on the verge of extinction—diversity of curriculum, instructional practices, and assessment. We are moving into an era that will link Common Core standards with a Common Core curriculum taught by teachers who will assess student learning through a slate of Common Core exams and be evaluated with a common rubric that uses scores on these exams as measures of teacher quality.

Some think this is progress. We don't. We think it deflects energy away from opportunities for building a collegial professional culture aimed at real teaching and learning. We think education is facing a crisis. The question is, Can we emerge from this crisis with a renewed focus on real teaching and learning and a wholesale rejection of standardization?

The Homepage of Real Learning

The Common Core standards themselves aren't the problem. In fact, the standards are aligned with the kind of constructivist teaching and learning observed in the classrooms of Cris Lozon and Lyndsay McCabe.

But the Common Core State Standards Initiative goes far beyond the content of the standards themselves. The initiative conflates standards with standardization. For instance, many states are mandating that school districts select standardized student outcome measures and teacher evaluation systems from a pre-established state list. To maximize the likelihood of student success on standardized measures, many districts are requiring teachers to use curriculum materials produced by the same companies that are producing the testing instruments, even predetermining the books students will read on the basis of the list of sample texts that illustrate the standard. The initiative compartmentalizes thinking, privileges profit-making companies, narrows the creativity and professionalism of teachers, and limits meaningful student learning.

The homepage of the Common Core State Standards Initiative (www.corestandards. org) declares the standards to be "robust" and "relevant to the real world." In our view, robust and relevant learning is determined by what occurs in classrooms among teachers and students, not by standardized curriculum content mandated from above. The homepage of learning isn't on the Common Core State Standards Initiative website—it is in the minds of individual students, supported by their teachers.

Good teachers set up classrooms rich in opportunities for students to construct integrated knowledge transferable across disciplines. They offer interdisciplinary, authentic investigations that provoke students to confront cognitive challenges in the pursuit of answers to their own questions. They invite students to think about ideas that matter to them and to resolve potential contradictions, and they help students develop the skills and dispositions to think about those ideas at increasingly deep levels.

This kind of classroom activity is tough intellectual work for both teachers and students. It's demanding —and it's energizing. The payoff is that it enables students to take ownership of their knowledge (Brooks, 2002, 2011; Brooks & Brooks, 1999).

Is the Common Core State Standards Initiative likely to promote this kind of teaching and learning? If experience is any guide, the answer is no. Martin Haberman (1991), in his hallmark study of the "pedagogy of poverty," identifies the prominent instructional practices observed in most high-poverty environments as one-way communication with rote memory activities. Under such a regime, students come to understand school as a place to obey, to repeat what the teacher tells them, and to seek high scores on tests. They do not experience the opportunity to build their repertoire for investigating, inquiring, and refining their understandings of literature, civics, scientific theories, or mathematical reasoning.

In an update of his study, Haberman (2010) found that the instructional methods that he decried in 1991 have not only become standard during the No Child Left Behind era, but have come to be regarded as best instructional practice. Particularly in high-poverty environments, our schools are narrowing, if not entirely eliminating, opportunities for students to develop the skills and dispositions associated with 21st century learning. Curiosity, exploration, perseverance, critical and creative thinking, and complex problem solving are being pushed aside and replaced with test preparation curriculums. The increased standardization promoted by the Common Core State Standards Initiative threatens to bring in more of the same.

The initiative is at least as likely to perpetuate the continuation of bad teaching as to increase good teaching. Excellent teachers, as they always have, will undoubtedly continue to engage in the practices that the Common Core standards endorse: balancing informational and narrative texts, helping students build knowledge within the disciplines, scaffolding complexity of text material, fostering rigorous conversations connected to the content, nurturing students' abilities to offer evidence in crafting an argument, and building academic vocabulary. But less-skilled administrators and teachers who interpreted the "old" state standards as directives and followed those directives with little thought will likely do the same thing with the "new" standards.

Real Learning, Committed Culture

Standards are not new, and they are not bad. They are old, and they are good. It is the Common Core State Standards *Initiative* that is miscast as the epicenter of education reform.

Meaningful education reform is not something you can mandate, standardize, or easily measure. It requires a collegial culture in which teachers are continually advancing their practice and making adjustments on the basis of their students' current levels of understanding, readiness, and responses to inquiry-based instruction. This is what good teachers have always known—and what good leaders encourage through shared leadership and shared accountability for student learning.

Reaching agreement on what constitutes effective instruction and what it looks like at the classroom, grade, school, and district levels is not easy. Educators may find themselves at odds with one another and those in authority when they honestly discuss issues such as, Is there a difference between achievement and learning? Can we invite students into self-directed inquiry without jeopardizing test scores? What is the relationship between teacher effectiveness and student test scores? These are the "fierce" and "truthful" conversations (Aguilar, 2011; Scott, 2002) that must occur to generate meaningful progress toward improved student learning.

The Common Core State Standards can play a helpful role in these conversations, as teachers and administrators analyze and apply them to their unique sets of needs (Dietz, 2008). An analysis of how these standards correspond to the current curriculum and instructional practices can be an important dimension of the change process, keeping in mind that the focus is on understanding the current level of readiness among students and on selecting and designing activities that invite curiosity, interest, and engagement (Lambert, 2008).

When we integrate new and compatible instructional practices into present repertoires or eject nonworking instructional practices and replace them with new ones, we are engaging in professional learning. Leadership teams must establish structures for professional learning that foster progress toward ever more effective teaching practices emerging from understandings of learning processes. Some examples of such structures include

- *Professional learning walks*, in which groups of educators move together through the school, taking individual notes in search of broad patterns related to deep questions about curriculum and instructional practices.

- *Tuning protocols*, through which everyone has a voice in the discussion and contributes in a structured way.

- *Lesson studies*, in which teachers come together to plan a research lesson that will be observed and analyzed by a small group of educators and reported on to the larger faculty, so all can benefit (Killion & Hirsh, 2011).

Teachers are the key players in this process, and their voices must be involved so it's not done *to* them, but *with* them.

Not from Above, but from Within

As management consultant Meg Wheatley (2009) wrote, "Change doesn't happen from a leader announcing the plan" (p. 25). Our education system can no longer tolerate the tyranny of unfocused, misguided, or reactionary leadership imposed through those outside the profession and promoted by government regulations, funding, and expectations. As education leaders, we need to self-organize and reorganize while listening to and learning from one another.

The Common Core State Standards Initiative is not the solution for what ails education; standardization can never be the solution. In place of the current initiative, we propose using the common standards to support cultures within schools that put teacher professionalism and student learning at the center. The standards themselves can enhance professional conversations about teaching and learning. The power and efficacy of the programs that schools offer students derive from the knowledge constructed in such conversations, and are built on trusting relationships that revolve around the core mission of schooling: to light up children's worlds with opportunities for learning.

Bibliography

Aguilar, E. (2011, April 6). Educational change starts with listening [blog post]. Retrieved from *Teacher Leadership* at www.edutopia.org/blog/educational-leadership-change-listening-elena-aguilar

Brooks, J. G. (2002). *Schooling for life: Reclaiming the essence of learning*. Alexandria, VA: ASCD.

Brooks, J. G. (2011). *Big science for growing minds: Constructivist classrooms for young thinkers*. New York: Teachers College Press.

Brooks, J. G., & Brooks, M. G. (1999). *In search of understanding: The case for constructivist classrooms*. Alexandria, VA: ASCD.

Dietz, M. E. (2008). *Journals as frameworks for professional learning communities* (2nd ed.). Thousand Oaks, CA: Corwin.

Haberman, M. (1991). Pedagogy of poverty versus good teaching. *Phi Delta Kappan*, 73(4), 290-294.

Haberman, M. (2010). 11 consequences of failing to address the "pedagogy of poverty." *Phi Delta Kappan*, 92(2), 81-87.

Killion, J., & Hirsh, S. (2011). Elements of effective teaching, *Journal of Staff Development*, 32(6), 10-12, 14, 16.

Lambert, L. (2008). *The constructivist leader* (2nd ed.). New York: Teachers College Press.

Lozon, C. (2012, May 4). Playing the curriculum. *Kinder News*, 23. Palos Verdes, CA: Chadwick School.

Scott, S. (2002). *Fierce conversations: Achieving success at work and in life, one conversation at a time*. New York: Penguin.

Wheatley, M. (2009). *Turning to one another: Simple conversations to restore hope to the future*. San Francisco: Berrett-Koehler.

Warning: The Common Core Standards May Be Harmful to Children

By Joanne Yatvin
Phi Delta Kappan, March 2013

The language arts standards of the Common Core in too many places are simply too difficult and/or irrelevant for elementary grade students.

When I first read the Common Core English/language arts standards for grades K–5, my visceral reaction was that they represented an unrealistic view of what young children should know and be able to do. As an elementary teacher and principal for most of my life, I could not imagine children between the ages of 5 and 11 responding meaningfully to the standards' expectations. But clearly I was in the minority. Forty-five states have adopted the standards without a murmur of complaint; writers and publishers are racing to produce materials for teaching them, and the teachers quoted in news articles or advertisements speak of the standards as if they are the silver bullet they have been waiting for.

Since then, I have read the English/language arts (ELA) standards many times; each time, they are more troubling. Some standards call on young children to behave like high school seniors, making fine distinctions between words or literary devices, carrying on multiple processes simultaneously, and expressing their understandings in precise academic language. Others expect them to have a strong literary background after only two or three years of schooling. Some standards are so blind to the diversity in American classrooms that they require children of different abilities, backgrounds, and native languages to manipulate linguistic forms and concepts before they have full control of their own home language. And, sadly, a few standards serve only to massage the egos of education elitists, but are of no use in college courses, careers, or everyday life.

To give you just an inkling of the problems in applying the ELA standards to young children, I offer a scenario of what might happen in a 1st-grade classroom when the following language standard is approached:

(L.1.1) Use the most frequently occurring inflections and affixes (e.g., -ed, -s, re-, un-, pre-, -ful, -less) as a clue to the meaning of an unknown word.

While reading aloud from a 1st-grade book, Zach stumbled over the word "recheck" and, although he eventually pronounced it correctly, his teacher felt that he did not fully grasp its meaning in the sentence. It seemed like a good time to make the class aware of the prefix "re" and how it works. So, she stopped the lesson and wrote these words on the white board: remake, rewrite, and retell. Then she asked the children to explain what each word meant. Several students raised their hands and answered correctly.

"What does the 're' part of each word tell us?" she then asked. The first student called on said "re" means to do something again. Nodding in approval, the teacher wrote "recheck" on the board leaving a space between "re" and "check." Then she asked, "So, what does 'recheck' mean?"

"To check something again," answered the class in chorus.

Since things were going well, the teacher decided to continue by asking students to name other words that worked the same way. Various class members confidently suggested, re-eat, re-dance, re-sleep, re-win, and others were waving their hands when she stopped them.

"Those aren't real words," she said. "We don't say, 'I'm going to resleep tonight.' Let's try to think of real words or look for them in our books." After giving the class a few minutes, she asked again for examples.

This time, the words were real enough: repeat, renew, reason, remove, return, read, and reveal, but none of them fit the principle being taught. Since it seemed futile to explain all that to 1st graders, the teacher did the best thing she could think of: "You reminded (uh-oh) me of 'recess,'" she said. "So, let's go out right now."

As they left the room, the children chatted happily among themselves: "We're going to 'cess' again!" "We'll 're-see' our friends." "I want to 're-play' dodge ball."

"Next time," thought the teacher, "I'd better try a different prefix." But then "un-smart" and "un-listen" popped into her head, and she decided to leave that particular standard for later in the year.

Although I could write scenarios for several other standards, they would make this paper much longer and not be as amusing as this one. Instead, I will present just a few standards that I find inappropriate for K–5 students along with brief explanations of their problems.

A Reading/Literature standard for 4th grade calls on students to:

> **(RL.4.4)** *Determine the meaning of words and phrases as they are used in a text, including those that allude to significant characters found in mythology (e.g., Herculean).*

I can't help wondering how 9- and 10-year-olds are supposed to do their "determining." Competent, engaged readers of any age do not stop to puzzle out unknown words in a text. Mostly, they rely on the surrounding context to explain them. But, if that doesn't work, they skip them, figuring that somewhere down the page they will be made clear.

Should students regularly consult a dictionary or thesaurus while reading? I don't think so. That's a surefire way to destroy the continuity of meaning. Nor would I expect them to recall an explanatory reference from the field of classic literature at this early stage of their education. Moreover, for each "Herculean" word that matches a literary character, there would be several like "cupidity" and "pander" that have strayed far from their original meanings.

In the Reading/Information category, I quickly found a standard with expectations far beyond the knowledge backgrounds of the children for whom it is intended:

> **(RI.2.3)** *Describe the connection between a series of historical events, scientific ideas or concepts, or steps in technical procedures in a text.*

Just assuming that 2nd graders are familiar with "a series" of historical events, etc., is simply unrealistic. But expecting them to "describe the connection between (sic) them" is delusional. Is there only one simple connection among a series of "scientific ideas"? How would you, as an adult, describe the connections among the steps in building a robot or even baking a pie?

In most of the Reading/Information standards, the same expectations for describing complex relationships among multiple items appear:

> **(RI.5.5)** *Compare and contrast the overall structure (e.g., chronology, comparison, cause/effect, problem/solution) of events, ideas, concepts, or information in two or more texts.*

For 5th graders, this standard would be even more difficult to meet than the previous one because it asks them to carry out two different operations on two or more texts that almost certainly differ in content, style, and organization.

In the Writing and Speaking/Listening categories, there are fewer standards altogether. Yet, some of these standards also make unrealistic demands. One asks 1st graders to:

> **(W.1.7)** *Participate in shared research and writing projects (e.g., explore a number of "how-to" books on a given topic and use them to write a sequence of instructions).*

Since this standard does not mention "adult guidance and support," as many others do, I assume that a group of 1st graders is expected to work on its own to digest the content of several books, prune it to the essentials, and then devise a well-ordered list of instructions. This would be a complicated assignment even for students much older, requiring not only analysis and synthesis, but also self-regulation and compromise. I cannot see 1st graders carrying it out without a teacher guiding them every step of the way.

Of all the ELA standards, the ones in the Language (i.e., grammar) category are the most unrealistic. I could cite almost all of them as unreasonable for the grades designated and a few as pointless for any grade. Here is part of a kindergarten standard that fits both descriptions:

> **(L.K.1).** *(When speaking) Produce and expand complete sentences in shared language activities.*

Most of the kindergartners I know have no idea what the term "complete sentence" means. Children and adults commonly speak short phrases and single words to each other. I can't imagine any kindergarten teacher insisting during a group language activity that children speak in "complete sentences" or that they "expand" their sentences. Those directions would in all likelihood end the activity quickly as most children fell silent.

Here is another unrealistic standard, this time designated for 3rd grade:

> **(L.3.1)** *Explain the function of nouns, pronouns, verbs, adjectives, and adverbs in general and their functions in particular sentences.*

Aside from the unreasonableness of expecting 7- and 8-year-olds to explain the use of grammatical terms, this standard has no applications in reading, speaking, or writing. Research has shown unequivocally that being able to name parts of speech or diagram sentences has no positive effect on students' writing. This standard wastes instructional time on a useless skill.

I cannot leave this critique of the ELA Standards without taking one more swipe at the Language category. Standard **(L.4.1)** asks 4th graders to:

> *Use relative pronouns (who, whose, whom, which, that) and correctly use frequently confused words (e.g., to, too, two; there, their) in speech and writing.*

Several of these words are ones that many educated adults use incorrectly all the time. In fact "who" is so often used in place of "whom" that it is widely recognized as correct. Why not hold adults accountable for meeting this standard before expecting 4th graders to do so?

In finding fault with so many of the K–5 ELA standards, my familiarity with children's abilities and educational needs have guided me. Standards advocates may well argue that I have offered no evidence and scant research to support my views. In rebuttal, I would argue that they are in the same position and that much of what they propose for children flies in the face of established learning theory and brain development research. The reality is that the standards' creators have laid out a set of expectations for America's children that are grounded only in an antiquated conception of education and their personal preferences. And their followers, bedazzled by the standards length and breadth, illusion of depth, and elitist aura, have fallen into line as if lured by the Pied Piper of Hamelin.

Do the Common Core State Standards Flunk History?

By Craig Thurtell
Social Science Docket, Summer/Fall 2013

By now, virtually every public school teacher has heard about the Common Core State Standards (CCSS). Set forth in their final version in May of 2010, they claim to "represent a synthesis of the best elements of standards-related work to date and an important advance over that previous work."[1] The CCSS have been adopted by 45 states so far. The Standards address English language arts (ELA) and mathematics primarily, but they fold other subjects, including history, into the ELA standards and assign responsibility for their implementation. As the Standards took shape, the National Council for the Social Studies expressed an understandable concern for inclusion of social studies, but made no objection to their basic approach to reading and writing.[2] The National Council for History Education was similarly concerned about the role of history, but concluded that "[t]he Literacy Standards for History/Social Studies focuses [sic] on deep and critical, discipline-specific reading, writing, and thinking at grades 6–12."[3] The National Council for Teachers of English (NCTE) has taken no official position, but favors local control of ELA curriculum. The NCTE president reported that 59 percent of its members support the Standards, in spite of their recommended shift away from fiction, drama, and poetry to nonfiction texts.[4] The American Federation of Teachers has endorsed the Standards as well.[5] In the states that have adopted them, school districts are in the midst of implementation.

The apparent inevitability of the standards notwithstanding, scholars and educators have raised a range of criticisms. In a series of critical essays on education reform in the *New York Review of Books*, Diane Ravitch has pointed out that the standards have never been field tested, making their effectiveness unknown and nation-wide implementation premature. Others have raised more specific objections, including the obvious role of poverty in diminishing student achievement, which challenges the putative need for new standards; the inevitable proliferation of new tests to measure performance; the deceptively central role of the US Department of Education; the insufficient rigor of the standards; the fallacies of the "career and college readiness" exit standard; and the problems with the emphasis on "informational texts," as the CCSS has termed the non-fiction reading material it favors.[6]

Aside from the NCHE's praise, however, few critics have evaluated the impact of the CCSS on teaching the humanities, or more specifically, on the teaching of history. It is my contention that the CCSS express an antipathy to the humanities in general and insensitivity to the practice of history in particular, and that this problem is closely related to their nonhistorical approach to historical texts. This approach also permits the allocation of historical texts to English teachers, most of whom are untrained in the study of history, and leads to history standards that neglect the distinctiveness of the discipline. If implemented as their authors intend, the CCSS will damage history education.

At the outset, I must note a few limits to my critique. I will discuss the impact of the Standards on history specifically, not the various disciplines that comprise social studies. Among these disciplines, history lays the strongest claim to membership in the humanities, but the problems I raise regarding the Standards and history have clear applications to the social sciences. Examples of the harmful consequences of the Standards for history education could be multiplied, but I will limit myself to one representative illustration.

Why study history? This pursuit serves many purposes, but surely one of its fundamental objectives is to make us more human. Sam Wineburg, in his essential book *Historical Thinking and Other Unnatural Acts*, argues that history both enables us to situate ourselves in the present by making sense of how we got here, while also acquainting us with the often jarring *strangeness* of the past.[7] This encounter with bizarre, brutal, and peculiar behavior humanizes by encouraging us to understand historical events and actors in their own terms and by leading us to the humbling recognition that, generations hence, we, too, may be regarded as curious, primitive, and benighted. It is uniquely the job of the historian to engage with the frailties as well as the strengths of historical actors, and to render the limitless past into understandable terms. These are eminently humanizing enterprises.

Such historical understanding results from the practice, or discipline, of history. The study of history requires the use of specific concepts and cognitive skills that characterize the discipline—concepts like evidence and causation and skills like contextualization, sourcing, and corroboration. These concepts and skills are largely distinct from those employed in literary analysis. Both disciplines engage in close readings of texts, for example, but with different purposes. The object of the literary critic is the text, or more broadly, the genre; for the historian it is, however limited or defined, a wider narrative of human history, which textual analysis serves. Historical thinking and humanizing outcomes are linked. As with literary skills, the more deeply history's concepts and skills are grasped the more profound are the humanizing consequences. And like the intellectual skills called upon in the study of literature, historical thinking skills are enduring, even more so because they are applicable to a wider field of contemporary issues.

To what extent do the CCSS incorporate these purposes and practices into their proposed curriculum? The answer is very little; their intentions lie elsewhere. The Standards adopt an instrumental approach: Their ultimate objective is not the development of sensitive and discerning citizens but rather a career-and-college-ready high school graduate. They refer to "discipline specific content," and "the norms and conventions of each discipline,"[8] but, the NCHE's statement notwithstanding, the actual *use* of discipline-specific *thinking* must often be inferred, and suffers from telling absences. In fact, the CCSS for ELA devote only a single, mostly non-discipline-specific page to reading in history and social studies,[9] and then apply their writing standards to history/social studies, science and technical subjects in common, as if these diverse fields share the same modes of written analysis.[10] Their explanations of skills standards are abstract and remote from the specific practices of the historian.

The standards contained on page 61 of the ELA Standards suggest an author or authors unversed in the practice of history. A close reading of the most advanced skills, for grades 11–12, reveals an uneven deployment of historical thinking skills, often to the point of disappearance. The first three standards, assembled under the vague heading "Key Ideas and Details," are non-history-specific. Number 1, for example, mentions the expectation that students will "Cite specific textual evidence to support analysis of primary and secondary sources, connecting insights gained from specific details to an understanding of the text as a whole," while numbers 2 and 3 ask students to "[d]etermine the central ideas or information of a primary or secondary source; provide an accurate summary that makes clear the relationships among the key details and ideas" and "[e]valuate various explanations for actions or events and determine which explanation best accords with textual evidence, acknowledging where the text leaves matters uncertain," respectively. These standards call for close reading and making connections, and refer to "primary and secondary" sources characteristic of history. But the first two skills suffer from an exclusion of sourcing and contextualization skills, typically the first cognitive actions taken by a historian examining a document. Number 3 focuses on the accuracy of a text, but not on how the text illuminates a broader question or narrative; there is no reciprocity between text and context. The standard is also not history-specific—"actions or events" could be studied by political scientists, economists, or anthropologists.

Standard 4, under "Craft and Structure," asks students to "[d]etermine the meaning of words and phrases as they are used in a text, including analyzing how an author uses and refines the meaning of a key term over the course of a text (e.g., how Madison defines *faction* in Federalist No. 10)." Once again, an exclusive focus on text prevents the standard from expressing a historical skill. To illustrate, Madison's understanding of "faction" in Federalist 10 was shaped by a shared discourse among the American political elite during and after the Revolution, culminating in the debate over ratifying the Constitution. Madison's essay was a part of that discussion, and "faction" consequently has a meaning that transcends Madison's use of the term in Federalist 10.[11] Confining students to an examination of his use and refinement of the term in the text of Federalist 10 amounts to little more than an intellectual exercise without this essential context—that is, without establishing its relationship to and significance for a larger narrative. The standard fails the "So what?" test.

Standard 5, under the same heading, asks for a similarly non-contextual, and therefore nonhistorical, reading, but standard 6—"Evaluate authors' differing points of view on the same historical event or issue by assessing the authors' claims, reasoning, and evidence"—offers greater possibilities for historical analysis. There is a specific reference to history, and context appears to come into play. But how should a student go about evaluating the claims, reasoning, and evidence? The standard fails to mention the critical skills involved in such analysis: sourcing, corroboration, contextualization, inference, and others. Most fundamentally, what is the purpose of the exercise—to develop a particular skill abstracted from historical content, or to develop that skill by applying it to a specific event in order to better grasp the event and the narrative of which it is a part? In other words, is the skill divorced from the content, in this case historical narrative, or integral to it? "So what?" must again be invoked.

The next three standards, under the heading "Integration of Knowledge and Ideas," are better, though still not specific to history. Number 7 asks students to "[i]ntegrate and evaluate multiple sources of information presented in diverse formats and media (e.g., visually, quantitatively, as well as in words) in order to address a question or solve a problem." This skill could apply to any discipline, though it is certainly useful to the study of history. But again, the specific skills called into play—comparison, corroboration, and inference, for example, go unmentioned. Number 8 asks students to "[e]valuate an author's premises, claims, and evidence by corroborating or challenging them with other information." This standard calls most clearly on the historical skill of corroboration, but sourcing—evaluation of the character and reliability of a source—is an essential, but, for this standard, unacknowledged element of corroboration. Finally, number 9 asks students to "[i]ntegrate information from diverse sources, both primary and secondary, into a coherent understanding of an idea or event, noting discrepancies among sources." This standard asks for synthesis, but one should hope that the discrepancies are evaluated and, if possible, resolved.[12]

The history standards state *what* students must do, but not *how*, because they do not engage the distinctive practices of the discipline of history. They require students to marshal evidence, engage in close reading, make connections, and corroborate evidence—all important skills and all important to the discipline of history. But they are so text-focused that for most of them document analysis becomes hermetic. Sourcing, that is, evaluating the character and reliability of the author of a document, is absent except by inference, as is the closely related practice of contextualization. Both require the application of knowledge external to the text under study in order to amplify its meaning, and both are indispensable to historical thinking. Concepts like causation and chronology and skills like periodization and assessing significance are all missing. Humanizing practices, like empathy, recognizing the limits of one's knowledge, and understanding the past on its own terms are nowhere to be found, even by generous inference. Although the CCSS must be credited with recognition of the crisis in literacy in the United States, their solution for history emphasizes a blinkered form of reading comprehension.

Why have the authors of the CCSS adopted this narrow approach? One of its sources may be found in the subject area designated for the page: "Social Studies/

History." The authors' approach suggests a confusion of purpose. "Social Studies" does not constitute a discipline; rather, it is a grouping of social science disciplines for K–12 grade levels that is rarely found in higher education. The combination has its origins in the Progressive era, a time when many, though not all, professional educators favored downgrading traditional areas of study like classical literature and history, as mass immigration transformed the US population and led to advocacy of a more "practical," less academic curriculum. Unfortunate consequences ensued, and now the CCSS has provided one more example.

Why do the CCSS lift history out of the collection of disciplines of which it has been a prominent part and separate it with a slash mark from that time-honored but problematic "field" of social studies? The authors of the Standards seemingly hope to achieve two purposes: They want to address the practices of history while at the same time applying those practices to the other social sciences. This explains, at least in part, the abstract and non-specific character of the Social Studies/History skills, and their remoteness from the habits of mind that characterize the discipline of history.

There is probably more to it, however. The authors of the Standards have concluded that "Students must be able to read complex informational texts in these fields [social studies/history, science, and technical subjects] with independence and confidence because the vast majority of reading in college and workforce training programs will be sophisticated nonfiction."[13] This fixation on textual comprehension may have caused them to lose sight of crucial understandings that lie outside of, but exist in reciprocal relation with, an assigned text. Their failure to acknowledge, in this statement or elsewhere, any distinctive, intrinsic value in the various disciplines reflects their utilitarian approach. "Informational texts" may be the Standards' signature contribution to education jargon, but to justify the recommended preponderance of such texts by citing the demands of career and college begs the question of the purposes of college and career (not to mention the question of which college and which career). The CCSS do not entertain the question, but one may fairly surmise the authors' response: to get a good job, and, perhaps, at a further remove, restore American prosperity. Good jobs are, of course, hard to find these days, and therefore to be prized, but to reduce education to job training will actually diminish the intellectual capacities of high school graduates by ignoring the value of the humanities and their characteristic critical thinking skills to a discerning citizenry.

The standards for social studies/history do not compare favorably with the new historical thinking skills developed by the College Board for its Advanced Placement history courses, created as part of the AP history program's new and welcome emphasis on historical thinking. Although the AP rubric concentrates on skills and neglects important historical concepts, it is firmly rooted in the practices of the historian.[14] Four broad skills are given substance through the articulation of their components. For example, Skill 1, "Crafting Historical Arguments from Historical Evidence," includes the components "Historical argumentation" and "Appropriate use of relevant historical evidence." Regarding the use of evidence the rubric explains:

> Historical thinking involves the ability to identify, describe and evaluate evidence about the past from diverse sources (including written documents, works of art,

archaeological artifacts, oral traditions and other primary sources), with respect to content, authorship, purpose, format and audience. It involves the capacity to extract useful information, make supportable inferences and draw appropriate conclusions from historical evidence while also understanding such evidence in its context, recognizing its limitations and assessing the points of view that it reflects.[15]

Unlike the CCSS for Social Studies/History, the AP expectations demonstrate familiarity with the work of historians and emphasize the importance of sourcing and contextualization. By noting the limitations on knowledge and interpretation and the irreducibility of conflicting views, the rubric also engages with the humanizing purposes of history. Skill 4, Historical Interpretation and Synthesis, confirms the integration of reading comprehension with historical understanding, at best a tenuous relationship in the CCSS treatment of history. The other two skills and subordinate components are similarly rich and integral to the study of history.

The CCSS's history standards may not be irretrievably flawed, however. Teachers familiar with the discipline of history will be able to infer and extrapolate from the generic formulations on page 61 to justify a rich and stimulating curriculum. Unfortunately, such a favorable outcome is not assured; the CCSS text is open to more than one interpretation. To assess the potential consequences of the Standards for history education, it is illuminating to examine how an adopting state has gone about implementing them. In New York, a state-sponsored website called EngageNY.org offers "exemplar" lessons in ELA and math, and workshops have been organized across the state to assist in the implementation of the Standards. The ELA exemplars demonstrate a careful fidelity to the CCSS.[16] In a piece published in the *Washington Post* last March,[17] Jeremiah Chaffee, an English teacher, explained his dissatisfaction with the lesson on the Gettysburg Address he and his colleagues were asked to develop using an EngageNY exemplar.[18] His complaints included the exemplar's scripted lessons and instructions to read the speech to students without affect, but his main objection was the exemplar's insistence that teachers permit no contextual knowledge to enter into student consideration of the Address. Indeed, the exemplar advises teachers that "This close reading approach forces students to rely exclusively on the text instead of privileging background knowledge, and levels the playing field for all students as they seek to comprehend Lincoln's address."[19] History teachers will quickly register several objections to this statement. Shouldn't contextual knowledge be valued, not derogated as "privileged"? Wouldn't student sharing of that knowledge "level the playing field"? As Chaffee asked, can students really be expected to forget their outside knowledge? And what if their contextual knowledge is inaccurate, in which case, shouldn't it be explored and clarified at the outset?

All the "Guiding Questions" provided on Lincoln's Address are "text-dependent," and most of them demand a literal, as opposed to interpretive, understanding of the text. A few examples illustrate the approach:

- "What does Lincoln mean by 'four score and seven years ago'?"
- "When Lincoln says the nation was 'so conceived and so dedicated' what is he referring to?

- "What if Lincoln had used the verb 'start' instead of 'conceive'?"
- "What four specific ideas does Lincoln ask his listeners to commit themselves to at the end of his speech?"
- "What does the word 'dedicate,' [sic] mean the first two times Lincoln uses it, and what other verb is closely linked to it the first two times it appears?"[20]

These questions reveal an aversion to interpretation of the speech's historical significance, consistent with the Standards' emphasis on information extraction.

A page of the exemplar is devoted to explaining why "non-text dependent questions" like "Why did the North fight the Civil War?" and "Did Lincoln think that the North was going to 'pass the test' that the Civil War posed?" divert students from text comprehension:

> Answering these sorts of questions require [sic] students to go outside the text, and indeed in this particular instance asking them these questions actually undermines what Lincoln is trying to say. Lincoln nowhere in the Gettysburg Address distinguishes between the North and South (or northern versus southern soldiers for that matter). Answering such questions take the student away from the actual point Lincoln is making in the text of the speech regarding equality and self-government."[21]

But the exemplar offers weak examples of "non-text dependent questions." The first one is too broad to be effective in the context of a discussion of this speech, and, if taught in a history class, would already have been addressed. The second question is unanswerable. There are, however, many obvious and important "non-text dependent" questions that would enhance student appreciation of the speech. For example, how might contextualization help explain what Lincoln meant by "a new birth of freedom"? This question might elicit discussion of how the Emancipation Proclamation, issued nine months earlier, invested the phrase—and the speech—with indispensable meaning. Such an approach should be apparent to US history teachers.

In fact, no historian or history teacher could read the Gettysburg Address in the manner insisted upon by the exemplar, which should, at minimum, remand it to the drawing board. Its admonitions against a historical approach reveal a disheartening ignorance of historical thinking. In the hands of the Standard's New York exemplarians, the Address is to be utilized as an "informational text." Here we come to a portentous implication of that term: the divorce of reading comprehension from historical meaning. This alienation of meaning opens the whole undertaking to a deadly tedium. Sequestered from historical meaning, what is there to remember from such a lesson? As Chaffee concluded, the Gettysburg lesson "was intellectually limiting, shallow in scope, and uninteresting."[22]

Situating the Gettysburg Address lesson in a US history class and employing the tools of the historian would offer students a far better opportunity to grasp the significance of the speech and make their own meaning out of it. History relies on chronology, which is essential for understanding causation. By the time of a

Gettysburg Address lesson, students would already be familiar with the causes and outbreak of the Civil War, and banishing this context would be absurd. A close reading of the speech could proceed with reference to this context, as well as the other skills of historical cognition like sourcing and corroboration. The Address offers dramatic evidence of how the war's aims had shifted from the limited objective of preservation of the Union to the revolutionary objective of preservation through emancipation. EngageNY's approach obstructs such an understanding.

Why does the CCSS assign history texts to ELA teachers? Chaffee, the English teacher who criticized the Gettysburg Address lesson, did not pose this question, but many English and history teachers have. Apparently, once texts are redefined as informational, they can be severed from their disciplinary moorings and moved around the curriculum like interchangeable parts. According to the CCSS, ELA teachers enjoy a "unique, time-honored place . . . in developing students' literacy skills,"[23] so the Standards simply assign them texts recognized as important by other disciplines. As part of ELA's new responsibilities for historical documents (for grade 11 only), the Standards mention *The Federalist Papers*, presidential addresses, Supreme Court opinions and dissents, 17th, 18th, and 19th century "foundational documents" including the Declaration of Independence, the Preamble to the US Constitution, the Bill of Rights, and Lincoln's Second Inaugural Address—all delegated to English teachers.[24] Only James Madison's "Federalist Number 10" is mentioned on the Social Studies/History page. For grades 9-11, Appendix B adds fifteen US history documents to the ELA list and three for Social Studies/History.[25]

This disproportionate delegation of responsibility endangers both disciplines. For history teachers, it means that English teachers who are untrained in the study of history will assume significantly greater responsibility for crucial historical texts. Because they need not concern themselves with teaching vast expanses of history, ELA teachers can devote more time to these documents than most history teachers can afford, and their lack of training in history combined with the Standards' emphasis on a historical reading comprehension risks student confusion.

English teachers should be disturbed, too. Most of them study and teach ELA out of a love of literature and the arts, but they will search the CCSS in vain for guidelines on symbolism, imagery, or metaphors. The Standards expect students to read widely in literature, but in the new world of the Common Core Standards, the dazzling turns and leaps of the human imagination are subordinated to the barren extraction of information. English teachers cannot find the prospect attractive.

The CCSS appear to be unstoppable, so how might teachers who object to them proceed? First, discontent with the Standards has apparently been strong enough to cause three states (Minnesota, Massachusetts, and South Carolina) to consider withdrawing from them.[26] Political options may remain viable. Exemplar lessons like New York's may be improved. As noted, history teachers can interpret the Standards to advance the aims of history thinking. But the Standards appear to leave little freedom to venture from their fundamental approach. Under the heading "What Is Not Covered by the Standards," the authors assure teachers that they do not specify how to teach, that content is still open, the suggested texts are incomplete, and so on.

Still, any improvisations must be "consistent with the expectations laid out in this document."[27] Teachers are capable of recalcitrance, however, especially when asked to inflict bad pedagogy on their students. History and ELA teachers may find themselves agreeing with Jeremiah Chaffee and his colleagues at the end of their training in New York's CCSS exemplars: "[W]hen it came time to create our own lessons around the exemplar, three colleagues and I found ourselves using techniques that we know have worked to engage students— not what the exemplar puts forth." But publicizing the Standards' fundamental flaws will remain crucial to any efforts at resistance and change.

Notes

1. Common Core State Standards Initiative, *Common Core State Standards for English Language Arts & Literacy in History/Social Studies, Science, and Technical Subjects*, 3, http://www.corestandards.org/assets/CCSSI_ELA%20Standards. pdf. Hereafter this source will be referred to as CCSS, with a page number. I would like to thank Jeannette Balantic for her helpful comments on the final draft of this article.

2. National Council for the Social Studies, "A State Led Effort to Develop Standards in Social Studies," 31 March 2011, http://www.socialstudies.org/ statecreatedstandards; NCSS, "2010 House of Delegates Resolutions," http:// www.socialstudies.org/about/2010_house_of_delegates_resolutions.

3. National Council for History Education, "FAQs: Common Core State Standards and History Education," http://www.nche.net/advocacy; http://www. nche.net/commoncore.

4. National Council for Teachers of English, "NCTE President Keith Gilyard Talks about NCTE and Common Core Standards," 9 February 2012, http:// www.ncte.org/standards/commoncore/kg_2-9-12

5. American Federation of Teachers, "Recommendations of the AFT Ad Hoc Committee on Standards Rollout," 19 May 2011, http://www.aft.org/pdfs/ teachers/reso_commoncorestandards.pdf; "Common Core Standards Inspire Hope Among Experts," 15 February 2012, http://www.aft.org/newspubs/ news/2012/021512commoncore.cfm.

6. Diane Ravitch, "Schools We Can Envy," *New York Review of Books*, 8 March 2012; *NYR*, "How, and How Not, to Improve the Schools," 22 March 2012, "Do Our Public Schools Threaten National Security?" *NYR*, 7 June 2012, and "In Mitt Romney's School Room," *NYR*, 12 July 2012; "Sunday Dialogue: Improving Our Schools, *New York Times*, 22 July 2012; Mel Riddile, National Association of Secondary School Principals, The Principal Difference, "PISA: It's Poverty Not Stupid," http://nasspblogs.org/principaldifference/2010/12/ pisa_its_poverty_not_stupid_1.html; Sandra Stotsky and Ze'ev Wurman, "Common Core's Standards Still Don't Make the Grade: Why Massachusetts and California Must Regain Control Over Their Academic Destinies," A Pioneer Institute White Paper, No. 65 (July 2010), http://www.pioneerinstitute. org/pdf/common_core_standards.pdf; Peter Wood, "The Core between the

States," *Chronicle of Higher Education*, 23 May 2011, http://chronicle.com/blogs/innovations/the-core-between-the-states/29511; Michael W. Kirst, "Statement About Common Core," http://whatiscommoncore.wordpress.com/2012/04/09/expert-testimony-about-common-core/.

7. *Historical Thinking and Other Unnatural Acts: Charting the Future of Teaching the Past* (Philadelphia: Temple University Press, 2001), 3-27.
8. CCSS, 60.
9. CCSS, 61.
10. CCSS, 63-66.
11. See the discussion in Gordon Wood, *The Creation of The American Republic, 1776-1787* (New York: Norton, 1969), 58-60, 402-403, 503-505, and passim.
12. I am ignoring standard 10, a generic reading comprehension skill.
13. CCSS, 60.
14. College Board, "Historical Thinking Skills," http://apcentral.collegeboard.com/apc/public/repository/WorldHistoryHistoricalThinkingSkills.pdf.
15. Ibid.
16. EngageNY, Curriculum Exemplars, "Gettysburg Address," http://engageny.org/resource/common-core-exemplar-for-high-school-ela-lincolns-gettysburg-address/. Future citations of this exemplar will refer to exemplar title and page number.
17. Jeremiah Chaffee, "Teacher: One (maddening) day working with the Common Core," *Washington Post*, PostLocal, 23 March 2012, http://www.washington-post.com/blogs/answer-sheet/post/teacher-one-maddening-day-working-with-the-common-core/2012/03/15/gIQA8J4WUS_blog.html.
18. EngageNY offers a disclaimer for its exemplars: "DRAFT – Awaiting review and improvement per the Tri-State quality review rubric."
19. Gettysburg exemplar, 3.
20. The quotations are from the Gettysburg exemplar, pages 4, 8, 9, 13, and 14-15 respectively.
21. Gettysburg exemplar, 19.
22. http://www.washingtonpost.com/blogs/answer-sheet/post/teacher-one-maddening-day-working-with-the-common-core/2012/03/15/gIQA8J4WUS_blog.html, 23 March 2012.
23. CCSS, 4.
24. CCSS, 40.
25. CCSS, Appendix B, 10-13.
26. http://chronicle.com/blogs/innovations/the-core-between-the-states/29511.
27. CCSS, 6.

Political Rivals Find Common Ground Over Common Core

By Eric Westervelt
NPR, January 28, 2014

Supporters of the new Common Core education standards adopted by 45 states say the standards hold American students to much higher expectations, and move curriculum away from a bubble-test culture that encourages test preparation over deeper learning.

But there's growing backlash to Common Core, and conservatives and liberals increasingly are voicing similar concerns: that the standards take a one-size-fits-all approach, create a de facto national curriculum, put too much emphasis on standardized tests and undermine teacher autonomy.

The mainstream business wing of the Republican Party strongly backs Common Core, arguing that raising standards is vital to creating the next-generation American workforce. But in an echo of the rifts in the GOP nationally, the Tea Party branch has been critical of the new standards.

Conservative broadcaster Glenn Beck has often led the push. On his show *The Blaze*, he often charges that Common Core will undermine student individuality and teacher autonomy, and that it marks a dangerous takeover of local control by federal bureaucrats pushing a leftist agenda.

"This is a progressive bonanza, and if it's allowed to be in our schools in any form and become the Common Core of America's next generation, it will destroy America and the system of freedom as we know it," Beck told his audience last year.

A small but growing number of liberal reformists have joined conservatives, agreeing on some of the key criticisms.

"It's fundamentally flawed because it was fundamentally undemocratic in the way that it was defined, rolled out, financed," says Stan Karp, a former high school teacher now with New Jersey's Education Law Center and the liberal reform group Rethinking Schools. He sees Common Core as the ideological stepchild of President Bush's No Child Left Behind Act: another high-stakes testing program, he says, imposed from Washington with big help from wealthy foundations and little help from teachers, parents and local communities.

"This is a set of standards that does not reflect the experience of many groups of students served by public education, does not reflect the concerns that many parents have for what they want to see in their education, and that really doubles down on a testing-and-punish regime that has proven to be the wrong approach to improving public education," Karp says.

The mutual criticism of Common Core extends to potential uses and abuses of data collection under the new standards. Both sides also say Common Core represents an end-run around federal prohibition against a national curriculum. And both argue that the new standards were not really state-driven. They say the Obama administration all but forced states into it by requiring adoption of the new standards in order to be eligible for more than $4 billion in federal "Race to the Top" grant money.

Anthony Cody, co-founder of the liberal reform group Network for Public Education, says he sees growing common-ground opposition to Common Core. He taught for nearly 20 years at a high-poverty middle school in Oakland, Calif.

"From the conservative side, there is an understanding of the dangerousness of standardization. And from sort of a libertarian perspective, there's suspicion of government control of what students learn that really resonates with me as a teacher who wants some autonomy," Cody says. "I don't want to be so tied to filling their heads with this predetermined list of things."

Worries about Common Core's content and accompanying tests also cross ideological lines. In one example, Cody points to Common Core's idea of emphasizing "close reading" of literature and nonfiction. Students will be given short passages of text to try to uncover "layers of meaning" and to encourage "deep comprehension." That sounds better than the bubble-test world of No Child Left Behind. But Cody worries that it will stifle free-flowing discussion by pushing teachers to prep kids for tests.

"These standards were built to be tested. . . . I want to have some autonomy as a teacher to do open-ended investigations, to explore things [the students] are curious about," he says. "And the more tightly this is tied to a predetermined list of outcomes and testing, the harder it is for me to do that as a creative teacher."

Advocates of Common Core reject the notion that it creates a national curriculum. They point out that teachers can pick their own materials as long as students know what the standards ask them to know by the end of the school year. Common Core, they argue, will do a lot to promote critical thinking and collaborative problem-solving while significantly raising the bar on what every student should know.

"I would encourage your listeners to take a hard look at the standards before they start believing some of the critics," says Dane Linn, vice president for education and workforce at the Business Roundtable. With the U.S. Chamber of Commerce, the Business Roundtable is rolling out a new national ad campaign to support Common Core.

Linn worked on Common Core when he directed the education policy arm of the National Governors Association and says the idea that it's a stalking horse for federal intrusion into local education is ludicrous.

"I was at that first meeting in Chicago with the state's governor's offices, state superintendents of schools, members of state boards of education. It was a state decision," Linn says. "Clearly, some of those critics of the standards have chosen to base their arguments on fallacies about both the development of the standards and the intention of the standards."

Meantime, many parents and teachers feel caught in the middle as they work to train up on and implement the new standards. Megan Franke, an education professor at UCLA, says her big worry is "that we're not going to support people and then we're going to say, 'See, the Common Core doesn't work.'"

And Education Secretary Arne Duncan has taken political heat and criticism, first for dismissing Common Core critics as fringe and then for suggesting the backlash was largely from embittered "white suburban moms."

It all goes to show that at the very least, the standards have a serious image problem. Tea Party conservatives, calling it "Obamacore," are planning a big march on Washington this summer to oppose the new standards.

But the growing number of liberal critics of Common Core aren't likely to join hands with them and march. They fundamentally disagree about how to reform public education and are alienated by marchers' other calls to abolish teacher tenure and the federal Education Department.

Standards Supporters Firing Back

By Andrew Ujifusa
Education Week, May 15, 2013

Supporters of the Common Core State Standards are moving to confront increas-ingly high-profile opposition to the standards at the state and national levels by ral-lying the private sector and initiating coordinated public relations and advertising campaigns as schools continue implementation.

In states such as Michigan and Tennessee, where Common-Core opponents feel momentum is with them, state education officials, the business community, and allied advocacy groups are ramping up efforts to define and buttress support for the standards—and to counter what they say is misinformation.

Supporters assert that the Common Core remains on track in the bulk of the states that have adopted it, all but four at last count.

But the pressure is on for Common-Core champions to make sure their message gets through. U.S. Secretary of Education Arne Duncan told the U.S. Chamber of Commerce in Washington last month that the private sector had to snap out of what he portrayed as its lethargy and to prevent states from reverting to inferior stan-dards, as he contended states did a decade ago under the No Child Left Behind Act.

"I don't understand why the business community is so passive when these kinds of things happen," he said.

On May 1, former Michigan Governor John Engler—now the president of the Business Roundtable, a Washington-based group of business leaders—took to the radio show of former Arkansas Governor Mike Huckabee, a fellow Republican, to defend the standards.

And soon thereafter, Michigan Governor Rick Snyder, another Republican, re-iterated his Common-Core support in an appearance in that state with Secretary Duncan.

"States are standing up for what's right, and organizations are supporting them," said Chris Minnich, the executive director of the Council of Chief State School Officers, which led the effort to develop and promote the standards along with the National Governors Association. "There are several types of organizations that are doing that."

"Start at Square One"

Critics have made several arguments against the Common Core. Some say the stan-dards are being crammed into classrooms by the federal government in a power grab of questionable legality. They and others say that the Common Core is a national curriculum in disguise, that claims about its rigor are inflated, or that it sets unrealistic expectations.

Criticisms also have arisen about the testing load the standards require, the timetable for implementation, and the pace of professional development for teachers.

Participating states are now implementing the standards, which cover English/language arts and math, and tests based on the Common Core are slated to begin in the 2014–15 academic year.

Perhaps the most prominent pushback has been in Indiana, where Governor Mike Pence, a Republican, is expected to sign a bill that would require a fiscal and policy review of the standards.

Michigan, Ohio, and Tennessee are among the other states that, to varying degrees, have dealt with growing political opposition to the Common Core. Conservative organizations and tea party groups have pushed bills opposing the standards at the state level, but groups skeptical about the role of standardized tests and the private sector in education have also made inroads among progressives.

American Federation of Teachers President Randi Weingarten, who says she continues to support the Common Core in principle, presented a critique on April 30 based on concerns about how quickly and effectively the standards are being implemented. In a speech to the Association for a Better New York, she called for a delay in attaching high stakes to results from tests based on the Common Core. Teachers should have more time to understand the standards and adapt instruction to fit them, she said.

Even as supporters say Common Core remains on track, they say they are taking its opponents seriously.

When the Tennessee education department started getting basic but increasingly frequent questions about the standards—along the lines of "Is the federal government now telling us what textbooks we have to purchase?"—supporters saw the need to act, said state Commissioner of Education Kevin Huffman.

"We realized that we had to start at square one and be able to start telling people, 'OK, this is the story of Tennessee's engagement with the Common Core,'" Mr. Huffman said.

In recent weeks, there have been renewed efforts in Tennessee from the State Collaborative to Reform Education, or SCORE, a nonprofit group led by former U.S. Senator Bill Frist that promotes college and career readiness, to counter foes of the Common Core in the state. Opponents began holding public forums last month where representatives from anti-Common-Core groups made their case.

On April 30, SCORE announced that more than 200 groups had signed on to its Expect More, Achieve More Coalition. The coalition, begun by SCORE in 2009 and revived last year to support the Common Core, includes state businesses and school districts and stresses what it says is the importance of the Common Core.

The coalition has geared up a social-media campaign to promote the standards. It also released a fact sheet and history that says in part, "Standards do not dictate curriculum (e.g., textbooks and reading lists) or prescribe a method of instruction."

Mr. Huffman said he's also lobbied to shore up Common-Core support among state legislators.

In an op-ed essay earlier this month in *The Tennessean*, in Nashville, state Senator Dolores Gresham, a Republican and the chairwoman of the Senate education committee, said the standards would reverse the state's history of having students perform well on state assessments but poorly on national tests that ask more of them.

Continue the Collaboration

States should remember how they collaborated to develop the standards and work to share best practices about keeping the standards politically viable and putting them into effect, argued Dane Linn, a vice president of the Business Roundtable who also oversaw work on the Common Core at the NGA.

"It's important to be patient, to not be alarmist, and to support states as they implement these standards," Mr. Linn said.

Still, the private sector is responding to what some supporters see as ominous developments.

For example, Business Leaders for Michigan, a nonprofit group of private-sector leaders in that state, sent an open letter to state political leaders on May 2, urging them to stand by the new standards, after the state House of Representatives passed a budget last month that would defund the Common Core.

"Adopting the Common Core gives us even a better way of seeing how well we're doing. And for the amount of money we're spending on public education, we should want that," Doug Rothwell, the president and CEO of Business Leaders for Michigan, said in an interview.

Both Mr. Rothwell and Mr. Linn said they were somewhat surprised by the ability of what they deemed small groups of opponents to get political traction. But groups outside the private sector are being proactive as well—before Mr. Snyder's May 6 remarks, Education Trust's Midwest affiliate, which advocates for a focus on transparent data and student achievement, also stressed in a May 2 statement the broad support for the standards, including the state PTA.

But supporters also were jolted by the Republican National Committee's decision last month to oppose the standards, said Chester E. Finn Jr., the president of the pro-Common-Core Thomas B. Fordham Institute in Washington.

"Some people have suddenly discovered that they might need a few people with at least faint Republican credentials besides [former Florida Governor] Jeb Bush to say that the Common Core is a good thing," he said. He added that he thought conservative efforts in state legislatures posed the bigger threat to the common standards, compared with opposition from the political left.

Drawing Connections

Standards supporters are also becoming more active on the airwaves.

Stand for Children Indiana, a pro-Common-Core group, which supports broad early-education opportunities and charter schools, released two different 30-second TV advertisements, one on March 5 and another on April 16, defending the standards. The campaign also included radio spots.

A spokesman for the group, Jay Kenworthy, declined to disclose how much it spent on the ads and said it hadn't decided whether to renew the public relations push when Common-Core hearings get underway in Indiana this summer.

That state is also ground zero for a pro-Common-Core argument aimed at a liberal audience: that many of the loudest Common-Core opponents hold other political views that the audience would find abhorrent.

For example, Larry Grau, the director of the Indiana affiliate of Democrats for Education Reform, or DFER, wrote on the group's blog April 23 that GOP Sen. Scott Schneider wants schools to teach creationism and has sought to make enforcement of President Barack Obama's Affordable Care Act a felony. DFER Indiana has also used language that warned about "bedfellows" in the anti-Common-Core movement that could cause someone to say, "I hate myself for this in the morning." Mr. Grau said he wanted the group's rhetoric to be "a little edgy."

He argued that Democrats suspicious of other policy proposals, like vouchers, should not let those views lead them to lash out at the Common Core. "They're not thinking before they're saying who they're partnering with on the Common Core," Mr. Grau said in an interview.

Others make an economic argument in favor of the standards. Legislators weighing whether to ditch the Common Core should keep in mind that education technology providers already have been designing products based on the standards, said Bob Wise, the former governor of West Virginia who is now president of the Washington-based Alliance for Excellent Education, which works to improve high school graduation rates.

He argued it would end up costing states more to backtrack than to implement the Common Core.

Opposition Persists

The federal government has provided $360 million to support two consortia of states developing Common-Core-based assessments.

But without new federal enticements to follow through and implement the Common Core, supporters don't have much gas left in the tank, argued Jim Stergios, the president of the Boston-based Pioneer Institute, which opposes the standards and has sent representatives to forums in Tennessee and elsewhere.

"Michigan wasn't even on our radar screen," he said. "A lot of representatives and senators are starting to feel the heat."

Parents, in particular, are also catching on to the "propaganda" coming from corporate and foundation-based Common-Core supporters, said Julie Woestehoff, a co-founder of the Chicago-based Parents Across America, a progressive-oriented group that is concerned about the Common Core's standardized-testing requirements. (She is also executive director of Parents United for Responsible Education, located in Chicago.) "What we're seeing are people with a lot of money throwing money at a PR problem that they see happening," she said.

But Mr. Minnich of the CCSSO maintains that there is a broad consensus in support of the Common Core that isn't fracturing and that wants implementation to continue.

On this front, the GE Foundation has traveled to districts to discuss work on the standards, and has helped the Erie school district in Pennsylvania, for example, travel to receive additional Common-Core training. (The GE Foundation provides grant support for *Education Week*'s coverage of college- and career-ready standards' implementation.)

"Implementation is critical. . . . Simply adopting a set of standards isn't going to make things better," Mr. Minnich said.

Cutting to the Common Core: Academic Language Development Network

By Susan O'Hara, Jeff Zwiers, and Robert Pritchard
Language Magazine, January 29, 2014

Susan O'Hara, Jeff Zwiers, and Robert Pritchard explain the mission of the Academic Language Development Network.

The Academic Language Development Network (http://aldnetwork.org) is a collaborative project, co-housed at the University of California Davis and Stanford University. The Network focuses on research-based teaching and assessment practices for developing the complex academic language, literacy, and thinking skills that support the learning of the Common Core State Standards, Next Generation Science Standards, and new ELD standards. One of the main purposes of this network is to share ongoing research and effective professional development resources for building system-wide capacity to meet the instructional needs of academic English learners. We currently collaborate on professional development and research efforts in multiple school districts, counties, and states.

The work of the ALD Network will be featured at the seventh annual Academic Literacy Summit co-hosted by the CRESS center (http://education.ucdavis.edu/cress-center) located within the School of Education at UC Davis. This year's summit, Keys to Unlock the Common Core: Academic Literacy for All, focuses on how teachers and schools can imaginatively adapt to the new California Common Core Standards in literacy across all subjects (http://education.ucdavis.edu/2014-summit). Jeff Zwiers, co-director of the ALD Network and senior researcher at Stanford University will deliver the keynote address, and teacher leaders who have been involved with the ALD Network will share practices from their classrooms. Teachers, coaches, and educators will, in 90 minutes, present workshops and share effective academic-literacy instructional and coaching practices aligned with Common Core State Standards. Below is an overview of the research and development work conducted by the ALD Network.

Introduction

The development of academic language and literacy is one of the most important factors in the academic success of English learners and has been increasingly cited as a major contributor to gaps in achievement between ELs and English-proficient students (Anstrom et al., 2010; Francis, Rivera, Lesaux, Kieffer, & Rivera, 2006). Some argue that "achievement gap," usually indicated by yearly test scores and/or graduation rates, is largely an academic language gap.

The Common Core State Standards (CCSSs) have added an exciting and challenging layer to the schooling of ELs. The exciting part is that many of the CCSSs focus on robust development of disciplinary thinking and communication skills, which better prepare all students for success in college. The challenging part is that meeting these new standards requires higher levels of receptive and productive academic language. The CCSS, for example, place a high emphasis on argument-based reasoning, writing and reading complex texts, and engaging in academic discourse across disciplines. Such skills demand much more advanced abilities to use academic syntax and communication skills than learning that is based on memorization. This situation is further complicated by a wide variety of English learner differences and needs, such as language and literacy levels in English, that are not addressed in depth in the CCSS.

Explicit attention to academic language instruction, coupled with extended opportunities for students to hear and use academic language, is needed in classrooms with English learners and other students who struggle to understand and use the language of school (Anstrom et al., 2010). Yet this is seldom the kind of instruction we see in classrooms with large numbers of ELs. One reason for this is the lack of clarity about evidence-based classroom practices. A second reason is the lack of support for teachers' growth in classroom instruction. Identifying classroom practices associated with academic-language-proficiency growth and then targeting these practices in professional development provides a potentially powerful approach for improving the quality of instruction for the nation's ELs.

The ALDN team has engaged in systematic research to identify essential practices that teachers can use to develop academic language that supports content learning across disciplines. The emerging data show that a small number of instructional practices can have a significant positive effect on students' development of academic language. However, the data are also showing that we cannot simply create a list of practices to check off when we observe or enact them.

In our reviews of the literature and classroom observation analyses, we synthesized the varying descriptions of academic language into three dimensions, each containing several features and skills. The dimensions are vocabulary, syntax, and discourse. See Figure 1 for a visual representation of the dimensions and their features and skills. The iceberg shows how the depth and complexity increase as one moves from looking at words to looking at how messages are put together for particular audiences.

A Delphi Panel Study of Expert Consensus[1]

In an attempt to move beyond the current research, which articulates broad sets of effective practices for academic-language-development, and in order to identify the most-essential and highest-leverage practices, we conducted an empirical study using a Delphi technique to answer the question: Which instructional practices

FIGURE 1: DIMENSIONS AND FEATURES OF ACADEMIC LANGUAGE

Dimensions	AL Features	AL Skills
Vocabulary	• Content terms and collocations • Figurative expressions and multiple-meaning terms • Affices, roots and transformations • General academic terms (aspects, consider, as long as, perhaps, evaluate)	• Figure out the meaning of new words and terms in a particular message, connect to underlying concepts and for comprehension of text • Use new words to build ideas or create products • Choose and use the best words and phrases to get the message across
Syntax	• Sentence structure and strength • Transitions/connectives • Complex verb tenses and passive voice • Pronouns and references	• Craft sentences to be clear and correct • Use a variety of sentence types to clarify a message, condense information and combine ideas, phrases and clauses
Discourses	• Organization and text structure • Voice and register • Density • Clarity and coherence	• Combine features to communicate, clarify and negotiate meaning • Create a logical flow and connection between ideas • Match language with purpose of message (clear complete, focused, logical and appropriate to the discipline)

are most essential and highest leverage for promoting the academic-language development of academic-English learners across disciplines? The methodology for this study was based in part on a Delphi study by Osborne et al. (2003), and was conducted in several steps. The final results of this Delphi panel suggest that there are three essential and high-leverage practices for the development of academic language of adolescent English learners in content-area classrooms: fostering academic interactions, fortifying academic output, and using complex text to develop academic language.

- **Fostering Academic Interactions** focuses on structuring and strengthening student-to-student interaction that uses academic language. Interaction consists of students responding to one another, building and challenging ideas, and negotiating meaning. The teacher provides and scaffolds multiple opportunities for students to interact with original, academic messages that require academic language (Cazden, 2001; Lemke, 1990; Long, 1981; Mercer & Littleton, 2007).

- **Fortifying Academic Output** focuses on structuring, strengthening, and supporting the quantity and quality of students' production of original, extended academic messages that require academic language (Cazden, 2001; Chafe, 1982; Mercer, 2000; Swain, 1985). The teacher provides and scaffolds multiple opportunities for students to communicate ideas in activities such as oral presentations and answering teacher questions. Output also includes producing complex texts such as essays, articles, web pages, and multimedia presentations. The teacher provides opportunities and supports students in using academic language (vocabulary, syntax, discourse) to produce texts that communicate clear, meaningful, and original academic messages (Harklau, 2002).

- **Using Complex Texts** focuses on utilizing texts to foster academic language and on developing students' overall abilities to practice with and process the language of complex texts (August, Artzi, & Mazrum, 2010; Wong, Fillmore & Fillmore, 2011). The teacher engages students in analysis of how a text's organization, syntax, and word choice combine to create meaning, and fosters analytical discussions of authors' use of language to convey certain meanings for given purposes. This practice develops students' overall academic language and metacognitive skills, while also strengthening their disciplinary thinking skills, comprehension habits, and content knowledge of specific texts (Urquhart & Weir, 1998).

Additional findings from this Delphi panel study suggest that these essential, high-leverage practices are central to effective academic-language instruction, but alone they do not get to the core of academic-language teaching. Effective academic-language teachers enact a set of dynamic instructional moves in support of these essential, high-leverage practices. In addition, these teachers negotiate these dynamic moves during instruction in the action of academic-language teaching (O'Hara et al., 2013). The analysis of the Delphi panel data suggests the foundational knowledge teachers need for effective academic-language instruction. It also suggests two categories of dynamic instructional moves that are key to enacting essential, high-leverage practices: (a) the art of scaffolding and guiding academic-language development; and (b) negotiating a balance between explicit and immersive academic-language instruction.

Upon further analysis of the Delphi study results coupled with additional observations of lessons, we realized that a list of practices with varying levels alone would not be enough to describe the model for effective, complex academic-language teaching. Therefore, we generated three initial combinations of practices, and instructional moves, that we call essential practice frames. (See Figure 2).

FIGURE 2

<table>
<tr>
<td rowspan="1">Core Practices, High Impact</td>
<td>

Fostering Academic Interactions

- (INT) Teacher provides opportunities for students to engage in extended interactions using target academic language that directly support content learning and are structured to encourage all students to participate.
- (COM) Teacher uses interaction opportunities to develop students' abilities to communicate with one another using discuorse moves, language, and thinking processes of the discipline and its experts.

Fortifying Academic Output

- (ORL) Teacher provides multiple and extended opportunities for all students to produce oral output using target academic language in meaningful ways.
- (PCT) Teacher provides meaningful opportunities for students to produce complex tasks to develop and use academic language.

Using Complex Texts to Build AL

- (TXT) Teacher engages students in analysis of how a text's organizational features, syntax, and word choice combine to create meaning; uses as opportunity to build disciplinary language, thinking, and comprehension.
- (RCT) Teacher provides extended opportunities for students to participate in engaging and language-rich tasks that depend on complex texts.

</td>
</tr>
</table>

<table>
<tr>
<td rowspan="1">Cross-Cutting Core Practices</td>
<td>

Modeling AL

- (MOD) Teacher clearly and completely models (and/or provides models of) target academic language that supports content learning.
- (DEC) Teacher clearly and completely deconstructs the language being modeled.

</td>
<td>

Making AL Input Comprehensible

- (INP) Teacher uses a variety of communication strategies that are appropriately differentiated for the mutliple levels of language proficiency represented in the class.
- (CHK) Teacher uses multiple approaches to check for academic-language comprehension, and appropriately adjusts instruction.

</td>
<td>

Guided Learning of AL

- (PRO) Teacher consistently prompts for and provides target academic language for the tasks at appropriate times.
- (FBK) Teacher consistently provides specific and helpful feedback on academic-language use; it appears to help student with the language demands of the activity.
- (MET) Teacher clearly engages in student activities in which they talk about academic language learning and how it accomplishes communicative purposes in the discipline.

</td>
</tr>
</table>

<table>
<tr>
<td rowspan="1">Foundational Core Practices</td>
<td>

Aligning and Designing Academic Language Development Activities

- (FAS) Teacher effectively and consistently assesses students' learning of target language and uses information to inform instruction.

- (MAT) Teacher uses support materials to make target academic language understandable or more accessible to use; materials are differentiated for multiple levels of language proficiency represented in the class.

- (AUT) Tasks are engaging and require students to authentically use the target academic language to understand and communicate meaningful and purposeful messages; deepen ideas and share perspectives.

- (OBJ) Teacher clearly communicates language objective(s), which clearly support(s) content objectives by addressing the main academic-language demands of the texts and tasks.

</td>
</tr>
</table>

Next Steps

For the observation tool, we have established inter-rater reliability and content validity. We are partnering with researchers at UC Davis, Stanford, and World-Class Instructional Design & Assessment (WIDA) at the University of Wisconsin in the design of a large-scale study to establish predictive validity of the Academic Language Development Network practices and tools.

Operationalizing the ALD Network Practices

We intend for this set of practices and tools to be used several ways.

First, we believe that they will support teachers in improving their teaching of complex academic language and implementation of the new standards. As we clarify the practices and tools that are most predictive of academic-language development, our team is developing a corresponding set of trainings, videos, tools, and materials to support and illustrate these practices.

Notes

1. Part of the academic-language work originated with CRESS Center executive director Susan O'Hara (principal investigator) and Jeff Zwiers (senior researcher) when they worked in Stanford's Center to Support Excellence in Teaching.

Indiana Replaces Common Core . . .
with Common Core

By Alex Newman
The New American, March 25, 2014

Celebrations by parents, teachers, and taxpayers across the political spectrum over the purported death of Common Core in Indiana may have been premature. When legions of outraged Hoosiers forced lawmakers to pass legislation dropping the Obama administration-pushed nationalization of K–12 education, which Republican Gov. Mike Pence signed on Monday, they thought that would be the end of the deeply controversial standards. However, now that drafts of Indiana's "new" standards have emerged, it is clear that they were largely copied and pasted from the scandal-plagued Common Core.

Officials still celebrated the bill, perhaps hoping nobody would notice or care. "I believe our students are best served when decisions about education are made at the state and local level," Gov. Pence claimed in a statement this week. "By signing this legislation, Indiana has taken an important step forward in developing academic standards that are written by Hoosiers, for Hoosiers, and are uncommonly high, and I commend members of the General Assembly for their support."

Despite the new law supposedly aimed at stopping Common Core in Indiana, though, suspicion and outrage is still building as Hoosiers learn about the supposedly "new and improved" standards. According to education expert Dr. Sandra Stotsky, who refused to sign off on the national standards while serving on the Common Core Validation Committee and was hired by Indiana to review the state's "new" proposed standards, what is happening is tantamount to "grand deception."

The retired University of Arkansas professor explained that the draft standards proposed as a replacement for Common Core in Indiana, in fact, are almost the same as the national scheme that sparked the public uproar in the first place. Incredibly, internal government documents actually reveal that as much as 90 percent of the "new" standards were taken from Common Core, meaning the "new" is essentially a repackaged version of the old.

Dr. Stotsky recently released an Indiana Department of Education report that blew the lid off what is happening. According to the document, cited in multiple news reports, more than 70 percent of the "new" Indiana standards for grades six through 12 were taken directly from Common Core. Another 20 percent of the standards were simply edited versions of Common Core. About half of the new standards from kindergarten through fifth grade were also lifted from the national scheme.

"It makes a fool of the governor," Dr. Stotsky, one of the premier national experts on Common Core, was quoted as saying by Fox News about Indiana's allegedly "new" standards. "The governor is being embarrassed by his own Department of Education if the final version is too close to Common Core." Based on the legislation rejecting Common Core, the Indiana Board of Education is set to vote on the proposed "new" standards in late April. It was not immediately clear whether they would be approved, but opposition is building as the public slowly realizes it has been taken for a ride.

Stotsky, the former 21st-century chair in teacher quality at the University of Arkansas's Department of Education Reform, also told *The New American* last year that Common Core standards should be scrapped entirely. Among other concerns, she said the national standards reduced opportunities for the development of critical thinking in students, scaled back literary study, and were "written hastily by people who didn't care how poorly written they were." The math subject-matter expert on the Common Core Validation Committee also refused to sign off on that component, citing, among other concerns, incorrect math.

Veteran Indiana educator Mary Black, who has been teaching for 40 years, also lambasted the attempted deception taking place in her state. "The truth about Common Core in Indiana is that we still have Common Core; it is just renamed," explained Black, who currently serves as Curriculum Director for FreedomProject Education, an online K–12 school dedicated to classical education and Judeo-Christian values. "The commission established to write the new Indiana standards 'by Hoosiers and for Hoosiers,' as Gov. Pence put it, was filled by publicly known proponents of Common Core."

One member of the commission, Black told *The New American*, was a representative of WestEd, a controversial organization connected to the federally funded Common Core testing regimes that also provides schools with a widely criticized data-collection scheme known as "Positive Behavioral Intervention System" (PBIS). In mid-April, meanwhile, the draft Indiana standards will go to an education "Round Table" which is expected to include representatives of the federally funded National Governors Association and billionaire Common Core financier Bill Gates—both of which played a key role, along with the Obama administration, in foisting the controversial standards on America.

"We have renamed Common Core standards, but are still bound to implement them by the federal government's waiver to [the unconstitutional federal education plot known as] No Child Left Behind, and have funding for the development of a state-wide data system for our schools," Black added, referring to the massive, federally funded information-collection regime targeting students. "Indiana has not dropped out of Common Core. Opponents of Common Core will have a difficult time convincing people that we have to get rid of it because so many have now been tricked into believing it is gone."

The education expert also offered some background on how it happened. The original legislation to stop Common Core in Indiana, she said, in addition to establishing a commission to create new standards, would have repealed the Obama administration's lawless waiver from the Bush-era No Child Left Behind mandate. As the bill worked its way through the legislature, however, the measure to repeal the NCLB waiver was dropped, causing the original author of the bill, State Senator Scott Schneider, to withdraw his support. He voted against the final version, too.

For the governor, it may be about slick politics. "Governor Pence, a neocon, is using this so-called victory over Common Core to deceive Hoosiers into thinking he took a stand against the standards for political gains," Black continued, adding that despite the rhetoric, the reality on the ground suggests the governor is just playing games with the public for his own purposes. "His ambitions to become president are well-known."

In 2010, Indiana became one of the first state governments in the nation to accept Obama administration bribes in exchange for foisting the controversial national standards on schools. It was done very quietly, and as in most of the 45 states that eventually capitulated to Washington, D.C., almost nobody noticed at the time. Once parents and teachers began catching on, though, Indiana, along with the rest of America, was in open revolt against the usurpation of education by unaccountable establishment forces.

The pressure to withdraw from the Big Business-and Obama-backed scheme eventually boiled over in Indiana, contributing to the fact that it became the first state to adopt Common Core and then "officially" withdraw. The process began last year, when lawmakers passed legislation to "pause" the implementation of the controversial education takeover. It all culminated with a bill this year that required State Board of Education officials to develop new benchmark standards for Indiana—standards that, again, were apparently copied and pasted from Common Core for the most part.

In signing the bill to formally kill the standards, Gov. Pence suggested other states would follow Indiana's lead. "I believe when we reach the end of this process there are going to be many other states around the country that will take a hard look at the way Indiana has taken a step back, designed our own standards and done it in a way where we drew on educators, we drew on citizens, we drew on parents and developed standards that meet the needs of our people," the governor was quoted as saying.

Indeed, Pence may be correct, although not in the way he presumably meant it. Across America, facing a tsunami of trans-partisan opposition, embattled state officials are desperately seeking to placate the outraged masses but, at the same time, keep the Obama administration bribes flowing and the pro-Common Core establishment happy. To that end, governors and policymakers are increasingly turning to deception rather than real action—in many cases simply slapping a new name on Common Core in an effort to deceive the public.

However, the American people may not be as gullible as the establishment believes, as evidenced by mounting outrage over Indiana's half-baked attempt to repackage the deeply controversial and poor-quality national standards under a new name. With the nationwide uproar against Common Core gathering momentum even in the face of a new Big Business propaganda blitz, officials in Indiana still have time to take real action against Common Core. In other states, meanwhile, as the battle between the public and the establishment intensifies, it will become increasingly difficult for officials to dupe the citizenry.

2

Public and Private:
The Class Gap

© Chris Clark/MLIVE.COM /Landov   © Stephen Flood/Express-Times /Landov

Left: Grand Rapids Public Schools students get on their bus on "count day," in Grand Rapids, Michigan.
Right: Eighth-grade students including Yaledy Charleus, center, 13, at Saints Phillip School in Phillipsburg, New Jersey.

2

Public and Private
The Class Gap

The Widening Gap

According to a 2011 research study from Stanford University, between the 1960s and the 2010s, class has become a more reliable determinant of a student's success than race. The income gap, defined by the difference in academic success between students from families in the higher income range and those from lower income families, is the result of many converging factors, including disparate access to educational resources, varying levels of supplemental education in the home, and an ongoing network of privilege that promotes the welfare of students in certain social groups.

The class gap in education is part of the ongoing struggle to balance the collective public benefit of an educated population with the market-driven model of American society in which the highest-quality goods and services are sold at the highest price. The educational economics of America are highly complex and the income gap in achievement is not a new feature of this ongoing debate. In the twenty-first century, the rise of for-profit education is another emerging feature of the debate, raising issues of exploitation as the crowded educational marketplace expands. In addition, as the quality of education is increasingly tied to price, the financial burden of affording educational advantages has become an important issue in the American debt crisis.

The Benefits of Income

Since the 1960s, sociologists have noted that students whose parents are educated perform better in most measures of academic achievement. A variety of theories have been proposed to explain this, including the fact that educated parents model and demonstrate the value of education and have the direct experience to help their children with schoolwork and to navigating educational culture. Parents in high-income families have an additional advantage, in that they are better able to invest money in educational aids like tutors, and to expose children to experiences, technology, and influences that play a major role in furthering knowledge.

The class gap begins at home, but deepens within the schools, as high-income families are better able to send their children to affluent public schools or private preparatory schools. An important portion of the funding for public schools comes from local property taxes and, for this reason, public schools in wealthy areas enjoy significantly higher levels of financial support. A 2013 article in the *New York Times* reported that New York's wealthiest public school districts spent almost twice as much per student as the state's poorest districts.

The disparity is even more pronounced when examining the difference between public and private schools. Tuition for private schools in many American cities matches or exceeds tuition for college, and this influx of revenue translates into the capacity to provide advanced resources to students, offer more extensive academic options, and attract highly trained staff. Statistics derived from the National Assessment of Educational Progress (NAEP) indicate that private school students enjoy an edge in achievement, as measured by SAT scores and other tests, when compared to students at public schools. This gap narrows when one compares students at private high schools with students at the nation's most affluent public schools, but still remains significant, indicating that the high price of tuition is providing students with a measurable advantage.

One benefit most private schools provide is smaller overall class size, which means more direct interaction between teachers and students. A 2011 article in *Education Week* analyzed statistics from a variety of sources indicating that students in smaller classes tend to retain more information and to perform better in evaluations. Another 2011 study from Tennessee's statewide assessment project found that students from impoverished families reaped the most pronounced benefits from learning in small classes. These studies indicate that smaller classes and more direct teacher interaction might be essential for improving education overall, and yet small classrooms are not the norm in most public schools.

Another advantage to private and high-income public education may lie in the diversity of educational options offered to students. A 2012 article in the *Village Voice* reported on unusual electives offered in some of New York's private schools, including Zen dance classes and Mandarin Chinese. While classes like these may seem like luxuries, especially as the nation increasingly moves towards federal guidelines stressing the importance of core curricula, it can be argued that diverse educational options are more engaging to a larger number of students. In addition, the diversity of elective options is a path toward cultural expansion, introducing students to aspects of foreign culture and experience that may prove useful as American students increasingly work in a globalized environment.

Culture and Academics

Many of America's private preparatory middle and high schools are part of an elite network of educational and commercial institutions tied together through mutual assistance and favoritism. Attending a well-known preparatory school carries a name recognition that can be as important in the college admissions process as a student's academic record.

A 2007 study in the *Wall Street Journal* showed, for instance, that the top ten schools sending students to Harvard and the nation's other most prestigious universities were all private schools. The prestigious Phillips Academy in Andover, Massachusetts, sends more students to Harvard per capita than any other school in the United States. The tuition at Phillips Andover in 2013 was $36,700 per year for day students.

In part, this phenomenon can be tied to the fact that students at private schools, on average, score better on college entrance exams, but this may not indicate higher academic quality through private education. In the 2013 book *The Public School Advantage*, University of Illinois researcher Sarah Theule Lubienski presents a detailed argument for the perspective that public schools are improving in academic quality faster than private schools and have begun faring better academically in several key areas.

While public schools may be equivalent or better in terms of advancing students on achievement tests, private school students continue to have an edge in SAT scores. Analyses indicate that achievement tests measure a student's capability to demonstrate memorized knowledge, whereas SATs measure applied or developed abilities. The private school edge in developed skills indicates that private education does more to encourage critical thinking, and this is perhaps related to the enhanced diversity of teaching resources and methods used at these schools, which are aspects of the curricula highly dependent on levels of funding and resources.

Profit in Education

The traditional college and high school model in the United States is based on the public and private nonprofit model. Public schools receive government funding and operate on a model where all revenues are invested in school development. Private nonprofit schools receive a majority of their income from tuition, but also operate on a model where excess revenues are returned to the school to fund improvements.

For-profit educational institutions, which have been part of the American education system since the nineteenth century, operate on a business model, where revenues from tuition and other sources constitute profits for shareholders and owners. Prior to the late twentieth century, for-profit schools mostly served as vocational programs, where students paid for training in skills needed for a certain career. However, the growth of the population and the advent of online education have resulted in a vast expansion in for-profit higher education. In 1980, around 1 percent of American students were enrolled in for-profit degree programs, whereas in 2008, this percentage had grown to more than 8 percent. The nation's largest for-profit school, the University of Phoenix, serves more than half a million students throughout the nation.

While for-profit schools are not eligible for direct federal support, an expansion of student aid programs in the twenty-first century enabled for-profit students to obtain federal financial aid. This means that for-profit schools receive billions in annual aid from the government in the form of tuition assistance for students. In 2012, a US Senate committee report indicated that students pay higher fees to attend for-profit schools than public universities and that for-profit schools spend less per student than private or public institutions.

Department of Education statistics released in 2013 indicate that students at for-profit institutions are borrowing at a higher rate and taking out larger loans as well, and thus incurring higher risk of extended debt. Across the board, 90 percent of for-profit students took out loans as compared to 72 percent of public university students. This investment does not seem to result in higher levels of occupational success, as a Harvard University study from 2012 indicated that for-profit students have higher unemployment rates compared to public university students and have lower income levels when employed.

While studies like these seem to indicate that the for-profit industry provides dubious benefits, the issue is more complex, as supporters of the industry, like the National Black Chamber of Commerce, argue that the for-profit sector is the only facet of the educational industry catering to the nation's most at-risk students. This includes minority students with poor academic backgrounds who have difficulty obtaining acceptance to traditional universities. For some students, therefore, for-profit education may provide the only option for continuing education and students with vocational or for-profit degrees may still have an advantage over students lacking any higher education.

Balancing Public and Profit

The American education system faces unique challenges due to the ongoing interplay of market-driven and public welfare–driven influences on the overall educational model. The American public has embraced the idea that a strong education system is one of the most important national goals, yet realizing this goal within the market-driven economy results in challenges that cannot be easily overcome.

For those who can afford the nation's top educational options, the income gap is a benefit, maintaining the name recognition of top-tier schools, which continues to proffer a significant advantage to graduates of these institutions. The modern trend in educational reform is to push core competency skills in an attempt to expand the benefits of what is deemed the most essential knowledge. However, public and private schools differ less in their presentation of core curricula and more in their use of personalized, comprehensive, and diverse educational exposure. Americans are faced with the task of determining whether it is possible not only to enhance the education system's ability to teach rote skills, but also to bring the benefits of comprehensive critical thinking to all levels of the educational spectrum. Achieving this more complex goal may mean a generation of students with a higher capacity for applied thought and thus a distinct advantage in using their education to advance in their lives.

Micah Issitt

Bibliography

Anderson, Jenny, and Rachel Ohm. "Bracing for $40,000 at New York City Private Schools." *New York Times*. New York Times, 27 Jan. 2012. Web. 2 June 2014.

Cloud, John. "Are Private Schools Really Better?" *Time Magazine*. Time, 10 Oct. 2007. Web. 2 June 2014.

Deming, David J., Claudia Goldin, and Lawrence F. Katz. "The For-Profit Postsecondary School Sector: Nimble Critters or Agile Predators?" *National Bureau of Economic Research*. Natl. Bureau of Economic Research, Dec. 2011. Web. 2 June 2014.

Gamerman, Ellen. "How to Get into Harvard." *Wall Street Journal*. Dow Jones, 30 Nov. 2007. Web. 2 June 2014.

Garland, Sarah. "When Class Became More Important to a Child's Education Than Race." *Atlantic*. Atlantic Monthly, 28 Aug. 2013. Web. 2 June 2014.

"Issues A-Z: Class Size." *Education Week*. Editorial Projects in Educ., 1 July 2011. Web. 2 June 2014.

Kingkade, Tyler. "Faculty Pay Survey Shows Growing Gap between Public, Private Colleges." *Huffington Post*. TheHuffingtonPost.com, 8 Apr. 2013. Web. 2 June 2014.

Kirkham, Chris. "For-Profit College Students Face Higher Debt, More Unemployment, Report Finds." *Huffington Post*. TheHuffingtonPost.com, 4 Jan. 2012. Web. 2 June 2014.

Porter, Eduardo. "In Public Education, Edge Still Goes to Rich." *New York Times*. New York Times, 6 Nov. 2013. Web. 2 June 2014.

Reardon, Sean F. "The Widening Academic Achievement Gap between the Rich and the Poor: New Evidence and Possible Explanations." *Whither Opportunity? Rising Inequality, Schools, and Children's Life Chances*. Ed. Greg J. Duncan and Richard J. Murnane. New York: Russell Sage Foundation, 2011. 91–116. Print.

Ryan, Julia. "Are Private Schools Worth It?" *Atlantic*. Atlantic Monthly, 18 Oct. 2013. Web. 2 June 2014.

Sheehy, Kelsey. "Student Borrowing Higher at For-Profit Than Public Colleges." *US News*. US News and World Report, 22 Aug. 2013. Web. 2 Jun 2014.

Smith, Jacquelyn. "The World's Most Reputable Universities." *Forbes*. Forbes, 14 Mar. 2012. Web. 2 June 2014.

"Why Do Americans Mistrust For-Profit Universities?" *Economist*. Economist Newspaper, 2 July 2013. Web. 2 June 2014.

Affirmative Inaction

By William M. Chace
The American Scholar, Winter 2011

Opposition to affirmative action has drastically reduced minority enrollment at public universities; private institutions have the power and the responsibility to reverse the trend.

In his 1965 commencement address at Howard University, President Lyndon Johnson declared, "You do not take a person who, for years, has been hobbled by chains and liberate him, bring him up to the starting line of a race and then say, 'you are free to compete with all the others,' and still justly believe that you have been completely fair." The affirmative-action approach President Johnson proposed in that speech was to be a moral and policy response to the losses, both material and psychological, suffered by African Americans during and after the time of slavery: "We seek not just freedom but opportunity—not just legal equity but human ability—not just equality as a right and a theory, but equality as a fact and as a result." Johnson's speech was followed in 1965 by executive orders aiming "to correct the effects of past and present discrimination." Universities and colleges across the land soon adopted affirmative-action policies. More than 45 years have passed since that June afternoon on the Howard campus. What is the fate of Johnson's triumphant vision in the world we now occupy?

If you listen to Roger Clegg, who heads up the Center for Equal Opportunity, a conservative think tank devoted to "colorblind public policy," the answer is that the practice of affirmative action in higher education has put the country on the path to grievous error. Clegg believes, as he said in a 2007 speech to the Heritage Foundation, that the policy "passes over better qualified students, and sets a disturbing legal, political, and moral precedent in allowing racial discrimination; . . . it stigmatizes the so-called beneficiaries . . . fosters a victim mindset, removes the incentive for academic excellence, and encourages separatism; it compromises the academic mission of the university and lowers the overall academic quality of the student body." He contends, as do his many allies, that anything diluting academic excellence hurts teachers and students alike because colleges and universities exist primarily to protect and exalt the life of the mind.

A very different response to Johnson's speech came, 38 years after its delivery, from within the chambers of the United States Supreme Court. In 2003, Justice Sandra Day O'Connor, having just voted on two cases involving the admissions

From *The American Scholar* 80.1 (Winter 2011): 20–31. Copyright © 2011 by Phi Beta Kappa Society. Reprinted with permission. All rights reserved.

policies of the University of Michigan, predicted that affirmative action would soon end because it would no longer be needed:

> *"Finally, race-conscious admissions policies must be limited in time. The Court takes the Law School at its word that it would like nothing better than to find a race-neutral admissions formula and will terminate its use of racial preferences as soon as practicable. The Court expects that 25 years from now, the use of racial preferences will no longer be necessary to further the interest approved today."*

We stand, as a country, somewhere amid President Johnson's vision, Roger Clegg's hostility, and Justice O'Connor's expectation. Anyone interested in higher education should want to contemplate, on behalf of colleges and universities, students and faculty, alumni and paying parents, the fate of affirmative action. How should it now play out on campus after campus? Will it continue until the year 2028? If not, why not? If so, should it then end? If not, for how long should it be sustained?

To begin to answer these questions, it is important to acknowledge the educational milieu in which affirmative action has been practiced. Two fundamental ambitions have long characterized the culture of our colleges and universities: they have sought to be meritocracies, and they have sought to be egalitarian communities. The first goal gives primacy to intellectual accomplishment, the second to community rapport. Students are prompted by the first to demonstrate their full mental powers, by the second to be citizens of what Plato's *Republic* as well as John Henry Newman's ideal university were to be: a model commonwealth. In his book *The Idea of a University*, Newman said, "I cannot but think that statesmanship . . . is learned, not by books, but in certain centers of education." The one is not the other. "Being as smart as you can be" is only hazily connected to "learning from each other in a mutually beneficial way." The tension between the two is never resolvable; that tension is where arguments about affirmative action find their campus home.

Those people who champion affirmative action assert that much of what education offers is social, participatory, and communal. Enrolling students of many different ethnic backgrounds and of unequal educational achievement, they say, only helps the institution and, again, its students. They believe that the educational process is itself corrupt if it does not bring together the full spectrum—the diversity—of American young people. Using the helping hand, they argue, means creating a better education for everyone and fulfilling a civic obligation to enroll a given number of students for the purpose of creating a stronger and more democratic society.

The history of affirmative action includes the graduation of thousands of young men and women who otherwise would not have passed within the gates of a college or university. Many of those graduates have gone on to professional careers where their success has helped to reinvigorate the American dream. They have become physicians, diplomats, lawyers, Army officers, stockbrokers, journalists, high government officials, scientists, and business leaders. Why, advocates of affirmative action now ask, should their number not be augmented?

But before all else, it's worth asking whether affirmative action is really needed. For all their differences, both critics and advocates acknowledge that some classes of students, particularly African-American and Hispanic, cannot gain admission to many colleges and universities solely on the basis of their academic preparation. They need preferential treatment to enter the model commonwealth. The College Board last measured mean Scholastic Aptitude Scores by Ethnicity in 2008; the results are sobering:

GROUP	CRITICAL READING	MATHEMATICS	WRITING
Asian	513	581	516
Black	430	426	424
Mexican American	454	463	447
White	528	537	518
All	502	515	494

In critical reading, African-American students scored, on average, 83 points below Asian-American students, who in turn scored less well, by 15 points, than white students. But in mathematics, Asian-American students trumped both whites and African Americans, by 44 points and 155 points respectively. In writing, whites did just about as well as Asian Americans (two points higher) and considerably better than African Americans (94 points higher). And in every category, Mexican Americans did less well than whites and Asian Americans but better than African Americans. With such dissimilar scores facing them over the years (the year 2008 being little different from the previous five years), admissions officers at colleges or universities have introduced handicapping measures in order to admit applicants with weaker scores. Those measures have hardly been trivial.

One important set of studies, by Thomas Espenshade of Princeton University and his colleagues, examined the records of more than 100,000 applicants to three highly selective private universities. They found that being an African-American candidate was worth, on average, an additional 230 SAT points on the 1600-point scale and that being Hispanic was worth an additional 185 points, but that being an Asian-American candidate warranted the loss, on average, of 50 SAT points.

What happens if the handicapping is taken away? The same authors found that the outcome would be dramatic, with acceptance rates falling for African-American applicants from 31 percent to 13 percent and for Hispanic applicants by as much as one-half to two-thirds; Asian-American applicants would occupy four out of five of the seats created by fewer African-American and Hispanic acceptances. The Asian-American acceptance rate would rise by one-third from nearly 18 percent to more than 23 percent. Most astonishingly, it turns out that—contrary to the assumptions of those who contend that affirmative action puts white students at a severe disadvantage—white applicants would benefit very little from the removal of racial and ethnic preferences; their acceptance rate would increase by less than one percentage point.

Given the probable results of eliminating affirmative action—a student body consisting almost wholly of whites and Asian Americans—no chief administrator of a respectable college or university would happily oversee the erosion of the presence of black or Hispanic students. That is why no such institution has volunteered to be first to proclaim that it will formally jettison affirmative action. In order to protect what they see as the positive results of the practice and also to protect themselves against litigation by a white plaintiff arguing that his or her chance of admission has been jeopardized, colleges and universities have increasingly relied on admissions standards that depend less on SAT scores and more on intangible and personal attributes: having leadership skills, having the strength to overcome social and economic circumstances, or being the first in the family to seek higher education. With such careful consideration, the candidates can then be admitted (or rejected) one by one.

But careful consideration of this sort is expensive. It requires many people to read, with sensitivity, thousands upon thousands of files, and to make judgments requiring a delicate understanding of the abilities and character, the social background and the hidden promise, of the young people represented by those files.

The two celebrated cases emerging from the University of Michigan, about which Justice O'Connor made her memorable remark, illustrate the situation faced by a leading public institution practicing affirmative action. The Supreme Court employed "strict scrutiny" in reaching its decisions. And, as the Court saw, when the university itself employed careful scrutiny in its admissions procedures, it was entitled to an important victory.

One case addressed the admissions policies of Michigan's law school (*Grutter v. Bollinger et al.*); the other addressed undergraduate admissions in its college (*Gratz et al. v. Bollinger et al.*). The former found for the university, declaring, "The narrowly tailored use of race in admissions decisions to further a compelling interest in obtaining the educational benefits that flow from a diverse student body is not prohibited by the Equal Protection Clause." The latter decision found against the university, noting that its "current policy, which automatically distributes 20 points, or one-fifth of the points needed to guarantee admission, to every single 'underrepresented minority' applicant solely because of race, is not narrowly tailored to achieve educational diversity."

For the Court, narrow tailoring was the factor on which its decisions turned. The Court asked the university if candidates for admission had been considered one by one ("holistically," in the parlance of admissions officers) or if each had been given a unique profile based on factors both quantitative and qualitative. The law school responded with a record of showing it had considered candidates one by one; the undergraduate college hadn't done so. The college automatically gave considerable weight to race, doubtlessly because of the number of candidates it annually faced, more than 25,000. Only by gross mechanistic methods could it pluck out those to be admitted from such a profusion of applicants. The applicant pool faced by the law school was much smaller and therefore greater care could be devoted to each dossier.

The distinction between the two cases is sharp, and the lesson deriving from it is crucial. First, the Court located a compelling constitutional interest in student diversity; race and ethnicity could be taken into account in admissions (provided that narrow tailoring is practiced) even when the government did not find specific discrimination. Moreover, the Court acknowledged that the composition of student bodies presents unusual, vital, and sensitive considerations. While it said that the big 20-point automatic advantage was no longer there for the taking, it also declared that colleges and universities could, if they wished, adhere to procedures both labor intensive and expensive, but neither mechanistic nor entirely quantitative, to arrive at the goal of genuine racial diversity.

Upon hearing these two decisions, the University of Michigan could declare a real, if partial, victory. But its satisfaction was short-lived. In the immediate aftermath of the Court action, the citizens of the state reared back and passed, by a decisive margin, the "Michigan Civil Rights Initiative," amending the state constitution to prohibit state agencies and institutions from operating affirmative-action programs granting preferences based on race, color, ethnicity, national origin, or gender. The amendment, having decisively passed with 58 percent of the vote, became law in December 2006.

Similar action had been taken a decade earlier in California. Citizens there voted Proposition 209 into law in November 1996, with 54 percent of the vote. It banned every form of discrimination on the basis of race, sex, or ethnicity at any public entity in California. Within little less than a decade, black enrollment in the freshman class at UCLA had dropped from 211 to 96 and at UC Berkeley from 258 to 140. In the state of Washington, Initiative 200, which passed in 1998, ordered public agencies to cease giving preferential treatment on the basis of race, sex, color, ethnicity, or national origin. It effectively ended affirmative action by state and local governments in hiring, contracting, and school admissions. This law was approved by 58 percent of the voters. Elsewhere and earlier (*Hopwood v. Texas*, March 1996), a federal circuit court had curtailed affirmative-action programs at public colleges and universities in three other states (Texas, Louisiana, and Mississippi). In Florida, Governor Jeb Bush simply issued an executive order banning affirmative action. In the California and Michigan cases, Ward Connerly, once a regent of the University of California system, led campaigns barring the use of racial preferences. Before the elections of November 2008, with the ambition of introducing legislation banning affirmative action across the country, he took aim at Nebraska and Colorado. In the former, a proposal to ban affirmative action passed handily; in the latter, a similar proposal failed by a very small margin. And in November of 2010, Arizona voters approved Proposition 107; it bans consideration of race, ethnicity, or gender by any unit of state government, including the state's public colleges and universities.

Referendums are one thing; public opinion is another. When it comes to what Americans feel about the practice, polls reveal that positive attitudes toward affirmative action in college admissions, while always in flux, are usually in jeopardy. Back in 2003, Gallup revealed that 69 percent of those asked thought that merit alone should be weighed in college admissions. Three years earlier, an Associated Press poll indicated that 53 percent of those polled thought affirmative action should be continued in admissions, with 35 percent saying it should be abolished. The same year, a *Time*/CNN poll showed 54 percent disapproval of affirmative action and 39 percent approval. A CBS News Poll in January 2006 revealed that 12 percent of those responding believed that affirmative action should be ended immediately; 33 percent said it should be phased out; and 36 percent believed it should be continued. The latest poll (from Quinnipiac University) reported in 2009 that affirmative action is opposed by 61 to 33 percent of those responding (with black voters supporting it by 69 to 26 percent and Hispanics by 51 to 46 percent). Such shifting attitudes provide nothing but chilly comfort to champions of affirmative action.

On a variety of fronts, then, the practice now faces more resistance in this nation than ever before. Should another affirmative action case be granted certiorari by the United States Supreme Court, there is every reason to think that it will meet determined resistance by all the conservative justices.

In the face of that resistance, colleges and universities themselves are silently backing away, bit by bit, from affirmative action. Data from more than 1,300 four-year colleges and universities in the United States show that the use of race and ethnicity in admissions declined sharply after the mid-1990s, especially at public institutions. The proportion of public four-year colleges considering minority status in admissions has fallen from more than 60 percent to about 35 percent. Among private institutions, the drop during the same years has been notable but less dramatic, from 57 percent to 45 percent. The major decline came after 1995, when the campaign against affirmative action intensified, and schools, particularly public ones, thrown on the defensive, retreated. They were reacting not only to actual litigation but also to its threat. While colleges and universities that are considered elite are more likely to have practiced affirmative action and to have been more protective of it, even they have retreated. Few innovative or vigorous forms of affirmative action are now in play in the face of courts and federal agencies exercising strict scrutiny when examining admissions procedures and in the face of an increasingly suspicious citizenry.

Another reality is redefining, and probably weakening, the meaning of affirmative action. Although few schools publicize the fact, one of the central historic principles giving rise to affirmative action is being undermined. President Johnson's speech assumed that affirmative action would help the descendants of former slaves (he made no mention of Hispanics). That assumption from yesteryear is out of sync with today's realities. Affirmative action more and more functions to open the campus not only to the descendants of former slaves but to black students with different cultural and political heritages. Once championed, as in Johnson's speech, as a means of reparation or restitution, affirmative action now turns out to be helping hundreds and hundreds of young people who have suffered the wounds of old-fashioned American racism little or not at all. More than a quarter of the black students enrolled at selective American colleges and universities are immigrants or the children of immigrants. African-American students born in the United States thus turn out to be more underrepresented (given their presence in the U.S. population) at selective colleges than one might imagine. At some of the most exclusive institutions (Columbia, Princeton, Yale, and the University of Pennsylvania), no less than two-fifths of those admitted as "black" are of immigrant origin. Such facts, as they come into view, blunt the force of arguments favoring affirmative action. Diversity and restitution are better reasons than diversity alone, but restitution seems less and less in play.

Diversity itself, moreover, seems weaker and weaker as an argument for affirmative action when many campuses now appear, at least to the public at large, more diverse than ever before. The increasing presence on campus of students from myriad ethnic groups (Indian, Vietnamese, Chinese, Korean, Iranian, and many others) and the consequent reduction of "white" students (witness student populations at the University of California at Berkeley, UCLA, Stanford, USC, Columbia, and other schools) undercut the notion that American higher education is still unfairly monochromatic.

Yet another reason lies behind the decline, in practice, of affirmative action: it is expensive—in more ways than one. A large proportion of students benefiting from affirmative action also benefit from financial aid. As administrators, facing breathtaking drops in endowment and thus endowment income, constantly scrutinize budgets to find ways to strip out costs, they look hungrily at the sizable amount of money that could come from tuition income (an asset) that is lost in financial aid (a liability). They remain aware of the institutional commitment to the social good of affirmative action and of the model commonwealth; but as officials responsible for the fiscal health of the schools where they work; they know the cost of supporting such a social good. The tension between doing what is right for society in the largest sense and keeping the school solvent bedevils such administrators. Nonetheless, as the tension is resolved, affirmative action is further compromised.

Facing this kind of opposition—legal, public opinion, and fiscal—what, then, is the likely future of affirmative action? We return to Justice O'Connor's remark about 2028. She was, I think, wrong if she was making a prediction. (And, indeed, she has backed off the remark.) Affirmative action will still be needed to fortify the model commonwealth, and it will still be needed given the continuing gap in tested academic preparation between black and Hispanic students and others. Thomas Espenshade, the Princeton professor who has studied admissions numbers, predicts that, given the slow rate of convergence in test outcomes between black and white students, "it is likely to take another century to reach parity." And for all that time, affirmative action will likely meet with opposition in the courts and in public opinion almost everywhere it is practiced. But the differences between public and private institutions suggest a solution to the legal and ethical challenge presented by affirmative action.

Public institutions, post-Michigan, will continue to confront vigilant and skeptical adversaries determined to discover if the admissions procedures at such places are flouting the law by allowing affirmative-action policies to fly below the radar. When Justice Ruth Bader Ginsburg dissented in *Gratz et al. v. Bollinger et al.*, she commented that there was one thing worse than racially divisive admission policies, and that was "achieving similar numbers through winks, nods and disguises." No public institution can now afford the slightest risk of contriving artificial and bad-faith circumventions of the law.

But private institutions are different, very different. Their relative insulation from courts (because they do not take much public money) and referendums allows them to protect affirmative action more steadfastly than public institutions can. One person at the center of the Supreme Court's decisions in 2003, Lee C. Bollinger, who was president of the University of Michigan from 1996 to 2002 and is now president of Columbia, a private university, told *The Chronicle Review* in 2007, "I am glad that independent institutions retain the autonomy to support diversity efforts that make our graduates more competitive candidates for employers and graduate schools, as well as better informed citizens in our democracy and the world." And former Justice O'Connor herself, perhaps imagining the years from now until 2028, observed in 2007 the irony that private colleges, not covered by state bans on preferences, may—by virtue of that autonomy—end up being more diverse in their enrollments than public colleges.

But oddly enough, private colleges and universities may turn out to be relatively less attractive targets than public institutions for some potential litigants. That is because anti-affirmative-action organizations, such as the Center for Equal Opportunity (led by Linda Chavez and Roger Clegg) or its companion-in-arms, the Center for Individual Rights (led by Terence J. Pell), which might be expected to bring suits pleading reverse discrimination against selective public and private institutions in equal measure, strongly favor individual rights and generally dislike intrusions on what they deem as institutions not established by the government. Jonathan Alger, senior vice president and general counsel at Rutgers University, follows these issues closely and has observed that public institutions, as taxpayer-supported entities, are often seen by such organizations as more attractive targets for litigation involving the application of federal anti-discrimination law.

Hence, if they are prepared to spend the money to admit students "holistically," one by one, and if they are comfortable with some admitted students whose board scores and grades are noncompetitive but whose individual promise is compelling, private schools can hold on to some level of affirmative action. Like public institutions, however, they cannot afford to disregard budgetary reality: affirmative action never comes free.

But why should private institutions and their leaders continue to carry the banner of affirmative action? The answer resides in the cultural and historical environment in which many of those schools were founded and in the separation from the world around them that they chose upon that founding. Many of them (Quaker, Roman Catholic, Methodist, and Presbyterian) grew out of deep religious or spiritual conviction; others were quickened by imperatives arising from the dreams of ambitious founders, such as Leland Stanford, John D. Rockefeller, and Ezra Cornell. Several of them—the Ivy League schools, Stanford, Duke, Rice, Chicago—are now among the most prestigious (and wealthiest) academies in the nation. Self-directed, they owe much of their success to the individual aspirations they have championed and cultivated. For schools with such histories, the appeal of marching to a drummer not put into position by the state will always prove attractive. To them, I believe, we must look not only to preserve the civic value of affirmative action, but to redeem it in the eyes of the nation.

But they are and will continue to be playing against the odds. While they can be comforted by their origins—secular or religious, but always independent—they will have to live with the fact that the public at large has an ever-declining interest in the central buttress for affirmative action: the model commonwealth. But for those living on campuses where different moral concerns resound, the formation and protection of that commonwealth has been an abiding goal, decade after decade. In response to those moral concerns, the private institutions must act, explicitly and publicly; their policies of recruitment and admission should be intentional, painstaking, and undertaken proudly.

Just how determined and tenacious will they have to be? Courageously so, for all of the reasons I have given. Moreover, they must be especially attentive to one particular chapter of American history—a distressing one—as it has unfolded in this country. That chapter, about African-American males, reveals just how difficult the future of affirmative action will be. The dwindling population of African-American males on college campuses over the last four decades marks the most stunning failure in sustaining the model commonwealth. It also illuminates how limited universities and colleges are in what they can do, even if unconstrained by courts and public opinion.

While the proportion of black students on American college and university campuses, both public and private, rose from 9 percent in 1976 to 13 percent in 2004 (with blacks continuing to represent about 12 percent of the national population), the proportion who were men was the same in 2002—4.3 percent—as it was in 1976. Thirty years ago, 43 percent of undergraduate degrees conferred on African Americans were won by males, but by 2002/2003 that percentage had dropped to 33 percent. Black women, however, continued an ascendancy uninterrupted for years. According to the Joint Center for Political and Economic Studies, black men represented 7.9 percent of the 18- to 24-year-olds in the U.S. population in 2000, but they constituted just 2.8 percent of undergraduate enrollments in 50 of the best public universities in the nation in 2004. In each of the 30 flagship universities, fewer than 500 black male undergraduates were enrolled that year.

Even after being enrolled, less than half of all black male students who start college at a four-year institution graduate in six years or less, a rate more than 20 percentage points lower than the white graduation rate. That is not good news: it is the lowest college completion rate among all racial groups for both sexes. Perhaps most striking about these discouraging figures is that many black male students at some of the best institutions would likely not be enrolled at all if they were not athletes. The same Joint Center study reveals that more than one out of every five black men at 21 flagship public institutions was a student athlete in 2004. At 42 of these universities, more than one out of every three football players was black. At 38 of those schools, 50 percent or more of the basketball team was made up of black men. A dispiriting way of putting this is to say that, without their presence on many campuses to field teams in basketball and football, black males would barely exist in the model commonwealth. One goal of affirmative action, then, a campus fully representative of the diversity of the nation, can be achieved only when black males are present as students in proportion to their presence in the nation as a whole, and not just as athletes who also happen to be students.

If African-American males are underrepresented in colleges or universities, they are overrepresented in federal, state, and county prisons, jails, and juvenile detention facilities. About one in three black men will go to prison in his lifetime, compared to one in 17 white males. One in three black men between the ages of 20 and 29 already lives under some form of correctional supervision or control. The Bureau of Justice Statistics reports that some 186,000 black males between the ages of 18 and 24 were behind bars in federal and state prisons and local jails in 2005.

No amount of affirmative action, at either private or public colleges and universities, will free these men from jail. Nor will affirmative action be able to reach into the homes, neighborhoods, and schools to rectify the distressing situations—poverty, drugs, families customarily without either husband or father—that once served such men, and will now serve others, so badly. Nothing that colleges and universities do will be enough to rewrite the history of racial inequality that has, for decade after decade, poisoned this nation's history. Black men in prison are a function of that poisonous history, and affirmative action is a societal antidote to this and other existing effects of racism. We must not forget that history. History matters.

Private universities and colleges now stand at the center of this national drama. The burden upon them is great, and so is the weight of energetically sustaining the ideal of a model commonwealth. Nothing less than the essential civic and moral meaning of these schools is at stake. They must, because they can, act in ways that public institutions of higher learning now seem precluded from doing. The way forward since 1964 has been difficult; the way forward from 2010 will be even harder. But this difficulty can be eased just as so many American problems have been eased in the past: with a combination of individual desire and private money. This approach can make the process of admission thorough, detailed, and vigilant in recognizing promise in the lives of the next generation of American young people.

Single-Minded: The Real Meaning of Privilege

By Helena Andrews
The Root, October 8, 2010

Helena Andrews re-examines her privileged private-school education after seeing the documentary Waiting for Superman.

Someone called me "privileged" the other day, and I took it as a backhanded insult. *How dare you!* Lucky? Sure. Grateful? Most days. But privileged? Those were the kids who didn't have to answer phones in the main office every summer to pay for thick copies of *The Odyssey* and *The Iliad*. Those were the kids who didn't get called out of Mr. Feinstein's math class and into the guidance counselor's office because, "Despite your A's, your mother owes us 800 bucks."

But after watching *Waiting for Superman*, David Guggenheim's documentary about the fissures in and possible fixes to this country's public education system, I understood more clearly what it means to be privileged. More than a shock, it was something closer to a slap in the face.

In *Waiting for Superman*, Guggenheim tells the story of "the statistics" through the plight of five kids looking to beat them. Anthony, Francisco, Bianca, Daisy and Emily are kindergartners and eighth-graders from disparate backgrounds: urban, suburban, black, white and Latino, from Silicon Valley to Harlem.

Each child's parents, feeling trapped by finances and location, turn to a lottery to rescue their kids from the schools that are failing them for a host of both unjustifiable and legitimate reasons that in the end don't matter. If your first-grader's teacher doesn't have time for a parent-teacher conference, then are you just supposed to stop asking?

The documentary exposes the lie that says that those silly Facebook groups— "I Went to Private School, Strumpet" and "I Went to Public School, Bitch"—are just for fun. Some of the country's best and brightest are products of a solid public education, the film makes clear. But what about the kids who need more class time, more one-on-one time—just more? For those students, the benefit of a private-like education is a privilege that should be a right.

"I don't care if we have to get up at 5:00 a.m. every morning," explains Maria, Francisco's mom, in the film, after she learns about the Harlem Success Academy, a public (i.e., free) charter school about 45 minutes by train from their home in the Bronx, N.Y. Francisco's teacher says that he's behind in reading, but Maria works with him every night and has even found him a free, one-on-one tutor at a local college.

Clearly he needs more out of his school—attention, time, etc. So she enters him in the lottery at Harlem Success. Francisco is one of 792 students applying for the remaining 40 spots in the second-grade class. He has a 5 percent chance of getting in. "I won't give up on my kids," says Maria, a social worker and the first in her family to graduate from college. "There's just so many different parents out there that want so much for the children."

Maria might have been talking about parents like Nakia, a single mother who pays $500 a month to send her only daughter, Bianca, to the parochial school across the street because she knows that the local elementary school simply isn't good enough. But when her hours at work get cut back, Nakia falls behind on tuition. Scholarships have dried up, and the school refuses to let Bianca graduate from kindergarten with the rest of her friends.

So instead of walking across the stage and posing for pictures, the 6-year-old is stuck looking out of her bedroom window at all the little girls and boys getting ready for the ceremony just on the other side of the street. "It's cruel," says Nakia, wiping tears from her eyes.

Gulping down the lump in my own throat, her tears reminded me of all the ones I must have avoided growing up. From eighth to 12th grades, I attended an expensive private school in downtown Los Angeles, and for years my mother, like Nakia's and Francisco's, fought hard for her magic.

Because a true professional never reveals her secrets—lunch money, new backpacks, bus passes, cheerleading uniforms and school trips—simply appeared without my knowing how. I knew full well that we weren't anything remotely close to rich (I arrived at class via the MTA, not a Mercedes), but somehow I still got to do everything all the other rich kids did, including being a smart-ass, with the grades to prove it.

Once, when I was a freshman in high school, I lost the $200 my mother gave me to pay off something important. Instead of getting mad, she got me a job, and from then on I realized that my charmed 8:00 a.m.-to-4:00 p.m. life wasn't free. Small class sizes, computer labs, books I still own today, a nurse with Advil at the ready and teachers who were visibly outraged by mediocrity all came at a price. I was privileged, but only because I had a parent, who, like the ones featured in *Waiting for Superman*, considered it her right to exploit every opportunity.

When my mother turned 50, we threw a party for her at the Compton Baptist church the Andrews family has attended since 1960. I knew I was supposed to make a speech, but I figured that winging it would work just as well as reading off a napkin. With the mic in my hand, tears gathering and a mind swimming with every amazing thing this woman had done for me over the last two decades, my first sentence was clear: "Thank you for being so dedicated to my education."

Why I Choose State Education over Private School

By John O'Farrell
The Guardian, July 30, 2012

John O'Farrell explains why he chose a state school to give his children the very best education.

Last week in *Education Guardian* Janet Murray wrote about why she sent her child to a private school. Within a few hours, 500 comments had been posted online, a number of them congratulating the *Guardian* on this brilliant satirical parody of the same article that we see on an annual basis from London journalists. I don't want to have a go at Janet Murray in particular, although *Education Guardian* does seem a curious gig for someone who didn't even try state education at nursery level. Instead, I would like humbly to suggest that Janet is wasting her money. But worse, she is doing her child a disservice. There are some things in this country where paying more actually gets you inferior results. And for me, private education is right up there with G4S security.

Twelve years of being deeply involved in education issues have taught me that no parent reacts well to being told they've made the wrong educational choice for their child. It suggests the subtext "I don't like the way your kids are turning out," which is never guaranteed to enamor you to old friends. A genteel social occasion in some middle-class home can turn in an instant. "So we were thinking of taking Timothy out of the local primary to get him ready for Common Entrance . . ." A couple of hours later, police sirens are flashing outside, yellow "crime scene" tape blocks off the entire road as dinner party guests are helped into ambulances clutching bleeding noses and fractured jaws.

But it's because this is very important and emotive stuff. It feels like the frontline in the eternal struggle between personal interests and what's best for society in general. Anyone can be leftwing if it means just reading the *Guardian* and voting Labor occasionally. But having enough faith in the public sector to entrust it with your child's welfare, that demands a confidence in the system and a confidence in your own children that many left-leaning parents do not seem to possess.

However, this is a false dilemma. In any choice between "my children" and "wider society" all of us would put our own kids first. My wife and I sent our kids to a state school because we wanted what was best for them. We wanted the very best education they could possibly receive. And guess what—it was all free! Imagine, we said to each other, if we didn't spend £10,000 a year each on school fees? That would be a six-figure sum by the time they go to university. How much better it would be if that money was put into a savings account for a down-payment on a flat each, or saved for even later when they were starting a family? Obviously we never did put the money away; I think I spent most of it on beer and curries, but the point still stands.

It's quite possible that if I had spent a fortune on them, they would have got an extra grade A GCSE here and there, and a rugger trip to Johannesburg along the way. But that's not the same thing as getting an education. My kids both walked to their local school with classmates they never would have met on the private bus to Dulwich College. (Top tip by the way, there is a London bus, free to children, that travels exactly the same route.) My kids rubbed along with classmates of all races and classes. They know the other people in their community, they are not frightened when they walk down the high street after dark, they have gained an understanding of how society works that you could never get in an institution from which most of society is excluded.

There is a world of difference between studying Islam and going to school with lots of Muslims. Sociology is a different subject when there are classmates missing the school trip because they can't afford a passport. (And please don't tell me how mixed your children's private school is, because believe me, it really isn't. When we drove past a prep school near where I live, my daughter said "I never knew there were so many blonde people in London.")

Such was my trust in the state sector that I very much left them to it. Oh, except for campaigning for this new school and then becoming its chair of governors for eight years. In fact, my involvement in the school only increased my admiration for the outstanding teachers my children encountered at Lambeth Academy. I am not quite naff enough to list their exam results here, but they and their friends did fantastically, despite a wobbly start when the school first opened. And that was without the misery of two or three hours of extra homework every night and school on Saturday mornings.

Obviously there is no way that Lambeth Academy will ever achieve the exam statistics of nearby private schools. But studying the results of schools with socially selective intakes is a bogus science. Children from advantaged backgrounds are going to do much better wherever they go to school—that is module 1 of a GCSE in The Bleedin' Obvious. If you read to your children from an early age, if the poor things are dragged round museums every other weekend, if you have the time and energy for them and are not leaving them at home alone every evening because you have a second job cleaning floors at Heathrow, then your children will do better academically. If your local comp got 50% five A–Cs including English and maths, that doesn't mean that your child has only a 50% chance of achieving that over-simplistic benchmark. What parents generally perceive as a "better school" usually means a school with an intake that is easier to teach.

Janet Murray was seduced by the idea of the extra attention that her daughter would get in a class of 11 (too small in my unprofessional opinion). But it's actually quite important to learn to wait your turn, to appreciate that everything in life is not handed to you on a plate, that it's down to you to make things happen. I wouldn't mind so much if the privilege and social advantage of Britain's most famous public schools led to extra respect for one's fellow man or woman, but it doesn't; it tends to teach rank snobbery and an unmerited sense of superiority. Private schools are always boasting about all those extra-curricular activities. It's a shame Eton doesn't offer after-school tuition in Humility.

So you don't have to send your children to private school if you want them to turn out a particular way. Far simpler to put a hundred grand on the barbecue and teach them to be rude to waiters yourself. Or spend 10 years putting £50 notes into the paper shredder while instructing them to be frightened of hoodies.

Not only is this divisive system bad for both sets of students involved, it is also bad for the country. The top tiers of our institutions and industries are packed with former public school boys, who are only there because of connections and an entitlement and self-confidence that is not matched by their ability to do an excellent job. George Osborne is not chancellor because he is a financial genius without equal in the United Kingdom. He is there because he is chums with the prime minister. When they all trashed restaurants together, maybe it was Osborne who produced the roll of notes to pay for the damage. "George seems pretty good with money—maybe he should be chancellor?"

But none of that matters as much as what is best for your child. There are all sorts of different children, and all sorts of different schools and I appreciate that not every child will thrive in every institution. But the moment you decide to pay, you are denying your child a basic education in what their own society is like. So don't be frightened of your own community; your children will amaze you with their resilience and adaptability and fluency in African-Caribbean swear words. One of the best lessons you can give them is demonstrating how much confidence you have in them. So be selfish. Put your children first. Send them to your local state school.

(Oh, but just a short PS to my own kids. In 30 years' time when it comes to choosing a residential care home for your aged father, disregard everything I've written here about the wonderful public sector. Feel free to spend a fortune on every private luxury available.)

Screw U: How For-Profit Colleges Rip You Off

By Yasmeen Qureshi, Sarah Gross, and Lisa Desai
Mother Jones, September/October 2013

The for-profit college industry makes a killing while handing out expensive degrees that fizzle in the real world.

The folks who walked through Tressie McMillan Cottom's door at an ITT Technical Institute campus in North Carolina were desperate. They had graduated from struggling high schools in low-income neighborhoods. They'd worked crappy jobs. Many were single mothers determined to make better lives for their children. "We blocked off a corner, and that's where we would put the car seats and the strollers," she recalls. "They would bring their babies with them and we'd encourage them to do so, because this is about building motivation and urgency."

McMillan Cottom now studies education issues at the University of California-Davis's Center for Poverty Research, but back then her job was to sign up people who'd stopped in for information, often after seeing one of the TV ads in which ITT graduates rave about recession-proof jobs. The idea was to prey on their anxieties—and to close the deal fast. Her title was "enrollment counselor," but she felt uncomfortable calling herself one, because she quickly realized she couldn't act in the best interest of the students. "I was told explicitly that we don't enroll and we don't admit: We are a sales force."

After six months at ITT Tech, McMillan Cottom quit. That same day, she called up every one of the students she'd enrolled and gave them the phone number for the local community college.

With 147 campuses and more than 60,000 students nationwide, ITT Educational Services (which operates both ITT Tech and the smaller Daniel Webster College) is one of the largest companies in the burgeoning for-profit college industry, which now enrolls up to 13 percent of higher-education students. ITT is also the most profitable of the big industry players: Its revenue has nearly doubled over the past seven years, closing in on $1.3 billion last year, when CEO Kevin Modany's compensation topped $8 million.

To achieve those returns, regulators suspect, ITT has been pushing students to take on financial commitments they can't afford. The Consumer Financial Protection Bureau is looking into ITT's student loan program, and the Securities and Exchange Commission is investigating how those loans were issued and sold to investors. (Neither agency would comment about the probes.) The attorneys general of some 30 states have banded together to investigate for-profit colleges; targets include ITT, Corinthian, Kaplan, and the University of Phoenix.

A 2012 investigation led by Sen. Tom Harkin (D-Iowa) singled out ITT for employing "some of the most disturbing recruiting tactics among the companies examined." A former ITT recruiter told the Senate education committee that she used and taught a process called the "pain funnel," in which admissions officers would ask students increasingly probing questions about where their lives were going wrong. Properly used, she said, it would "bring a prospect to their inner child, an emotional place intended to have the prospect say, 'Yes, I will enroll.'"

For-profit schools recruit heavily in low-income communities, and most students finance their education with a mix of federal Pell grants and federal student loans. But government-backed student loans max out at $12,500 per school year, and tuition at for-profits can go much higher; at ITT Tech it runs up to $25,000. What's more, for-profit colleges can only receive 90 percent of their revenue from government money. For the remaining 10 percent, they count on veterans—GI Bill money counts as outside funds—as well as scholarships and private loans.

Whatever the source of the funds, the schools' focus is on boosting enrollment. A former ITT financial-aid counselor named Jennifer (she asked us not to use her last name) recalls that prospects were "browbeaten and hassled into signing forms on their first visit to the school because it was all slam, bam, thank you ma'am." The moment students enrolled, Jennifer would check their federal loan and grant eligibility to see how much money they qualified for. After students maxed out their federal grants and loans, there was typically an outstanding tuition balance of several thousand dollars. Jennifer says she was given weekly reports detailing how much money students on her roster owed. She would pull them from class and present them with a stark choice: get kicked out of school or make a payment on the spot. For years, ITT even ran a (now discontinued) in-house private loan program, known as PEAKS, in partnership with Connecticut-based Liberty Bank, with interest rates reaching 14.75 percent. (Federal student loans top out at 6.8 percent.)

Jennifer, who had previously worked at the University of Alabama, says she felt like a collection agent. "My supervisors and my campus president were breathing down my neck, and I was threatened that I was going to be fired if I didn't do this," she says. Yet she knew that students would have little means to get out from under the debt they were signing up for. Roughly half of ITT Tech students dropped out during the period covered by the Harkin report, and the job prospects for those who did graduate were hardly stellar. Even though a for-profit degree "costs a lot more," Harkin told *Dan Rather Reports*, "in the job market it's worth less than a degree from, say, a community college."

Jennifer says the career services office at her campus wasn't much help; students told her they were simply given a printout from Monster.com. (ITT says its career counselors connect students with a range of job services and also help them write résumés, find leads, and arrange interviews.) By the time she was laid off, Jennifer believed the college "left students in worse situations than they were to begin with."

It's not just whistleblowers who are complaining about ITT. There's an entire website, myittexperience.com, dedicated to stories from disappointed alumni. That's how we found Margie Donaldson, a 38-year-old who says her dream has always been to get a college degree and work in corporate America: "Especially being a little black girl in the city of Detroit, [a degree] was everything to me."

Donaldson was making nearly $80,000 packing parts at Chrysler when the company, struggling to survive the recession, offered her a buyout. She decided to use it to get the college degree that she never finished 13 years before. Five years later, she is $75,000 in debt and can't find a full-time job despite her B.A. in criminal justice from ITT. She's applied for more than 200 positions but says 95 percent of the applications went nowhere because her degree is not regionally accredited, so employers don't see it as legitimate. Nor can she use her credits toward a degree at another school. Working part time as an anger management counselor, she brings in about $1,400 a month, but there are no health benefits, and with three kids ages 7, 14, and 18, she can barely make ends meet. She has been able to defer her federal student loans, but the more than $20,000 in private loans she took out via ITT can't be put off, so she's in default with 14.75 percent interest—a detail she says her ITT financial-aid adviser never explained to her—and $150 in late fees tacked on to her balance each month. Donaldson says she has tried to work out an affordable payment plan, but the PEAKS servicers won't agree until she pays an outstanding balance of more than $3,500—more than double her monthly income. "It puts me and my family, and other families, I'm sure, in a very tough situation financially," she says.

Donaldson says she didn't understand how different ITT was from a public college. If she had attended one of Michigan's 40-plus state and community colleges, her tuition would have been roughly one-third of what it was at ITT. Now, she says, all that time and money feels wasted: "It's almost like I'm like a paycheck away from going back to where I grew up."

❖

Study Haul
How for-profit schools leave their students high and dry.
- **96%** of students at for-profit colleges take out loans. **13%** of community college students, **48%** of public college students, and **57%** of nonprofit private college students do.
- For-profit colleges enroll **13%** of higher-education students but receive **25%** of federal student aid.
- The **15** publicly traded for-profit colleges receive more than **85%** of their revenue from federal student loans and aid.
- **42%** of students attending for-profit two-year colleges take out private

student loans. **5%** of students at community colleges and **18%** at private not-for-profit two-year colleges do.

- **1 in 25** borrowers who graduate from college defaults on his or her student loans. But among graduates of two-year for-profit colleges, the rate is **1 in 5**.

- Students who attended for-profit schools account for **47%** of all student loan defaults.

Sources: Sen. Harkin, Consumer Finance Protection Bureau, Education Sector

What College Can Mean
to the Other America

By Mike Rose
The Chronicle of Higher Education, September 16, 2011

It has been nearly 50 years since Michael Harrington wrote *The Other America*, pulling the curtain back on invisible poverty within the United States. If he were writing today, Harrington would find the same populations he described then: young, marginally educated people who drift in and out of low-pay, dead-end jobs, and older displaced workers, unable to find work as industries transform and shops close. But he would find more of them, especially the young, their situation worsened by further economic restructuring and globalization. And while the poor he wrote about were invisible in a time of abundance, ours are visible in a terrible recession, although invisible in most public policy. In fact, the poor are drifting further into the dark underbelly of American capitalism.

One of the Obama administration's mantras is that we need to "out-innovate, out-educate, and out-build" our competition in order to achieve fuller prosperity. The solution to our social and economic woes lies in new technologies, in the cutting edge. This is our "Sputnik moment," a very American way to frame our problems. However, the editors of *The Economist* wrote a few months back that this explanation of our economic situation is "mostly nonsense."

Instead, the business-friendly, neoliberal magazine offered a sobering—at times almost neo-Marxist—assessment of what it considers the real danger in our economy, something at the core of Harrington's analysis: chronic, ingrained joblessness that is related to our social and economic structure. We are looking toward the horizon of innovation when we should be looking straight in front of us at the tens of millions of chronically unemployed Americans and providing comprehensive occupational, educational, and social services. Otherwise, to cite an earlier issue of *The Economist* that also dealt with American inequality, we risk "calcifying into a European-style class-based society." For people without school or work, we already have.

There are a few current policy initiatives that are aimed at helping the disadvantaged gain economic mobility, mostly through some form of postsecondary education. Sadly, the most ambitious of these—the federal American Graduation Initiative—was sacrificed during the health-care negotiations, although some smaller projects remained in the stimulus package and the Department of Education.

Private foundations, notably Gates and Lumina, have been sponsoring such efforts as well. These efforts reach a small percentage of poor and low-income Americans and, on average, are aimed at the more academically skilled among them—although many still require remedial English and mathematics. A certificate or degree alone will not automatically lift them out of hard times—there is a bit of magic-bullet thinking in these college initiatives—but getting a decent basic education could make a significant difference in their lives. At the least, these efforts are among the few antipoverty measures that have some degree of bipartisan support.

For the last year and a half, I have been spending time at an inner-city community college that serves this population, and I have seen firsthand the effects of poverty and long-term joblessness. Although some students attend the college with the goal of transfer, the majority come for its well-regarded occupational programs. More than 90 percent must take one or more basic-skills courses; 60 percent are on financial aid. A fair number have been through the criminal-justice system.

As I have gotten to know these students, the numbers have come alive. Many had chaotic childhoods, went to underperforming schools, and never finished high school. With low-level skills, they have had an awful time in the labor market. Short-term jobs, long stretches of unemployment, no health care. Many, the young ones included, have health problems that are inadequately treated if treated at all. I remember during my first few days on the campus noticing the number of people who walked with a limp or irregular gait.

What really strikes me, though, is students' level of engagement, particularly in the occupational programs. There are a few people who seem to be marking time, but most listen intently as an instructor explains the air-supply system in a diesel engine or the way to sew supports into an evening dress. And they do and redo an assignment until they get it right. Hope and desire are brimming. Many of the students say this is the first time school has meant anything to them. More than a few talk about turning their lives around. It doesn't take long to imagine the kind of society we would have if more people had this opportunity.

But right at the point when opportunity is offered, it is being threatened by severe budget cuts in education and social services. For several years, the college—like so many in the United States—has been able to offer only a small number of summer classes, and classes are being cut during the year. Enrollment in existing classes is growing. Student-support services are scaled back. And all the while, more people are trying to enroll at the college; some will have to be turned away, and those who are admitted will tax an already burdened system.

Given the toll the recession has taken on state and local governments, policy makers face "unprecedented challenges" and say they "have no other choice" but to make cuts in education. Secretary of Education Arne Duncan, borrowing a now-ubiquitous phrase, has called the necessity to do more with less "the new normal."

I don't dispute the difficulty of budgeting in the recession, nor the fact that education spending includes waste that should be cut. But we need to resist the framing of our situation as inevitable and normal. This framing makes the recession a catastrophe without culpability, neutralizing the civic and moral dimensions of both the causes of the recession and the way policy makers respond to it.

The civic and moral dimensions also are diminished by the powerful market-based orientation to economic and social problems. Antigovernment, anti-welfare-state, antitax—this ideology undercuts broad-scale public responses to inequality.

If the editors of *The Economist* are right, the deep cuts in education—especially to programs and institutions that help poor people connect to school or work—will have disastrous long-term economic consequences that far outweigh immediate budgetary gains. And rereading *The Other America* reminds us that the stakes go beyond the economic to the basic civic question: What kind of society do we want to become? Will there be another Michael Harrington 50 years from now writing about an America that has a higher rate of poverty and even wider social divides?

Private Schools in Poor Countries Offer Crucial Escape from Inept Public Systems

By Charles Kenny
Today's Zaman, March 21, 2014

When Americans think about private education, what likely comes to mind are posh-sounding names like Milton or Collegiate, where the elites of Boston and Manhattan—for the low, low price of $40,000 a year—send their offspring to give them a small leg up in the race to Harvard or Yale.

But in developing countries, private schools are a big deal too, and they play a very different role: For just cents a day, they're giving some of the world's very poorest children a chance to escape the absolute deprivation their parents have suffered their whole lives. And by showing what can be achieved in schools where teachers actually make an effort to teach and where principals actually care about results, they're laying the basis for a revolution in global education.

For many countries in Africa, Latin America and Asia, one of the most dramatic changes over the past couple of generations has been the number of children who go to school. Take the West African country of Guinea-Bissau, where practically all of the country's primary-school-age kids had entered the formal education system in 2010 and nearly two-thirds were completing the full six years of primary school. That's up from around a quarter completing only a decade earlier. Across sub-Saharan Africa as a whole, the percentage of children completing primary school has climbed from 54 percent in the early 2000s to 69 percent in 2011.

But enrollment doesn't tell the full story.

Although more and more kids worldwide are making the walk to school every morning, it's not at all clear that they're actually learning something in class. In Guinea-Bissau, independent surveys suggest only about a quarter of children are able to do even the most basic addition, let alone handle fractions. Less than one-fifth of Bissau-Guinean schoolchildren can read and comprehend simple words. It isn't just small African states: In India, only around one in four 10- and 11-year-olds (most of whom completed their primary education) can read a simple paragraph, perform division, tell time and handle money—all skills they should have learned after just two years of schooling. It's a global problem: From Panama to Tunisia, Brazil to Indonesia, average scores on international math tests would put students from developing countries among the bottom tenth of Danish pupils, according to analysis from Harvard University's Lant Pritchett. (Denmark has typical scores on these tests among countries in the Organization for Economic Cooperation and Development, making it a good developed-world comparison.)

There are lots of reasons why kids aren't learning—especially in poorer countries. Many arrive at school malnourished or have illiterate parents who can't help with homework. The schools themselves lack books, desks, even basic supplies. All too often, they lack teachers. In some countries, as many as 25 percent of teachers don't even show up for work on a regular basis. But perhaps the biggest problem is that teachers and principals face little incentive to help kids learn. They're paid to get through the syllabus—not to ensure their pupils retain any of it.

The good news, however, is that across the developing world, tens of millions of parents are refusing to accept that their kids sit in class day after day learning nothing. Instead, they're moving their children to private schools. And these aren't just wealthy parents. Extremely poor mothers and fathers are taking some of their limited income and using it to ensure that their kids can have a better life through higher-quality education.

In India, as many as two-thirds of urban kids and 28 percent of rural children attend private school. The median per-person income is about $565 per year, and the poorer districts and states have more rural private schools than the richer ones. In Pakistan, roughly one-third of children attend private primary school. Parents there spend about 10 cents a day on private education—sure, that's less than one-thousandth of what it costs to attend Phillips Academy in Andover, Mass., but it's a lot of money in a country where more than half the population subsists on less than $2 a day.

The investment is paying off. Kids in private schools are learning far more than their friends stuck in government-financed classrooms. In the Indian state of Andhra Pradesh, for example, the government used a lottery system to hand out vouchers to some parents to cover the costs of private school attendance. Analysis by economists Karthik Muralidharan of the University of California, San Diego, and Venkatesh Sundararaman of the World Bank shows those students saw significantly higher test scores in a number of subjects than their peers who remained in public schools. This happens despite the fact that education costs per student were one-third of those in government schools—and teacher salaries were only one-fifth as high. But maybe the biggest endorsement is this: Four out of five public school teachers in India send their own kids to private school.

The pressure on developing-country education systems to deliver learning results is growing. They are shamed by published test results from international organizations like the OECD and by local civil society groups like Uwezo in East Africa and Pratham in India. And it doesn't look good for elected politicians when parents start voting with their feet—abandoning free public education in favor of fee-based private schooling.

But when it comes to reforming education systems, the answer isn't necessarily mass privatization. Remember, the principle of universal access to free primary education is enshrined in the UN's Universal Declaration of Human Rights. That means governments should be paying the tab for primary school—either public or private—and making sure that teachers and principals are put on notice: Either shape up or ship out. The real test is whether students are learning anything, not just attending.

Private Schools Exploring Blended Models

By Benjamin Herold
Education Week, January 29, 2014

Since becoming one of the first Roman Catholic elementary schools in the country to adopt a blended learning program, Mission Dolores Academy has boosted enrollment by 16 percent, cut per-pupil operating costs by one-third, and generated encouraging academic results.

Now, the 250-student school here wants to take the next step.

"Figuring out how to get data that people find reliable and actionable so that we can adapt our curriculum," said Principal Dan Storz, "has become kind of the Holy Grail."

Most observers agree that Catholic and other private or independent schools are several years behind public schools when it comes to embracing blended learning. If they adopt blended programs at all, the focus tends to be on cutting costs and expanding course offerings rather than rethinking how education is delivered.

But some advance-guard private and independent schools, like Mission Dolores, are beginning to leverage blended learning data to make strategic schoolwide decisions or overhaul their school's culture.

Others are looking to technology to provide students and teachers with more collaborative, engaging experiences. Private schools are forming consortia to share resources and ideas and encourage the creation of new blended learning materials.

They're all signs that nonpublic schools want to be leaders in the nascent blended learning movement, said John E. Chubb, president of the National Association of Independent Schools, or NAIS, in Washington.

"Our schools want to be producers, not just consumers, of online content," Mr. Chubb said. "They deserve credit for that level of entrepreneurship, and I think we'll see more."

According to the National Catholic Education Association, based in Arlington, Va., K–12 Catholic school enrollment has declined from a peak of 5.2 million students in 1965 to 2 million today. More than 2,000 Catholic schools have either closed or been consolidated in the past 13 years. NAIS member schools, which serve 569,000 students, according to the organization, have also struggled in recent years, in large part due to the shaky national economy.

Power through Data

Hit by those trends, Mission Dolores merged with a nearby school, Megan Furth Academy, in 2011. The school then received a $500,000 grant from various sources to work with a New York City-based nonprofit, Seton Education Partners, to go blended. The goals were to reduce costs by pushing class sizes higher and to bolster academic performance and relevance.

"The two go hand in hand," said Mr. Storz, the principal. "No matter how much money blended learning saves, your cost structure is going to be bad if you don't have families willing to pay tuition."

Located adjacent to a historic church in the heart of the gritty Mission District here, the academy uses a "classroom rotation" model in which groups of about 15 students cycle throughout the day between classroom computers and time with their teacher. The program has generated signs of positive growth in students' reading levels and math achievement.

One key has been granting teachers access to the "back end" of the software programs Mission Dolores uses.

"I understand the data now. Before, I had no clue what [students] were doing on computers," said Michelle Escobar, who teaches 7th and 8th grade reading.

The difference, she said, is that now she's able to more frequently regroup her students based on skill level and more regularly reteach the content or skills that students struggle to grasp.

Assistant Principal Paul F. Recktenwald said Mission Delores Academy administrators are trying to extend that approach by attempting to analyze school-level data from different software programs, two sets of standardized assessments, and more. Among other things, they hope to identify gaps in the school's curriculum and uncover inconsistencies in teachers' grading. Such sophisticated data use would put the academy at the cutting edge of blended learning programs, regardless of sector.

"We need to synthesize information to be more strategic," Mr. Recktenwald said.

Another Seton Education Partners elementary school, the DePaul Catholic School in Philadelphia, is using blended learning data to gauge students' noncognitive skills, part of an effort to emulate the "no excuses" culture favored by charter school networks such as KIPP—the Knowledge Is Power Program. At DePaul, students of all skill levels are rewarded for completing 85 percent of the online content that is difficult but doable for them—a sign of persistence.

Such networks and consortia are also supporting efforts by some nonpublic schools to use blended approaches to rethink the classroom experience.

The nonprofit Jesuit Virtual Learning Academy, based in Omaha, Neb., has for the past six years provided online coursework to students in some of the country's 60 Jesuit secondary schools. Now, the group is piloting an effort to create new blended approaches in subjects like history and theology and to connect students and teachers around the country.

"It's about digging deeper and finding ways of delivering collaborative experiences for students," said Jeffrey L. Hausman, the Jesuit academy's founder and executive director.

Another group, the Affordable Jewish Education Project, based in New York City, provides similar support to Jewish day schools.

And five independent high schools in Northern California recently formed the Bay Area Blend-Ed Consortium. That undertaking will focus on helping "students prepare for the changing methods of instruction and communication they will see in college and the workforce" while preserving the culture that lies "at the core" of their educational missions, the group said in a statement.

"It's a particularly valuable approach for these schools because they tend to be so small," said John Watson, the founder of the Evergreen Education Group, a Colorado-based online-learning consulting group involved in the consortium.

A Leadership Role

Elite private schools, meanwhile, are "infusing their programs with technology," said Mr. Chubb of the independent schools association, but the extent to which they are changing instruction is less evident.

That's partly because such schools are widely perceived to be working well. Families also expect those schools to provide intense student-teacher interaction in small classes.

But the dynamics of higher education are instructive, said Mr. Chubb. Elite institutions were slow to enter the online and blended arena but later quickly assumed a prominent role.

"We have an opportunity to [provide] some leadership in the field," he said. "The next step in all this, and where these schools are beginning to experiment, is re-thinking how students should learn."

3

Affordable Education: Majoring in Debt

Raeshel Smith receives her masters of arts in education from Washington State University at Tri-Cities during graduation ceremonies at Toyota Center in Kennewick, Washington.

The New Cost of Education

Student Loan Debt Reaches New Highs

As of 2014, approximately forty million Americans hold a combined $1.2 trillion in student loan debt—nearly triple the amount held ten years prior. Even worse, default rates are at their highest level in two decades. According to research by the New York Federal Reserve, delinquency rates actually improved for most types of loans during 2013, with student loans being the one major exception. Economists suspect this is because consumer loans such as credit cards, auto loans, and mortgages became more difficult to obtain following the 2008 financial crisis, while student loans remained readily available.

Different types of student loans have different terms with varying repayment timelines and interest rates. Some are backed by the federal government, while others are backed by private companies and banks. Federal student loans often have terms to ease the repayment burden, such as income-contingent payments, extended time for repayment, or deferral if the borrower returns to school or becomes unemployed. Some federal loans can even be "forgiven" if the borrower works in a community aid–related position for several years. Private lender loans are often, although not always, less accommodating. They tend to have higher interest rates than federal loans, and only some allow refinancing to help borrowers take advantage of improved interest rates.

Additionally, unlike other forms of debt, student loans are only discharged in bankruptcy under extreme circumstances. The government can garnish wages, Social Security disbursements, disability payments, and income tax refunds if a borrower defaults on a federal loan. Parents who cosign any type of loan on behalf of their children can receive the same penalties if the child defaults because cosigning is legally the same as if the parents had taken out the loan themselves.

Default Rates Rise

As of the end of 2013, about 11.5 percent of student loan balances were delinquent or in default. By contrast, credit card debt—traditionally the type of debt on which borrowers are most likely to default—had only a 9.5 percent default rate. And as high as student loan default rates seem, analysts worry that the number present an incomplete picture: the data does not include borrowers with loans that are not currently in repayment, either because they are still in school or because they are enrolled in a deferment program for financial reasons.

Interestingly, studies show that borrowers with larger student loan debt are less likely to default than those with smaller debt. Analysts from the Consumer

Financial Protection Bureau suspect this could indicate that borrowers with smaller student loan debt did not complete their degrees: as a result, they still need to repay the loan, but do not receive the higher salary that often comes with degree completion. These borrowers could make up a significant portion of student loan debt because the National Center for Education Statistics reported that, in 2011, only 59 percent of full-time, first-time undergraduate students who began a bachelor's degree program completed their degree at that institution within six years. Degree completion is the key to earnings increase, regardless of the degree program. According to the Bureau of Labor Statistics, individuals who complete an associate's degree have higher median weekly earnings and lower unemployment rates than those who attend some college but do not graduate, even if both individuals spent two years in school.

Changing Economic Landscape

During the temporary economic boom of the mid-2000s, students borrowed money to finance their degrees because job prospects looked promising. Few students worried about finding employment with a salary adequate to repay their loans. But when the bubble burst just as these students entered the job market in the late-2000s, the picture abruptly changed. Unemployment and underemployment rates rose significantly, and recent graduates found it difficult to find jobs at all, let alone ones that paid well enough to be able to afford their student loan bills.

But rather than seeing a decline in borrowing during the recession, the amount of student loan debt continued to increase. Many people went back to school to improve their employment prospects or wait out the recession. Some already had an undergraduate degree and took on additional debt to pay for graduate school, while others completed their first degree.

Additionally, the cost of undergraduate and graduate degrees has been steadily rising for the past few decades, and tuition rates have increased faster than inflation. And while the rate of tuition hikes is finally slowing, prices are still increasing, with published tuition and fees increasing by 2.9 percent in 2013. Since financial aid in the form of grants and scholarships has not kept up with tuition increases, students are bearing a higher percentage of college costs than in previous years.

The For-Profit Education Revolution

Despite the rising cost of college, enrollment at for-profit education institutions skyrocketed in the past decade. Many of these schools are significantly more expensive than traditional two- and four-year colleges, and the federal government is concerned about the financial repercussions these programs have for their students and for the federal loan program as a whole.

As of 2010, for-profit schools enrolled about 11 percent of college students, but received 26 percent of all federal student aid. Studies such as those conducted by the Center for Analysis of Postsecondary Education and Employment (CAPSEE) show that students attending for-profit colleges have higher debt loads and default rates than their counterparts at public and not-for-profit institutions. They are also more likely to be minorities, older students, single parents, and from lower income households, and have a GED than students attending traditional two- and four-year programs. And while their graduation rates are higher than students with similar backgrounds attending community colleges, they are more likely to experience long-term unemployment, and more likely to report being dissatisfied with their education several years after enrollment.

The US Department of Education is trying to intervene, especially as for-profit schools fail to deliver on promises of future employment, leaving students heavily burdened with student loan debt and few prospects for paying it back. Specifically, the government wants to restrict access to federal student loan money for any school whose graduates are consistently unable to obtain jobs sufficient to pay off their loans. But any attempt to restrict access to federal student loans raises important questions: Would this unfairly prevent low-income students from receiving a higher education? Or would it help nontraditional or disadvantaged students avoid being exploited for the financial gain of a for-profit education company?

Broader Economic Effects

Growing student loan burdens can significantly affect young adults' abilities to settle into postcollege life. Studies such as the 2013 report by the Consumer Financial Protection Bureau suggest that large monthly loan payments are one reason why many young adults return to living with their parents after college. They simply cannot afford to live on their own while repaying their loans with the salaries they receive. Even more troubling for long-term prospects is the fact that today's young adults contribute very little to retirement accounts early in their careers, likely for the same reason.

Rising student loans also impact the American economy as a whole. According to the New York Federal Reserve, until 2009, young adults with student loan debt were actually more likely to own homes and cars than their non-indebted counterparts. Analysts suspect that, prior to the recession, student loan debt correlated with individuals who had a college degree, and thus higher-income jobs and better credit that allowed them to afford these purchase and obtain favorable mortgages. Since 2009, however, the opposite has been true: individuals with student loan debt are now less likely to make these major purchases than their less-indebted counterparts.

Attempted Solutions

In light of its significance to young voters, rising student loan debt is one of the few issues that both political parties agree must be addressed. Republican Senator Marco Rubio and Democratic Senators Elizabeth Warren and Kirsten Gillibrand have discussed the need for student loan reform, but it remains to be seen whether political leaders can reach a bipartisan consensus on a solution.

Business analysts propose their own solutions to the growing crisis, largely placing the burden on the student to avoid borrowing too much. Some suggest requiring periodic written loan repayment plans that force students to reassess their future repayment abilities in light of their realistic earning potential, while others suggest that qualification for further loans should be tied to students' academic performance.

By contrast, government agencies want to place the burden on the colleges and universities. The US Department of Education proposed a rule requiring schools to prove that their degree programs provide students with employment opportunities sufficient to repay their loans in order to qualify as a recipient institution for federal loan money. However, the rule was defeated through a lawsuit filed by the Association of Private Sector Colleges and Universities, who argued that it unfairly cut off their institutions—and therefore their students—from the more favorable borrowing terms provided by federal loans. However, the self-interest is evident: as of 2012, about three quarters of the revenue of for-profit educational institutions arrived in the form of federal student loan disbursements, so any restriction on these loans would severely impact their bottom line.

Other educational policy commentators suggest applying an incentive program directly to the schools themselves. Institutions whose students have a high rate of loan default would be penalized financially, while those whose students have solid repayment histories would receive a financial reward in the form of grant or scholarship money. Proponents of this system believe that forcing the school to have a financial stake in the loan process would deter them from pushing expensive programs that do not benefit students. Detractors believe this system—or any similar rules that restrict access to federal student loan money—would make it harder for students with financial needs to attend college, or would require such students to take out more private loans with unfavorable repayment terms.

Going Forward

Concern over growing student loan debt and default rates understandably leads to the question of whether college is worth the cost. But despite the risks, research overwhelmingly suggests that it is. According to both the US Department of Labor and the Economic Policy Institute in Washington, DC, in 2013, Americans with a four-year college degree made almost twice as much as those without a degree. This percentage increased over the past three decades, from 64 percent in the early 1980s, to 85 percent in the early 2000s, and finally to 98 percent in 2013. Economist David Autor of the Massachusetts Institute of Technology (MIT) says that, over the course of a lifetime, college graduates come out ahead by about half a million dollars, even after accounting for the cost of tuition. However, other research shows a significant earning discrepancy based on undergraduate major. For example, US Census Bureau data from 2011 showed that, while the median salary for a petroleum engineering major was $120,000, the median salary for a counseling-psychology major was only $29,000.

Ultimately, the biggest problem seems to be the willingness of lenders—both public and private—to lend large amounts of money to students to finance their education without any real consideration of future ability to repay the loan. One significant obstacle is that, unlike a mortgage or home equity loan, it is nearly impossible to accurately determine a student's future earning potential before that student even begins his or her studies, in order to gauge how much is appropriate to lend. By contrast, the loan amount and interest rate of mortgages and home equity loans are heavily based on the borrower's salary and creditworthiness at the time of the loan. This information is simply not available for students. While economists, politicians, and educators have proposed several different solutions, so far, none have seemed viable, and the burden remains on the student to gauge how much student loan debt is appropriate given a best-guess estimate of future career prospects and earnings.

Tracey M. DiLascio

Bibliography

Bhatia, Pooja. "Of Debt + Degrees." *Ozymandias Online*. OZY Media, 1 Mar. 2014. Web. 3 June 2014.

Bidwell, Allie. "The Rise in Tuition Is Slowing, But College Still Costs More." *US News & World Report*. US News and World Report, 24 Oct. 2013. Web. 3 June 2014.

"Employment Projections: Earnings and Unemployment Rates by Educational Attainment." *Bureau of Labor Statistics*. US Bureau of Labor Statistics, 24 Mar. 2014. Web. 3 June 2014.

"Fast Facts: Graduation Rates." *The Condition of Education 2013*. US Dept. of Educ., Natl. Center for Educ. Statistics, 2013. Web. 3 June 2014.

Headlee, Celeste. "The Hard Truth About Defaulting On Student Loans." *NPR*. NPR, 21 Jan. 2014. Web. 3 June 2014.

Leonhardt, David. "Is College Worth It? Clearly, New Data Say." *New York Times*. New York Times, 27 May 2014. Web. 3 June 2014.

"Median Earnings by Major and Subject Area." *Chronicle of Higher Education*. Chronicle of Higher Educ., 23 May 2011. Web. 3 June 2014.

Norris, Floyd. "The Hefty Yoke of Student Loan Debt." *New York Times*. New York Times, 20 Feb. 2014. Web. 3 June 2014.

"Quarterly Report on Household Debt and Credit." *Research and Statistics Group, Microeconomic Studies*. Federal Reserve Bank of New York, Feb. 2014. Web. 18 May 2014.

Stacey, Georgia West. "For-Profit College Students Less Likely to be Employed After Graduation and Have Lower Earnings, New Study Finds." *CAPSEEcenter. org*. Center for Analysis of Postsecondary Educ. and Employment, 21 Feb. 2012. Web. 3 June 2014.

The Student Loan Crisis and the Future of Higher Education

By Michael Wenisch
The Catholic Social Science Review, 2012

The crisis in student loans has grown to the point that outstanding student loan debt will likely exceed $1 trillion in early 2012. Yet employment prospects for college graduates have grown alarmingly bleak, particularly since 2008. The downturn in the world economy since 2008 is itself, in substantial measure, the outcome of the historic peaking of world oil production rates within the past six years. With the onset of permanent oil production rate declines within a few years' time, the world economy faces an epoch of contraction destined to last decades. These broader economic developments are setting the stage for a tragic bursting of the bubble in student loan debt. The situation also raises acute moral questions revolving around a basic conflict between the interests of the institutional complex of higher education and the masses of students who financially sustain that complex.

The crisis in student loans has been relatively little noted in public discourse, yet it has already reached epidemic proportions and continues to expand. Total outstanding student loan debt will likely exceed $1 trillion early in 2012, and continues to grow at alarming rates. The total amount of loans taken out just for the year 2010 exceeded $100 billion, and total outstanding debt has doubled in just the past five years.[1] One can get some sense of the breadth and depth of the crisis by noting that $1 trillion is enough money for 20 million individuals to be carrying a balance of $50,000 each.

At the same time, however, millions of student loan borrowers are finding it difficult if not impossible to service their debt. This is principally due to the fact that the current and recent annual cohorts of graduating college students, especially since 2008, face the bleakest employment prospects in decades. A recent study of 667,000 students who entered repayment in 2005 found that 15 percent of students in that cohort defaulted outright, and another 26 percent became delinquent in their payments.[2] Another recent study documents the bleak state of the labor market for more recent college graduates. According to this study, only 56 percent of the graduating class of 2010 had held at least one job by the spring of 2011. This is a drastic drop of the 90 percent figure for graduates holding a job in their first year following the classes of 2006 and 2007.[3]

The tragedy of the unfolding student loan crisis is greatly compounded by developments in the student loan industry over the past twenty years that have rendered student loan debt the most malignant and predatory of any class of legally enacted loans.[4] The original foundation of the present student loan borrowing system was part of the Higher Education Act (HEA) of 1965. Among other things, this law made provision for federal loan guarantees to be extended to private lenders so as to encourage them to lend funds for the specific purpose of financing post-secondary education. Subsequently, in 1972, the Student Loan Marketing Association, more commonly known as Sallie Mae, was created as a semi-private Government Sponsored Entity (GSE) in order to provide a secondary market for student loans.

Yet in 1996, with congressional approval, Sallie Mae quietly initiated the transition from a GSE to a privately held, publicly traded corporation. Within just a few years, Sallie Mae had succeeded in establishing itself as one of the most successful publicly traded companies. Its stock skyrocketed in value even during the dot-com market collapse of 2000, and leading company executives such as CEO Albert Lord accumulated personal fortunes of hundreds of millions of dollars.

Since its original enactment in 1965, Congress has voted into law six amendments to the aforementioned HEA. For the most part, these amendments must be understood in the context of this too-little-known transition in the organization and mission of Sallie Mae, and to a lesser extent of other players in the industry. The most important of these amendments became law in 1998. One of its provisions established that all federally guaranteed student loan debt is non-dischargeable in bankruptcy in perpetuity. In 2005, this provision was extended to private, non-federally-guaranteed educational loans as well.

Other important aspects of the 1998 amendment to the Higher Education Act, and to a lesser extent of other federal legislation, stripped away most of the basic consumer protections from student loans that are taken for granted in all other legal forms of debt. The provisions enacted in this regard include the following:

- The elimination of the borrower's right to refinance following loan consolidation;

- The specific exemption of student loan debt from usury laws enacted at the state level, as well as from the federally enacted Truth in Lending Act;

- The power to secure payment on outstanding student loans through the garnishment of wages. Social Security and disability disbursements, and seizures of tax returns—all without the requirement of a court order;

- The ability to penalize delinquent borrowers with the stripping of state-issued professional licenses and the termination of public employment;

- The permission to assess substantial penalties and fees in the event of delinquency or default, to the extent that the original outstanding principal on a consolidated loan in default can easily double or even triple.

In order to understand the full implications of the student loan crisis, it is necessary to situate understanding of it within the context of a broader phenomenon currently playing itself out in world industrial civilization, namely, "Peak Oil," and the permanent cessation of economic growth that this historic turning point in energy availability entails. On July 12, 2008, the price of a barrel of oil reached nearly $150 per barrel for the first time in history, closing the day at $147.[5] This event may be regarded as the climactic moment of what is almost certainly the peaking of worldwide oil production rates at a plateau of 82 million barrels per day over the time period spanning early 2005 into the present, following approximately 150 years of nearly continuous annual increases in production rates.[6] As a result, currently, in late 2011, oil prices are hovering in the $100 per barrel range even in the absence of significant worldwide economic growth.

Historically, there has existed a strong correlation between oil price increases and the suppression of economic growth. With regard to the operative causal connections, one may profitably quote words written approximately thirty years ago by the currently most prominent anti-Peak Oil controversialist:

> Any price increase has immediate, undesirable effects on all oil-importing nations, causing a direct loss in national income. If the price rise is very gradual over a period of many years, thereby allowing the oil-importing nations a gradual adjustment, the direct effects might then be the main ones.
>
> A large, sudden increase in oil prices would [however, in addition,] have serious indirect effects. It would exacerbate inflation, place further strains on the international monetary system, and sharply contract the demand for goods and services, further reducing national income. In short, the economic consequences would likely be a major recession, or possibly even a depression.[7]

These brief paragraphs, written in 1983 by Daniel Yergin, provide a very apt description of the nature of the role played by the international oil markets in severely damaging the world economy during the recent years encompassing the worldwide peak in oil production rates. Originally, Yergin's words were intended to describe the effects of the oil shocks of the 1970s on the world economy. These oil shocks, as Yergin himself noted at the time, were themselves substantially precipitated by the peaking of U.S. domestic oil production in 1970.[8] The applicability of Yergin's analysis to the situation that has prevailed in the period extending from 2005 to the present has been confirmed in a number of more recent studies of the effects of precipitously rising oil prices on the broader economy.[9] Once the world begins to experience the onset of permanent declines in annual oil production rates, within a few years' time at most, a long-term process of contraction in world economic activity is sure to ensue.

Both the peaking of world oil production in the first decade of the new millennium and the peaking of U.S. oil production in 1970 constitute important remote factors contributing to the financial collapse of 2008 as well as the coming financial collapse imminently heralded by the European sovereign debt crisis. The inevitable onset of permanent declines in oil production rates renders any sustained economic growth, let alone the torrid rates necessary to service the European sovereign debt in any credible fashion, very unlikely. In the most fundamental sense, the widely expected resumption of long-term future economic growth serves as the collateral guaranteeing current debts, and the peaking of world oil production has objectively eliminated that collateral.

In a more proximate sense, however, the most significant underlying cause for both the student loan bubble collapse and the broader financial collapse, in whose train it will follow, will likely consist in a broad-based loss of confidence. The loss of confidence in question concerns the aforementioned expectation of future economic recovery and subsequent sustained growth. Eventually, this loss in confidence will extend to a critical mass of participants in world financial markets and the broader world economy sufficient to trigger a wave of defaults and market collapses. Currently, a degree of that confidence sufficient to prop up precariously the world financial system continues to persist, indicating that the subjective perceptions of the future prospects for sustained growth in the world economy continue to lag well behind the objective realities. Inevitably, however, the still widely-held illusion that sustained economic growth is shortly to resume will continue to evaporate. The imminent wave of defaults on European sovereign debt is destined to constitute a particularly dramatic episode in the evaporation of that illusion.

That same broad-based loss of economic confidence will likely also translate into the beginnings of a wholesale abandonment of higher education by prospective students. In the case of the student loan collapse, this loss of confidence will take the specific form of the realization on the part of a critical mass of actual and potential students that a college degree no longer translates upon graduation into a decent middle-class job. At that point, the currently still-expanding student loan bubble will burst. It is quite likely that the broad-based onset of the triggering realization may be relatively sudden, and constitute an effect of the same dramatic loss of economic confidence that will also drive the events surrounding the coming wave of European sovereign debt defaults.

The bursting of the student loan bubble will also have portentous implications for the complex of institutions of higher learning in the United States. With the exception of a handful of extremely wealthy universities, institutions of higher learning are for the most part substantially dependent on student tuitions, and thus also on student loans, in order to operate. Without the continuing growth of the student loan bubble, it is foreseeable that many colleges and universities will be forced to declare bankruptcy and cease operations over the next ten years.

What are the implications of the rather ominous picture that has just been briefly sketched? On a practical level, any current or prospective college student should take careful stock of the current economic realities in relation to his or her personal circumstances. The critical question to ask is whether incurring substantial amounts of student debt, with all the particular sorts of dangers this type of debt entails, is fundamentally warranted at all. On an ethical level, the situation calls for careful reflection in light of Catholic social teaching. Central to the necessary analysis is the recognition of a basic conflict of interest that the student loan bubble creates. This conflict pits the interests of those employed in the higher education sector—including professors, administrators, and various support personnel—against those of students. The former require the continued infusion of student tuition and student loan money to support their livelihoods, while decisions on the part of the latter to shoulder the financial burdens necessary to sustain these infusions may well prove personally disastrous.

Notes

1.   Cf "Loan Volume Outstanding," at www.finaid.org/loans/ (accessed December 14, 2011) for an estimated breakdown of the numbers. The $1 trillion milestone received widespread publicity earlier this year due to Dennis Cauchon's article, "Student Loans Outstanding; Will Exceed $1 Trillion This Year," in *USA Today* (October 19, 2011) (accessed December 14, 2011, at http://www.usatoday.com/money/perfi/college/story/2011-10-19/student-loan-debt/50818676/1).

2.   Alisa F. Cunningham and Gregory S. Kienzl, *Delinquency: The Untold Story of Student Borrowing*, published March 2011 by the Institute for Higher Education Policy (accessed December 14, 2011, at http://www.ihep.org/ assets/files/publications/a-f/Delinquency-The_Untold_Story_FINAL_March_2011.pdf), 4-5.

3.   Jessica Godofsky, Cliff Zukin, and Carl Van Horn, *Unfulfilled Expectations: Recent College Graduates Struggle in a Troubled Economy*, published May 2011 by the John J. Heldrich Center for Workforce Development, Rutgers University (accessed December 14, 2011, at http://www.heldrich.rutgers.edu/sites/default/files/content/Work_Trends_ May_2011.pdf), 2-3.

4.   The following history and data on student loan legislation are derived from Alan Michael Collinge, *The Student Loan Scam, the Most Oppressive Debt in U.S. History—and How We Can Fight Back* (Boston: Beacon Press, 2009): chap. 1, "The Rise of Sallie Mae and the Fall of Consumer Protections," 1-22; and chap. 2, "Who Benefited?," 22-36.

5.   Kathryn Hopkins, "Fuel Prices: Iran Missile Launches Send Oil to $147 a Barrel Record," in *London Guardian* (July 12, 2008) (accessed December 15, 2011, at http://www.guardian.co.ukybusiness/2008/jul/12/oil.commodities).

6.   Euan Meams, "Peak Oil—Now or Later? A Response to Daniel Yergin," *The Oil Drum* (September 22,2011) (accessed December 14,2011, at http://www.theoildrum.com/node/8391).

7.   Robert Stobaugh and Daniel Yergin, "The End of Easy Oil," in *Energy Future: Report of the Energy Project at the Harvard Business School*, ed. Robert Stobaugh and Daniel Yergin (New York: Vintage Books, 3rd ed. 1983), 14-15. Yergin is currently chairman of IHS Cambridge Energy Research Associates, and recently published "There Will Be Oil," in *The Wall Street Journal* (September 17, 2011), defending the proposition that the peak and decline of world oil production lies decades in the future.

8. Stobaugh and Yergin, "End of Easy Oil," 13.
9. One comprehensive recent study of the causal connections between the rise
    in oil prices and the subsequent collapse in the broader economy is by econo-
    mist James Hamilton, "Causes and Consequences of the Oil Shock of 2007-
    08," in *Brookings Papers on Economic Activity*, ed. David Romer and Justin
    Wolfers (Spring 2009) (accessed December 14, 2011, at http://eepurl.com/
    cSPu). For a detailed study of the direct causal connection between rising oil
    and gasoline prices and the historic reversal in housing price trends, see Joe
    Cortright, "Driven to the Brink: How the Gas Price Spike Popped the Hous-
    ing Bubble and Devalued the Suburbs," Discussion paper, *CEOs for Cities*
    (May 2008) (accessed December 14, 2011, at http://www.ceosforcities.org/
    nles/Driven%20to%20the%20 Brink%20FINAL.pdf). Since oil is the basis of
    95 percent of the world's transport fuel, the impact of the Peak Oil-related
    oil shock on the transportation sector of the economy has been particularly
    harsh. For a discussion of this issue in relation to the aviation industry, see
    U.S. Government Accountability Office Report to Congressional Requesters,
    *Commercial Aviation: Airline Industry Contraction Due to Volatile Fuel Pric-
    es and Falling Demand Affects Airports, Passengers, and Federal Government
    Revenues* (April 2009) (accessed December 14, 2011, at http://www.gao.gov/
    products/GAO-09-393).

Student-Loan Rates Become Hot Political Topic

By Caralee Adams
Education Week, May 9, 2012

Maybe it's because of the election year. Perhaps, it's the loud voices of student activists. Otherwise, the student-loan rate-hike debate might have taken center stage politically because it's a relatively easy concept to grasp: Interest rates will double in July on subsidized student loans unless action is taken to stop it.

Who wants to go on record in favor of higher college costs?

Whatever the confluence of factors bringing the issue to the forefront, Stafford Loan rates have become the higher education issue of the day—and, political observers say, may be one of the last to be resolved before November.

Without congressional intervention by July 1, students who take out new federally subsidized, need-based loans will pay 6.8 percent rather than 3.4 percent in interest. That means six months after graduation, the 7.4 million students expected to take out new Stafford Loans next academic year (one in three undergraduates) will pay 20 percent more in fees, or an average of $1,000 more per year in fees. The neediest students would pay $5,000 more over their repayment period.

"I'm not sure if I'll have a job when I graduate, or if I'll be making enough for the payments," said Faith Nebergall, a junior studying journalism at Indiana University in Bloomington, who estimates she'll pay about $400 a month for at least 15 years to pay off the $40,000 she expects to owe when she graduates.

"I want to get my own place and be independent, but with those huge payments," she said, "it might be hard to obtain."

Where's the Money?

While some contend finance charges aren't critical to access, they are part of the affordability puzzle that others say can make a difference to students deciding on whether to enroll. Loan debts recently surpassed $1 trillion nationwide. The average student graduates with about $25,000 in debt.

A consensus on Capitol Hill is emerging in support of passing a measure to keep the rate at 3.4 percent for another year, but differences remain on how to come up with the estimated $6 billion to pay for it.

President Barack Obama made the college-affordability issue a part of his State of the Union address in January. In late April, it was the focus of one of his weekly radio addresses, and he took the message on the road to college campuses in Iowa, North Carolina, and Colorado.

Soon after, presumptive Republican presidential nominee Mitt Romney came out in favor of lower rates—but in a statement, he added a critical reference to the president's handling of the economy, asserting the relief was needed to help college graduates because of "the bleak job prospects that young Americans coming out of college face today."

Not wanting to appear to be against help for students struggling with debt, congressional leaders in both parties in late April rallied behind efforts to keep the interest-rate cut from expiring, but proposed different routes to get there.

On April 27, the U.S. House of Representatives passed the Interest Rate Reduction Act along party lines, by a vote of 215–195. But the idea of paying for it with money set aside for a preventive program in the 2010 health-care law sparked intense criticism from Democrats and a veto threat from the White House. Congressional Democrats would rather come up with the money by requiring more from the wealthy in the Social Security and Medicare payroll taxes.

The Senate is discussing its own proposal to pay for the lower rate and is scheduled to vote on its version early this month.

"Clearly, everyone has agreed on the policy. Interest rates cannot double," said Rich Williams, a higher education advocate for the U.S. Public Interest Research Group, a consumer-advocacy group in Washington that has mobilized students to lobby lawmakers.

"Now, the struggle is working out the details with each other in Congress," he said.

Deadline Looms

The saga of student loans can be traced back to the College Cost Reduction and Access Act of 2007. Congress agreed to phase in lower rates on subsidized Stafford Loans to 3.4 percent by 2011–12, but then have them revert to 6.8 percent for the 2012–13 academic year.

The loans are awarded on the basis of financial need. The maximum amount a dependent undergraduate student can take out in subsidized loans is $23,000. The lifetime limit for an independent undergraduate is $65,000.

"Congress only acts when there is a perceived crisis," said Stephen Burd, a senior policy analyst with Education Sector, a nonprofit think tank in Washington. "It's an easy issue for people to understand. I'm not surprised with the attention. But it is amazing to see how quickly Republicans caved."

Earlier this year, the budget proposed by U.S. Rep. Paul Ryan, R-Wis., the chairman of the House Budget Committee, contained no changes in loan-interest rates.

"Politicians pay attention to the polls," said David Hawkins, the director of public policy and research for the National Association for College Admission Counseling, or NACAC. "Obviously, the student-loan issue has polled off the charts; otherwise, we would not have both parties floating bills."

Attention to student debt by the Occupy Movement and lawmakers in campaign mode also has fueled the debate, said Neal McCluskey, the associate director for the Center for Educational Freedom at the Cato Institute, a think tank in Washington with a free-market orientation.

"Nobody wants to go on record, especially now, as a person who would double interest rates on students," said Mr. McCluskey. He added that Republicans generally are not against student aid, but want to find a responsible way to pay for it.

Jim Miller, a former president of NACAC and the coordinator of enrollment services at the University of Wisconsin-Superior, said it would be politically difficult for Congress not to lower the rates.

"Student financial aid has always been a way that policy has tried to recognize the shared benefit and responsibility to go to college. It has a personal benefit and a public one," he said.

While there is a groundswell of support for lower interest rates, some in higher education circles contend that this is a relatively small issue on which to use up political capital, without having much direct impact on college access.

Priority Level

Matthew M. Chingos, a fellow at the Brookings Institution, a Washington think tank, argues that since blocking the interest-rate increase would only affect interest rates after students leave college, it wouldn't provide relief for current students struggling to afford college. He suggests it would be better to put more federal money into grants to benefit students immediately and decrease the cost of attending college, rather than give a subsidy down the road.

Mr. McCluskey of Cato agrees there is too much attention being spent on a minor issue that fixes the problem only for one year. "What they need to do is rethink the whole idea of the federal government providing aid for students going to college," he said. "Aid is what drives ridiculous college cost inflation."

Mr. McCluskey contends that cheap access to college aid is leading to an overconsumption of higher education, pushing too many students into college who are unprepared, can't afford it, and do not finish.

Mr. Burd, of Education Sector, said that while it's admirable that lawmakers want to help student borrowers, there are more far-reaching issues that should be addressed, such as helping borrowers who are dealing with unmanageable debt and stuck in default.

"It's a good sign that the administration and Congress are concerned about student debt," he said. "I hope that we can build on this, but I worry that people will say this solves the student debt problem."

Young people, too, would like to see a larger solution to problems of college affordability, but action to limit the interest-rate increase would be a step, said Andy MacCracken, a student leader and one of the founders of the National Campus Leadership Council, a new group of college student-body presidents that formed last fall. The group has organized students to speak up on this issue and on May 1 released an open letter to lawmakers signed by 205 student-body presidents representing nearly 3 million students.

"We are very excited this is being talked about and getting the attention it deserves," said Mr. MacCracken, 23, a part-time graduate student at American University, in Washington, who himself anticipates $70,000 in student-loan debt after finishing graduate school. "It affects everyone and has major ramifications for the economy and our nation down the road."

Student Debt: Your Threat

It Can Have an Impact on the Entire Economy

By *Consumer Reports*, May 2012

Mortgage foreclosures and credit-card debt have drawn the spotlight since the financial collapse of 2008. But there's another type of debt that could have potentially crippling ramifications for the U.S. economy: student debt.

How bad is it? The amount of student debt owed by Americans exceeded outstanding credit-card debt for the first time in 2010. Two-thirds of college graduates carried some debt at commencement, and the Class of 2010 had an average of $25,250 in student debt, up 5 percent from the previous year, according to The Institute for College Access & Success (TICAS), a nonprofit policy research group in Oakland, Calif. All in all, it's estimated that Americans owe more than $900 billion in federal and private loans.

At the same time, the depressed job market makes repaying those loans harder than it has been in decades. Two-year default rates on all student loans hit 8.8 percent for those starting repayment in 2009, with 15 percent defaulting at for-profit institutions, according to the Department of Education. Unlike most consumer loans, student debt generally can't be discharged by declaring bankruptcy. Lenders can recover the funds by garnishing wages, tax refunds, even part of Social Security checks.

All of this has consequences not just for graduates but also for the larger society. Some economists fear that lingering student debt will force many young adults to delay or defer important milestones, such as marriage and starting a family, which can impede a full economic recovery. Young workers with wrecked credit from unaffordable student loans, for example, won't be able to get mortgages to purchase homes, which could make it even tougher for retirees and others to sell theirs.

Why So Bad?

Jeff Macaluso, 42, a website designer from Dobbs Ferry, N.Y., says his student debt, about $59,000, is "like a prison sentence." His monthly payment is $430 under an income-contingent repayment option for a federal consolidation loan he took out about a decade ago, although he tries to pay $630 a month to keep the interest down.

Macaluso, who earned a master's degree in fine arts in 1997, says he's happy with the career opportunities his education afforded him. But paying off the debt is preventing him from saving for retirement and might deter him and his wife from buying a home. The debt, with more than 6 percent interest, "just grew and grew and grew," he says, "and I'm saddled with it unless I make twice as much as I'm making."

Student indebtedness has been rising sharply since the early 1990s. Skyrocketing college tuition and fees, which have risen faster than inflation, are factors. And government grants and scholarship aid haven't kept pace with costs, resulting in a greater reliance by students and parents on borrowing to fill the gap. And in recent years, as home values have declined, more families that may have relied on home equity for financing are looking to student and parent educational loans from government and private lenders.

TICAS estimates that at least 22 percent of student debt from nonprofit four-year colleges for the Class of 2010 was composed of private loans outside the federal student loan program. Those private loans often come with high variable interest rates, additional loan fees, and strict repayment requirements, even if borrowers are unemployed or can't afford the payments.

Spiraling student debt is also linked to the growing number of for-profit colleges, whose students have a much higher rate of borrowing than those at public and private nonprofit institutions and are more likely to be steered to private lenders. In 2011 the National Consumer Law Center addressed why students at for-profit colleges defaulted on their debt at a higher rate than those at other types of educational institutions. The NCLC attributed this to poor academic completion and job placement rates at many for-profit schools.

Whatever type of college students attend, they don't always understand what they're getting into when they take out loans. Kristine Beckford, 22, a senior majoring in communications at Lehman College in the Bronx, N.Y., part of the public City University of New York, says she already owes $60,000 to $70,000 in student loans for two other colleges she attended before transferring to Lehman. She's not certain whether they are federal or private loans ("What's the difference?" she asked). The first in her family to attend college, Beckford says she received virtually no financial-aid counseling.

Getting Out from Under

For the more than 36 million people saddled with federal student debt, what's the best strategy for digging out of the hole? "There are ways to manage it in tough times if you don't stick your head in the sand," says Lauren Asher, president of The Institute for College Access & Success.

Complicating matters is the fact that the various types of student loans have different repayment options. Most federally backed student loans must be repaid starting six months after the borrower leaves school or drops below half-time status. Some private loans and unsubsidized federal loans require interest payments even while the student is still enrolled.

The average college student has eight to 12 loans for his undergraduate education, says Mark Kantrowitz, publisher of FinAid.org, a financial-aid website, and

Fastweb.com, a scholarship-information site. Borrowers can begin to get a handle on their debt by following these steps:

1. Find out how much you owe and to what lenders. Upon graduation or sooner, line up all your student loans and determine the loan servicers, balances, interest rates, repayment options, and grace periods. You might have a combination of private loans and those that are backed by the federal government. If you don't know the types of loans you have, call or write to the student-aid office at your college or your lenders, or go to *nslds.ed.gov*, the website of the National Student Loan Data System, a database of federal loans (private ones aren't included).

2. Choose a repayment option. Federal loans, which include Perkins and Stafford loans and Direct PLUS loans (usually taken out by parents), offer several repayment options. The standard term is 10 years, and the minimum monthly payment is $50. Stretching out your payments over a longer period reduces the monthly amount but results in higher total interest expenses over the life of the loan.

Take a hard look at your financial situation and your income potential for the next few years. You'll save money and get out of debt faster by paying off your highest-interest loans as quickly as possible, which you can do by making the largest payments you can afford each month and applying extra to the principal.

If your total debt exceeds your first-year income after graduation, you probably won't be able to afford payments under the standard 10-year repayment plan. In that case, you may want to consider these repayment options, which result in smaller, more affordable monthly payments:

Graduated repayment. Payments start small and increase every two years, which could be a good option for those who expect their income to increase steadily over time, such as some physicians.

Extended repayment. If you're at least $30,000 in debt and didn't have a loan before October 7, 1998, you can choose this option, which gives you up to 25 years to repay your loans. You can choose fixed or graduated payments.

Income-contingent repayment. Your payments are calculated annually on the basis of your adjusted gross income (plus your spouse's income if you're married), family size, and the total amount of direct loans over a 25-year maximum repayment schedule. After 25 years of payments, any unpaid balance will be discharged, but you might have to pay taxes on it. This option is for direct loans only.

Income-based repayment. Monthly payment is based on your income (and your spouse's if you file together) and family size, and is adjusted annually. Last fall President Obama made a proposal to improve this type of payment for many borrowers sooner than the current program will do under an initiative called Pay As You Earn. The current program caps monthly payments at 15 percent of adjusted gross income and forgives remaining loan balances after 25 years. Pay As You Earn would cap monthly payments at 10 percent of adjusted gross income for some borrowers and forgive remaining loan balances after 20 years, but they might have to pay taxes on the discharged debt. The Department of Education says the new rules would apply to borrowers who took out their first federal loan in 2008 or later, but borrowers must also take out a new loan in 2012 or later to be eligible.

3. Explore options if you can't afford payments. For federal loans, you can request a deferment or forbearance. Under a deferment you may be permitted to stop making payments temporarily if you meet certain requirements. Under forbearance you may be allowed to stop making payments temporarily, make smaller payments, or extend the time for making payments if you don't qualify for a deferment. Forbearance is for a maximum of three years at the discretion of the lender, and you must reapply each year. "This is a last resort before default or for short-term financial problems," Kantrowitz says.

Most private loans don't offer deferment, and forbearance terms are limited. Quarterly fees may also apply, and interest accrues during the forbearance.

Don't reduce or skip payments without permission or you might be reported delinquent or in default. National credit bureaus could be notified of your default, which would adversely affect your credit score and also prevent you from qualifying for additional federal student aid.

4. Consider jobs or volunteer programs that qualify for deferment or forgiveness. Certain public-service and nonprofit-sector careers, such as teaching, police and fire services, working in public-interest law or public health, or joining the military, may qualify you for cancellation of federal loans. Generally, if you make 120 on-time payments, you might be eligible to have the outstanding loan balance (principal and interest) forgiven, and you could be exempt from taxation on the discharged amount.

You can find more information on the Department of Education's Public Service Loan Forgiveness page on its financial-aid website. Co to *studentaid.ed.gov*, click on "Repay Your Loans," then click on "Public Service Loan Forgiveness." Not all federal loans are eligible.

5. Consider loan consolidation. You can combine loans into one payment, which is more of a convenience than a cost savings, unless you still have unconsolidated loans that originated before 2006. Students and parents can't combine their loans; only loans taken out by the same borrower can be consolidated. And private student loans usually can't be consolidated with federal student loans.

6. Think twice about going back to school to avoid unemployment. College enrollment increases during recessions as young adults seek additional degrees and others seek retraining. But incurring more student debt might not pay off.

Erin Button, 23, of Chicago, an administrative assistant at the Public Interest Research Group, is rethinking plans to go to law school after graduating from Cornell University last year with $78,000 in private and federal loans for her bachelor's degree in anthropology. She gets a repayment benefit of $200 a month from her nonprofit job and pays $450 a month in debt service, more than she pays in rent. Button, who earns less than $25,000 a year, carries five loans with interest rates ranging from 3.8 percent to 6.8 percent and terms of 10 to 30 years. "It's daunting," she says, "but I'm taking it one month at a time."

7. Contact your lender immediately if you can't pay. Skipping out on a student loan won't solve the problem. Defaulting will add late fees and collection costs to your outstanding balance. Parents or grandparents who want to help recent graduates should consider helping to pay back loans instead of giving cash.

Of Debt + Degrees

By Pooja Bhatia
OZY, March 1, 2014

WHY YOU SHOULD CARE

Whether you're considering taking out student loans, still paying them off or blessedly in the black, the $1.2 trillion Americans hold in student-loan debt is a problem for all of us.

Only in post-recession America could the indebted masses become a constituency—and a potential market.

Call them Generation Overleveraged. A whopping 40 million Americans owe an even more whopping $1.2 trillion in student-loan debt. The amount surpasses every other type of household debt except mortgage debt.

While the federal government has enacted laws that will ease future graduates' debt burdens, plenty of 20- and 30-somethings are still in the lurch. And at last these red-ink-stained wretches are garnering some attention from policymakers, politicians and bankers. Eyeing voters, politicians on the left and right have highlighted the issue, while banks are beginning to broaden their reach to refinancing student loans. It's not clear whether true relief or reform is on the way, but there's no denying that momentum has built along with the debt.

The main reason for rising student debt is this: In the halcyon years before the Great Recession, millions of young Americans took out loans to get through university, only to graduate into an economy that didn't need them as badly anymore. They're finding it harder to pay off their loans than they likely anticipated.

That's not to say there hasn't been profiting at their expense. Federal loan interest rates remain high relative to other types of government-backed lending, and private loan rates tend to be even higher. Beneficiaries include for-profit secondary institutions, private lenders and good ol' Uncle Sam.

The Debt Vote

Their rising numbers have turned student-loan holders into a fledgling constituency. Student debt has become a marquee issue for both Republicans, like Sen. Marco Rubio, and Democrats, like Sens. Elizabeth Warren and Kirsten Gillibrand. There's even the hint of bipartisan consensus on the issue. Organizations that face off on other issues, like the conservative American Enterprise Institute and the liberal

Center for American Progress, are finding common ground on policy solutions like income-based repayment and refinancing.

To be sure, Rubio has long considered student debt an important issue—the 42-year-old paid off his own loans only last year, with some publicity. And Warren has devoted most of her career to debt.

But the sheer numbers have garnered new attention. Over the past 10 years, the amount of student loan debt has nearly tripled, while defaults are at a two-decade high, with nearly 15 percent of borrowers defaulting within three years. As an illustration, some 600,000 borrowers who started paying federal student loans in 2010 had defaulted two years later. Defaults on private loans, which are less subject to regulation than government loans, are likely worse.

It's Still the Economy . . .

Headlines are prone to describe student debt as the next coming bubble, but economists say defaults probably won't trigger a financial collapse. Student loans were never securitized to the extent that mortgage debt was.

That doesn't mean student loans aren't a drag on the economy as a whole. Analysts say that student loan debt has had widespread economic repercussions. In a report published last year, the Consumer Financial Protection Bureau said student debt is one reason that 20- and 30-somethings seem to be living a prolonged adolescence, including living with their parents, failing to contribute to retirement accounts and postponing big consumer purchases such as cars.

"Rising student debt burdens may prove to be one of the more painful aftershocks of the Great Recession, especially if left unaddressed," said the bureau's student-loan ombudsman, Rohit Chopra, in a speech in November.

Student-loan debt also has warped the economy, contributing to a shortage of primary-care doctors—highly indebted med-school graduates are more likely to specialize in big-bucks sectors like dermatology and radiology—and has stymied entrepreneurship. The National Association of Realtors reported in July that nearly half of Americans describe student loan burdens as a huge obstacle to homeownership: "It proves to be a real detriment across the board."

Buddy, Can You Spare a Re-fi?

What solutions exist? Historically, it's been much harder to refinance student loan debt than to refinance, say, mortgage debt. But that is starting to change. Over the past couple of years, several big banks have gotten into the student-loan refinance game, including RBS Citizens and SunTrust.

"It's common to hear about refinancing your mortgage, but this is a relatively new practice for educational debt," says Dan Macklin, co-founder and vice president of SoFi, a startup that has refinanced about $400 million in student loans since 2011. Lack of awareness is the biggest challenge in reaching the refinancing market, he says. And it's a huge market, in SoFi's estimation: Some $350 billion could be addressed, Macklin says.

But not everyone in student-debt distress is eligible for refinancing. Generally, you need to be in a better economic position, with a better credit score, than you were when you took out the loan. Lack of awareness about federal loan deferral and forgiveness is also a problem.

The Way Forward

One area of emerging consensus is that lenders should stop making loans without consideration of borrowers' ability to repay. Clearly, it's difficult to measure a 17-year-old's earning potential, but, analysts say, that doesn't preclude responsible lending. The debate lies in how to do it.

Some would put the onus on the student. They should write and amend loan repayment plans, argued one analyst, which would make them reassess their earning potential and career path periodically. Or they should be prequalified based on their academic record, others argue.

In contrast, a proposed rule by the Department of Education would put the onus on universities and colleges, making them show that a degree from them will provide gainful employment. (Its first attempt to put the rule through was scuttled when the Association of Private Sector Colleges and Universities sued.)

With competing interests and a still-evolving economy, the future of student lending and debt relief remains uncertain. But the issue has gained traction, and that should be a relief to us all, debt-burdened or not.

Student Loans I: Yes, Something Is Wrong

By Karen Gross
Inside Higher Ed, March 21, 2014

The student loan problem seems clear enough on the surface: students are incurring oversized student debt, and they are defaulting on that debt and threatening their ability to access future credit. The approaches to student loan debt collection are fraught with problems, including improper recovery tactics and informational asymmetry regarding repayment options.

But the current public policy conversations miss key issues that contribute to the debt mess, leading to proffered solutions that also miss their mark.

Start with these key facts about student loans:

The reported student debt loans represent averages, yet the amounts owed can differ dramatically from student to student. That is why solutions like the mandated debt calculator on college websites or the current College Scorecard do not resolve the issues; the disclosure of generic information does not impact student choice meaningfully.

Many of the problematic student loans are held by individuals who left college before graduation, meaning they have incurred "debt without diploma." This reality distorts default statistics, making their indicia of school quality misleading. The cost of education is not necessarily commensurate with the quality of the education received, meaning some students pay more and get less, and we do not have an adequate system for measuring educational quality other than accreditation, which is a deeply flawed process.

Finally, students and their families are woefully unaware of the myriad repayment options, and therefore forgo existing benefits or are taken advantage of by loan servicers. This occurs because we de-link conversations of "front-end" costs of higher education from "back-end" repayment options and opportunities; students and their families are scared off by the front end without knowing that there is meaningful back-end relief.

Given these facts, it becomes clearer why some of the current government reform suggestions are misguided. Two illustrations:

First, evaluating colleges on a rating system based on the earning levels of their graduates assumes the overwhelming majority of students graduate and that the employment chosen will be high-paying. But we know that not to be true, and for good reason: some students proudly enter public service or other low-paying but publicly beneficial employment. And, in today's economy, not all students can find employment directly correlated to their field of study.

We also know that those from high-income families have greater networking opportunities, given family connections. Yes, some schools offer degrees with little or no value, but the solution to student loan indebtedness does not rest on an earnings threshold.

Second, looking at loan default rates as a measure of the success of a college misses that many colleges welcome students from lower income quartiles, and these students have less collegiate success—understandably, although obviously many are working to improve these statistics. The fact that some of these students do not progress to a degree is not a sign of institutional failure any more than student success at elite institutions is a guarantee of those institutions' quality. One approach to consider is linking default rates with the types of students being served by an institution. But one thing that should not change, to the dismay of some: many of the government student loans should not be based on credit worthiness.

Not that many years ago, private lenders dominated both the student lending and home mortgage markets. This created obvious parallels between lending in these two spheres. Lenders overpriced for risk, provided monies to borrowers who were not credit-worthy, and had loan products with troubling features like sizable front-end fees, high default interest rates and aggressive debt collection practices.

In both markets, there was an embedded assumption: real estate values would continue to rise and well-paying employment opportunities would be plentiful for college graduates.

Then several things happened. The federal government took over the student loan market, cutting out the private lender as the middleman on government loans on both the front and back end. The economy took a nosedive that led to diminished home values and lower employment opportunities. And, when the proverbial bubble burst in the home lending markets, lenders sought to foreclose, only to find that their collateral had diminished in value.

For student loans, the bubble has not burst and, despite hyperbole to the contrary, it is unlikely to burst because the government—not the private sector—is the lender. Indeed, this market is intentionally *not* focused on credit worthiness; if anything, it awards more dollars to those who have weak credit, specifically to enable educational opportunity.

And while Congress can debate the interest rates charged on student loans, the size of Pell Grants and the growing default rates, it is highly improbable that the student loan market will be privatized any time soon.

But, for the record, there are already signs that private lenders and venture capitalists have re-entered or are ready to re-enter this market, for better or worse. And if the government's financial aid offerings are or become less beneficial than those in the open market, we will see a resurgence of private lending offered to students and their families. One caution: history tells us that the risks of the private student loan market are substantial; all one has to do is look at lending improprieties before and since the government became the lender-in-chief and the non-student loan predatory lending that targets our least financially stable borrowers.

There are things that can and should be done to improve the government-run student-lending market to encourage our most vulnerable students to pursue higher education at institutions that will serve them well. Here are five timely and doable suggestions worth considering now:

(1) Lower the interest rates on government-issued subsidized Stafford loans. The government is making considerable profit on student loans, and we need to encourage quality, market-sensitive, fiscally wise borrowing, most particularly among vulnerable students. Student loans to our most financially risky students should remain without regard to credit worthiness (the worthiness of the academic institution is point 2). Otherwise, we will be left with educational opportunity available only for the rich.

(2) Improve the accreditation process so that accreditors assess more thoughtfully and fairly the institutions they govern, whether that accreditation is regional or national. Currently, there are vastly too many idiosyncrasies in the process, including favoritism, violation of due process and fair dealing, and questionable competency of some of the accreditors. And the government has not been sufficiently proactive in recognizing accreditors, despite clear authority to do so.

(3) Simplify (as was done successfully with the FAFSA) the repayment options. There are too many options and too many opportunities for students to err in their selection. We know that income-based repayment is under-utilized, and students become ostriches rather than unraveling and working through the options actually available. Mandated exit interviews are not a "teachable moment" for this information; we need to inform students more smartly. Consideration should be given to information at the time repayment kicks in—usually six months post-graduation.

(4) Incentivize colleges and universities to work on post-graduation default rates (and repayment options) by establishing programs where they (the educational institutions) proactively reach out to their graduates to address repayment options, an initiative we will be trying on our own campus. Improvement in institutional default rates could be structured to enable increased institutional access to federal monies for work-study or SEOG, the greater the improvement, the greater the increase.

The suggestion, then, is contrary to the proffered government approach: taking away benefits. The suggestion proffered here uses a carrot, not a stick—offering more aid rather than threatening to take away aid. Importantly, we cannot mandate a meaningful minimum default rate because default rates are clearly correlated to the vulnerability of the student population, and we do not want to disincentivize institutions from serving first-generation, underrepresented minority and low-income students.

(5) Create a new financial product for parents/guardians/family members/ friends who want to borrow to assist their children (or those whom they are raising or supporting even if not biological or step children) in progressing through higher education, replacing the current Parent Plus Loan. The current Parent Plus Loan product is too expensive (both at initiation and in terms of interest rates) and more recently too keyed to credit worthiness. The individuals who most need this product are those who are more vulnerable. And the definition of "parent" is vastly too narrow given the contours of American families today.

Home ownership and education are both part of the American dream. Both benefit the individuals and larger society. How we foster both is, however, vastly different. We need to stop shouting about the shared crisis and see how we can truly help students and their families access higher education rather than making them run for the proverbial hills.

College Catastrophe

By Charles Scaliger
The New American, August 20, 2012

By encouraging government student loans, and then charging higher tuition, colleges and universities have not only created an economic bubble, they've changed the culture.

Last year, America's student loan sector swept past two important milestones in rapid succession, milestones with ominous portent. Sometime in the spring of 2011, the amount of total student loan debt surpassed the amount of total credit card debt for the first time ever. Toward the end of the year, total student loan debt appears to have breached the $1 trillion mark, prompting warnings of another asset bubble poised for a calamitous bursting.

Overcharged or Underpaid?

The numbers associated with student debt tell a sobering tale. Since 1999, student loan debt, adjusted for inflation, has risen by more than 500 percent, while other forms of personal debt have increased by "only" about 100 percent. The average college graduate now carries more than $25,000 in debt, an obligation that often takes decades to pay off.

A large percentage of college graduates find themselves underemployed, often with jobs that they might have been able to find without the vaunted college degree. A few cases in point: According to data gleaned from the Bureau of Labor Statistics, 21.62 percent, or 482,784, of all customer service representatives have a college degree; alongside them are 13.4 percent of waiters and waitresses (317,759), 16.64 percent of secretaries and administrative assistants (559,571), 5.01 percent of janitors (107,457), and 5.09 percent of truck drivers (85,205). Hundreds of thousands of others with college degrees are tending bar, preparing food, manning concession booths, clerking at hotel desks, and performing a very wide range of important, useful, and perfectly dignified forms of work—work that pays too little to allow realistic repayment of gargantuan student loans, and for which a four- or five-year undergraduate degree is completely unnecessary.

The Great Recession has been driving such figures for years now, but Americans' appetite for the mythic college degree continues unabated, seemingly without concern for the cost. Will this state of affairs ever change, and what will be the outcome?

College educations have always been a time of frugality and penury. Historian Charles Homer Haskins, the distinguished Harvard historian who was America's first medievalist, in his path-breaking early study on medieval universities, *The Rise of Universities*, published several specimens of medieval students' letters home to their parents, in which the students complain about the difficulty of the courses and the inadequacy of their living conditions—and ask for more money to be sent! Little has changed over the centuries, except that nowadays, instead of studying canon law and Latin, typical college students can choose from menus of hundreds of different courses ranging from the hard sciences and mathematics to modern conceits like gender studies. And medieval universities like Oxford, Bologna, and the Sorbonne, whatever their other considerable inadequacies, did not impose punitive costs for tuition and other fees that kept their graduates in financial bondage for most of their productive years.

Until comparatively recently, college degrees, both graduate and undergraduate, were designed for a fairly elite slice of society that genuinely desired academic advancement beyond normal societal expectations and intended to become teachers, professors, researchers, and practitioners of a few exclusive professions like medicine, law, and engineering. A college education came with few frills other than the chance to learn at the feet of some of the world's elite minds, and was correspondingly priced so that most students could pay for their education by working odd hours during the school year, or at most borrow from the bank a sum that could easily be repaid within a few years of graduation. Well do I remember a particular professor from my undergraduate years, who got his Ph.D. from the University of Pennsylvania, the Ivy League school founded by Ben Franklin, who told me that his tuition bill back in the early '50s was around 50 dollars per semester (roughly $450 in today's currency). He informed me that a part-time job during the school year and summer employment was more than adequate back then to cover all the costs of a college degree.

My own parents both attended the expensive and fairly elite Bucknell University back in the late '50s and early '60s. They married a year before my father finished college, and finished paying back their college loans only 10 years later, an event in my young life that I remember well. And they did it despite having three children and living on a single, very average income (my father's).

Such a scenario, except for the very few fortunate enough to earn an athletic or academic scholarship or whose parents are able and willing to pay the tab in full, is unthinkable nowadays. (Full disclosure: This author was the beneficiary of a "faculty brat" steep tuition discount as an undergraduate, and was blessed to graduate without debt of any kind.) The cost of four years' worth of tuition (not to mention room and board, textbooks, and the myriad steep fees universities routinely assess for parking, use of athletic facilities, and the like) has soared far beyond the means of any student to pay at the time they are assessed. Tuition for in-state students at large land-grant universities—which are usually reckoned among the better bargains—ranges from around $7,000 per academic year (the University of Wisconsin-Madison, for example) to just shy of $17,000 per year for Penn State University, the most expensive land-grant institution in the country. Textbooks routinely cost hundreds of dollars apiece, and additional fees can run into the hundreds of dollars per semester. Room and board, whether in warren-like dorms with no semblance of curfews or quiet hours or in blocks of off-campus "student housing," where students often crowd in four or six per apartment in order to afford high rentals, will cost tens of thousands more. And because few college students possess skills that will earn them more than entry-level work waiting tables, stocking shelves, or doing janitorial work, even students who forgo the parties, road trips, and other distractions of student life for part-time or even full-time work will not be able to avoid borrowing money to finance their education.

And this is bargain-basement higher education. Many private "liberal arts colleges" and Ivy League schools charge tens of thousands of dollars per year for undergraduate tuition. Postgraduate tuitions are steeper still, with even middle-tier law schools and MBA programs typically charging tens of thousands of dollars per year for tuition. Medical schools, of course, are more expensive still, usually leaving freshly minted M.D.s with hundreds of thousands in debt. And a coveted M.D. or J.D. is no guarantee of success, as many bankrupt doctors and lawyers eventually discover. Many of them spend decades paying off towering debts; President Obama himself has admitted to carrying significant debt from his own law school days.

Student loans, once incurred, can almost never be discharged by bankruptcy, unlike nearly all other forms of debt. This was not always the case; legislation passed in 2005 turned even private student loans into no-risk ventures for banks, whereby borrowers could be compelled by almost any means possible to repay them, and no amount of personal hardship of the sort that usually drives otherwise responsible people into bankruptcy—serious health problems, accidents, business failures, and so on—could bring any relief to the debtor.

Blowing up College Costs

This state of affairs has only been a few decades in the making, and has come about as a direct consequence of government interference in the higher education market on a massive scale. The federal government's first foray into higher education was with the post-World War II G.I. bill, which conferred benefits on military veterans wishing to attend college. The Servicemen's Readjustment Act of 1944 offered World War II veterans cash payments covering both college tuition and living expenses. By 1956, more than two million war veterans had taken advantage of the bill, a government program that most Americans, grateful for the sacrifices of the World War II generation, perceived as beneficial and morally defensible despite its dubious constitutionality.

Also in the 1950s, the federal government began offering loans to certain select students, mostly in engineering, science, and education, under the National Defense Education Act of 1958 (NDEA). This act, driven in part by American fears that the United States was falling behind the Soviet Union technologically (*Sputnik* had been launched the previous year), required all recipients to produce an affidavit denying any belief in the overthrow of the U.S. government. Despite its distinctly anticommunist tone, the NDEA represented the first concrete steps to bring American colleges and universities under federal control, by manipulation of the student loan market.

It was President Lyndon Johnson's "Great Society" cluster of new government programs in the 1960s, however, that permanently entrenched the federal government in the dubious business of subsidizing college educations. The Higher Education Act of 1965 (HEA) created a range of new scholarships and introduced subsidies for student loans. Title IV of this act provided for several categories of loans, now known as Stafford, Perkins, and PLUS loans. The former two were and are loans issued to students to help defray the cost of college up to certain limits, and subject to lax eligibility requirements. The Stafford loan, in its fully subsidized variety, is the most popular, since it allows students to borrow up to a total of more than $50,000 without having any interest accrue until after the end of a six-month grace period following graduation, dropping out, or going to less than full-time student status. Not only that, repayment (and the accrual of interest) on such loans can be deferred if the student continues with graduate-level studies. A student thus can borrow tens of thousands of dollars to finance an undergraduate education, and then defer payment and interest accrual on the loan for years afterwards while working on a J.D., Ph.D., and so forth. Taxpayers must cover the interest accrued on such loans during periods of interest deferral. PLUS loans, meanwhile, allow parents to borrow government money to pay for their children's college education. PLUS loans ordinarily require repayment to begin within 60 days of issuance, but they may also be used to cover part-time as well as full-time schooling.

Since 1965, the HEA has been reauthorized nine times, each time with more and more aid monies and education benefit programs superadded. Federal student loans and grants have always been billed as a tool to keep college education affordable, but in the nearly 50 years since HEA was first passed, they have done precisely the opposite. This is because government manipulation of the credit markets, ostensibly to keep borrowing rates affordable for the "little guy," always does the opposite. By driving interest rates below what the market would otherwise set, such government actions not only encourage excessive borrowing, they also drive costs up. Put otherwise: In the college education market, potential customers (students and their parents) know they will have access to credit on terms far laxer than what they would get if they borrowed from a private party without government subsidies, underwriting, or guarantees. This makes them more willing to borrow than would otherwise be the case, and allows colleges and universities to charge more for tuition, fees, and other services, because they know this artificial credit market can bear it, at least in the short run. It also allows others participating in the college education marketplace—textbook publishers, for example—to charge vastly more for their products than they could possibly get for comparable markets outside of the higher education sector. Thus a hardcover non-textbook volume of 500 pages, with color pictures and a dust jacket, that might retail for $40 on Amazon.com, would cost several hundred dollars if repackaged and sold as a course textbook. Of course, college textbooks are often written and edited by large teams of authors and printed on glossy, very high-quality paper when compared with the latest mass-market history tome by David McCullough. But that's precisely the point: While there is no reason a physics or economics textbook could not be authored by one person and printed on the same type of paper, and with the same proportion of illustrations, as any other hardcover, they are not, because those who manufacture and market textbooks are well aware that market distortions allow students (or their parents) to pony up $500 to $1,000 per semester for textbooks.

And this same type of distorted pricing is found in many parts of the higher education sector. When I was an undergraduate in the 1980s, for example, students were allowed to use swimming pools, weight rooms, racquetball courts, and the like for free, as long as they could flash a current student ID. Today, at the very same institution, students are charged a fee every semester for use of such physical-fitness facilities, which typically ranges from $50 to $100.

Costs Lead to Cultural Changes

For those of us associated with higher education for decades, the vertiginous rise of tuition rates and the proliferation of fees have wrought a wholesale transformation in the culture of higher education. For one thing, because a college education has become prohibitively costly, a higher and higher proportion of students, understandably worried about their ability to repay debts, are focusing more and more on degree tracks that will maximize their training and earning potential in areas like business management, accounting, and computer technology. A four-year college degree, after all, costs the same whether it is in history or in nursing—but in bottom-line terms, the latter is a far better investment.

Students who perceive a college education as merely a glorified license to practice accounting, hotel management, or information security tend to regard required courses in history, writing, mathematics, art, foreign languages, culture, and the like as pointless encumbrances foisted on them by an outdated system of educational values, and complain ceaselessly about being "forced" to take courses that will have nothing to do with running a hotel or analyzing a corporate balance sheet.

Colleges and universities, in their turn, are responding to students' demands by deprioritizing and defunding programs in the humanities and in other traditional areas where student demand has fallen. My employer, a large land-grant university that was founded in the mid-19th century primarily to promote agricultural research and development, has responded to budget shortfalls during the Great Recession by making massive cuts in what was once its flagship program, the College of Agriculture—this because relatively few students want to pursue a career in agriculture anymore.

Colleges and universities everywhere have been moving aggressively to restructure along corporate lines, with legions of bureaucrats tasked with writing and enforcing volumes of administrative protocol. In other words, American colleges and universities are transforming into behemoth business, trade, and technical schools, and moving away from the relatively exclusive model of liberal education that animated their founders. Men like Eli Yale, Benjamin Franklin, Thomas Jefferson, and

Ezra Cornell, all of whom founded elite universities that today service tens of thousands of American students, perceived universities as institutions dependent on endowments and donations by wealthy idealists who wished to further cultural advancement in areas where innovation would not necessarily be profitable—in mathematics, in philology, in the study of history, and the like. Such institutions were designed primarily for the comparatively few individuals interested in becoming either academics—scientists, teachers, and researchers—or quasi-academic, highly skilled professionals in law, medicine, and a few other areas. In such a context, early American universities were indeed centers where learning advanced. Men like Harvard's Benjamin Peirce, America's first mathematical physicist and astrophysicist, and Albert Michelson, a physicist at the Case School of Applied Science at Cleveland, and the first American scientist to receive a Nobel Prize, once defined the American academic landscape. Such innovators are still to be found, especially in enclaves of high-level theoretical science like Cal Tech and the Princeton Institute for Advanced Study, but today's universities are dominated by legions of students putting in their time in exchange for a coveted admission ticket to a remunerative profession or trade, and by unwieldy bureaucracies dedicated to getting them there at an inflated cost.

Another consequence of this new higher education market has been the well-documented "dumbing down" of standards. Because 21st-century college education comes with the expectation of optimal employability with minimal effort, and because colleges and universities are no longer competing merely for elite students desiring an education for its own sake but for masses of businessmen and accountant wannabes, college faculties are under withering pressure to make sure that coursework does not inconvenience tuition-paying clients.

Yet another consequence is the politicization of college curricula, especially in the humanities, where, given heavy dependence on government funding and subsidies, outlandish modern disciplines like Lesbian and Gay Studies enjoy clout all out of proportion to the actual validity of program content or demand among college students. Absent shrill special interest groups lobbying politicians on behalf of such programs, it is inconceivable that colleges and universities would go to the trouble to sustain them—this, while degree programs in the likes of classical studies and philosophy are jettisoned almost routinely.

Traded In for Trade Schools

All of this—skyrocketing costs, dumbed-down curricula, a de-emphasis on more traditional fields in favor of professional certification and programs promoting radical social agendas, and top-heavy administration and bureaucracy—is the consequence of decades-old systemic market distortions created by federal government interference in higher education, especially with subsidized student loans and grants. As with all other asset bubbles, this one is about more than just astronomical prices; the entire makeup of the system has changed (indeed, the fact that it can be characterized as a "system" in the first place is indicative of central planning). Probably the most pernicious of all side effects of this bubble is the transformation of colleges and universities into trade schools issuing degrees that, in more levelheaded times, would be deemed a waste of money. Why, after all, should someone intending to inherit the family business have a college degree? Or, for that matter, an insurance salesman, investment advisor, accountant, hotel manager, or any of a host of other entrants in well-paid professions, let alone the overwhelming majority of America's entrepreneurial class? It is no accident that many of America's most successful individuals, like Kirk Kerkorian and Bill Gates, do not possess college degrees. Nor, once in the not-so-recent past, was a college degree deemed a necessity for the multitudes of people who perform much of America's most important work. Even with a college degree, prospective insurance salesmen or financial planners, for example, must still undergo rigorous training and licensing designed to acquaint them with the intricacies of their field. Such people, understandably, have little use for a freshman writing course. So why insist on college at all?

The hard truth is that the pre-World War II way of doing things, in which higher education was divided between colleges/universities on the one hand and trade and business schools on the other, with huge numbers of successful professionals neither wanting nor needing a college education at all, was far more beneficial than what we have today. Many of America's most successful men from that era, including inventors Thomas Edison and the Wright brothers, journalist H. L. Mencken, and entrepreneurs like Henry Ford and John D. Rockefeller, never got a college degree (Rockefeller founded two universities but never attended one; probably the richest American in history, Rockefeller's exposure to post-secondary education was limited to a 10-week course in business). All of which is to say that success is not necessarily measurable in terms of credit hours.

None of which is to disparage commendable research into business, accounting, and management by competent researchers. Most business students, however, do not aim to become professors at Wharton; they instead seek a basic knowledge of the trade, which usually can be more efficiently provided by America's many excellent business schools and for-profit universities (like the University of Phoenix), without the costly frills of a university B.A. or B.S.

And the time is fast approaching that American parents and their college-age children will come to this realization, in droves. As the economic slowdown drags on with no rebound in housing or employment, more and more will perceive the inflated costs of a college degree as a hindrance to success. They will discover that their tastes and talents are better served by entrepreneurial activity, or by pursuing a vocational or business degree at cheaper community colleges, trade schools, and online programs.

Just as America is learning to adjust to new realities occasioned by bursting bubbles in stocks and real estate and to long-term high unemployment, so too will our country soon recalibrate its cultural expectations regarding college educations. In coming years, look either for college enrollments to decline sharply or for colleges and universities to make massive cuts in expenses, including faculty pay and benefits, administrative costs, and building construction, among many other things.

The distortions brought about by government interference in higher education, and especially the subsidizing of student loans, have had every bit as far reaching an effect on the higher education sector as government subsidies and other distortions of the real estate sector have had on the housing market, and the outcome will be no less wrenching. But as with the rupturing of the real estate bubble, the coming agonizing return to sanity brought about by the collapse of the student loan house of cards will lead in the long run to a more reasonable balance between costs and benefits. In the short run, America's colleges and universities face a painful day of reckoning, but in the long run, they will move toward providing the higher-quality, more affordable education that academically inclined Americans used to enjoy.

I Owe U

By Kristina Dell
Time, October 31, 2011

Like many of the protesters at Occupy Wall Street in New York City, Amanda Vodola is young, underemployed and loaded with student debt. She spends her days running around, helping organize the movement, and her evenings bussing tables at a dine-in movie theater in Brooklyn. Last spring, Vodola, 22, graduated from Fordham University with a degree in English. "I grew up with this narrative that to get a good job I need to go to school," she says. But the job she has "is not enough to pay the bills." And the bills she's dreading most are the ones tied to that narrative: the $30,000 she owes in college loans.

In November, when their six-month grace period runs out, Vodola and millions of other students who graduated in May have to start repaying their loans. Repayment requirements for private loans kick in regardless of whether borrowers have found jobs. Since employment rates for recent college grads have plummeted in the past two years, as have starting salaries, the possibility of a sharp rise in student-loan delinquencies has led some analysts to predict that this could be the next subprime-mortgage crisis, rippling into the wider economy. Total U.S. student-loan debt, which exceeded credit-card debt for the first time last year, is on track to hit $1 trillion this year.

The members of the class of 2011 have a frightening footnote on their diplomas: Most Indebted Class Ever—and this year's seniors are on track to surpass them. Average student-loan debt for new graduates has reached $27,300, according to Mark Kantrowitz, publisher of FinAid.org and FastWeb.com, sites that help students plan and pay for college. Add the loans parents took out for their children's education, which students frequently pay back themselves, and the number rises to $34,400. That's a nearly 8% increase over last year and a 36% hike (adjusted for inflation) from 10 years ago. And with student loans, unlike real estate or business debts, you can't walk away through bankruptcy as General Motors did.

But neither these statistics nor the voices of students, crushed by debt, at protests in cities and on campuses throughout the nation are likely to keep the families of high school seniors from seeing a brand-name education as a ticket to a better life. They've long been told that higher education, much like buying a house, is an investment in the future—even as the cost of college has soared 538% over the past 30 years. That's more than four times the growth of consumer prices and almost twice the increase in health care costs. Meanwhile, says Lawrence Mishel, president of the nonpartisan Economic Policy Institute, "the wages of those with a college degree have been roughly flat for 10 years, and it's not really improving relative to those with less education." In other words, all those tuition hikes aren't necessarily leading graduates to better paychecks. That letdown, coupled with rising debt loads, could stunt economic growth in the long term if today's grads end up being too poor to start a business or buy a house or send their own children to university.

What's Your Major?

Two years ago, president Obama challenged Americans to increase the number of college graduates from 40% of young working adults (ages 25 to 34) to 60% by 2020, which would be the highest proportion in the world. The goal is to help the U.S. compete globally. The problem is that the country doesn't have jobs for all its recent college grads—many of whom are now back home living with Mom and Dad—let alone the additional 5.5 million bachelor's-degree holders that Obama's plan calls for. There's also the problem of what those graduates studied. The U.S. isn't producing enough science and math majors, so high-paying positions in related fields are going either unfilled or to foreign applicants. A liberal-arts education, the pride of the American undergraduate system, increasingly looks like a road to financial distress.

Although the U.S. Bureau of Labor Statistics doesn't parse its data by graduating class, it does show that the unemployment rate for 16-to-24-year-olds with a B.A. or higher who are no longer enrolled in school was a whopping 13.2% in July—the highest to date for this cohort and almost double the rate from five years ago, before the Great Recession hit.

A faster growing economy could absorb more of those graduates, but the fear is that too many students are spending too much on degrees that may never generate the expected return on investment. A Harvard diploma is still going to open doors. But what about a degree from a less well endowed school, like Bates or Sarah Lawrence, that doesn't offer the generous grants the elite ones do? "These colleges are expensive," Kantrowitz says, "and that's where you hear kids going $100,000 in debt to graduate with religious-studies or theater majors."

Some students' debt burdens are so big, you wonder what bank would approve the loans or what parent would be willing to cosign them. Lyndsey P. (who did not want *Time* to include her full name) amassed an astounding $169,934 in debt while studying documentary filmmaking at New York University. Like many teenagers, she was so excited about getting into a top-tier school that the cost didn't keep her from enrolling. "You can't imagine the emotional darkness that descended when I started to understand the full extent of the debt situation I was going to be in," says Lyndsey, who graduated from NYU with honors in 2007.

To keep up with her $1,269 monthly payments, she spent the past two years working 9 a.m. to 5 p.m. as a lab technician and then rushing home to do phone support for a software company from 7 p.m. to 10:30 p.m. She got so burned out from the long hours that she quit the lab job this fall and doesn't know how she's going to fulfill the loan terms, which require her over the next 26 years to pay a total of $350,000, including accrued interest. "It feels absolutely hopeless. I don't know what I will do in the future if I want to get married or have kids," she says. "It's a huge burden to bring to a relationship. I am basically coming with a house on my back that we can't live in."

It's these costs, both personal and societal, that worry economists. More than two-thirds of all college students borrow to pay for school, and 10% to 20% borrow excessively, which is defined as having monthly loan payments that exceed 10% of a person's gross income. According to a study published in March by the Institute for Higher Education Policy, 41% of borrowers who began repayment in 2005 became delinquent or defaulted within five years. Repayments—and the often severe penalties that accumulate if borrowers fall behind—kick in regardless of whether students leave school with a degree, which points to another big problem: the connection between college dropouts and crippling debt. Barely half the students who start college get a degree within six years, and graduation rates at less selective colleges often hover at 25% or less.

More Toxic Than Mortgages

It's nearly impossible to discharge federal or private student-loan debt in bankruptcy, unless you meet the incredibly harsh "undue hardship" standard. In 2008, for example, only 0.04% of student-loan recipients who filed for bankruptcy succeeded in getting their college loans dismissed. Meanwhile, the government can garnish up to 15% of your take-home pay, dock your disability benefits and even deny you a security clearance, all in the name of student-loan payback. Defaulting will torpedo your credit rating to the point where for years to come you'll have a tough time getting a credit card, let alone a car or home loan. "Student debt is more toxic than mortgages," says Mark C. Taylor, a religion professor at Columbia University and the author of the higher-education critique *Crisis on Campus*, "because you can't walk away from it."

Given the dire consequences of defaulting, the government recently created an income-based repayment plan for federal-student-loan borrowers whose debt at graduation exceeds their starting salary. Monthly payments will be lower than they would be under the standard 10-year repayment plan, and although users may end up paying more interest over the life of their loans, anything still owed after 25 years will be written off. Another new program forgives federal loans for borrowers who spend 10 years working full time in public service.

But these options apply only to federal loans. To try to help people like Lyndsey who took out massive private loans, Fordham law-school grad Robert Applebaum started ForgiveStudentLoanDebt.com, which champions erasing student debt to stimulate the economy. (This is not an unheard-of strategy even on a national scale. Bono has been promoting the same idea for sub-Saharan African countries for years.) Applebaum has already secured the more than 25,000 signatures needed to deliver his petition to the President through the White House's We the People program. He has also amassed many followers on Facebook and at least one fan in the House of Representatives. This summer Michigan Democrat Hansen Clarke introduced a bill that includes a provision about forgiving student loans.

Getting the latter provision passed is a long shot, which helps explain why many higher-education advocates are encouraging the next generation of students to borrow less money in the first place. To help prospective applicants compare the costs of attending different schools, all colleges as of October 29 must include a net-price calculator on their websites. The calculator asks families for detailed financial information and then provides customized estimates of what they will likely pay out of pocket. Industry experts are also focusing on improving the information applicants receive once they are accepted. Kantrowitz testified before a congressional advisory committee that in an online survey last year of some 580,000 students and parents, 61% of respondents said the financial-aid-award letters they received did not include basic information about loan terms like interest rates or monthly payments. Some didn't even use the word *loan,* referring instead to a "subsidized Stafford," which families might confuse with a grant. (It's actually a loan whose interest is paid by the federal government while the student is in school.) Hence the Department of Education's current push to standardize financial-aid-award letters so people won't get lulled into overborrowing.

At the same time, more financial-aid offices are trying to help families maximize their use of federal loans, which have fixed interest rates, unlike private loans, which can have uncapped, variable rates that often go up after the first year. Lenders reel in families by advertising low rates, but usually only people with stellar credit qualify. Private loans—which make up 20% of outstanding education loans—also lack certain consumer protections, like the ability to write off the balance if the borrower dies. In 2006, Alison Rabil, then director of financial aid at Barnard College, started a policy of contacting families whenever she received requests from lenders to certify private loans. After one year of explaining why federal loans were the better option, Barnard saw the school's private-student-loan volume drop from $1.6 million in 2005–06 to $400,000 in 2006–07. Many other schools both big and small have since adopted similar procedures. Last year San Diego State started requiring students to go through an online counseling process before it would certify private loans.

Nina Marks, president of Collegiate Directions, a nonprofit that provides college counseling for low-income students, recommends that families drill deeper and ask financial-aid officers such questions as, If a college's cost of attendance increases each year, will financial aid go up too? What percentage of students graduate in four years? A fifth or sixth year could significantly increase debt load.

Early Decisions

Some high school guidance counselors encourage students to start at a more affordable state school or community college and then transfer to a more impressive (read: higher priced) institution to get their diploma. Other counselors suggest smaller ways to skimp. "You can lower the price of the second year by adjusting the meal plan," says John Boshoven, a counselor at Community High School in Ann

Arbor, Mich. "A lot of kids don't eat breakfast or can save money by eating cereal in their rooms."

Every little bit helps. But it's the bigger issues of which school students should attend and what they should major in that are much more difficult to address. Nanette DiLauro, who succeeded Rabil as Barnard's director of financial aid, recalls one student who wanted to go to Barnard—where the sticker price, including fees and housing, is $55,566 per year—so much that she begged the school to certify her private loans. The student, whose parents weren't willing to contribute, would have had to borrow $140,000. "That was a crazy amount," says DiLauro, who gave counsel with a candor that is perhaps all too rare. "I advised the daughter not to do it." The student ultimately chose to go somewhere else.

It's hard to tell teenagers to pass up their dream school and harder still to get them to make a serious effort to map out their future. Bob Giannino-Racine, CEO of ACCESS, a Massachusetts-based nonprofit that gives free financial-aid advice to students, counsels high schoolers to think about the long term. "If you have $50,000 or more in debt from undergrad, you will have a hard time paying for graduate school," he says. That might be helpful for aspiring bankers and lawyers to know. But what about the kids who can't see that far down the road?

Kantrowitz advises setting an undergraduate debt ceiling of $45,000 as a safe burden for someone who plans to earn a degree in engineering, computer science or business. He suggests lowering that cap to $35,000 for a student likely to choose a liberal-arts major. But he and other experts warn that the lesson is not to forgo college. Don't go overboard. College grads still have roughly half the unemployment rate of those without degrees, and their median earnings are about $21,900 more per year, which translates into almost $1 million more over a lifetime.

Students also need to make smarter choices. Too many are committing to expensive schools or completing lengthier programs than they need to. Bill Symonds, director of the Harvard-based Pathways to Prosperity Project, worries that many policy advisers are fanning the college-for-all flames when vocational training or a two-year associate's degree would be a better fit. "If you go to a four-year college and get a degree and can't use it in the labor market, you're not getting much of a return on that investment," he says.

It's advice current debt holders wish they had heard earlier. Jeri Leigh McDowell graduated third in her high school class in 2006 and passed up a free ride to the University of Texas to accept a spot at New Orleans' more illustrious Tulane University, which offered her a $22,000 scholarship. How she would come up with the rest of the $53,000-a-year tab for tuition and living expenses was a problem for another day. The anthropology and history major skated through Tulane in 3 years, but she now struggles to pay back the $90,000 she owes.

The teaching job she thought she had found last October never materialized. Today McDowell lives with her mother in Burleson, Texas, while dodging calls from a collection agency. She works a $9.50-an-hour job at a hotel. "I wish to God I had gone to the state school," she says. "Everyone at my high school was super impressed when I got into Tulane, and I thought it would open doors. I was an idiot."

Academic Freedom and Indentured Students

By Jeffrey J. Williams
Academe, January/February 2012

Discussion of academic freedom usually focuses on faculty, and it usually refers to speech. That is the gist of the 1915 *General Report of the Committee on Academic Freedom and Academic Tenure*, appearing in the inaugural AAUP *Bulletin* as a kind of mission statement. The report invokes the ideals of the German tradition, "*Lehrfreiheit* and *Lernfreiheit*," or freedom of teachers and freedom of students, in the first sentence, but the remainder of the document talks about the freedom of professors. That is because its authors were responding to their particular situation, notably the firing of Professor Edward A. Ross from Stanford University for his statements about railroad monopolies, as well as to the position of US college students, who were not subject to state control as they were in the German system. Given the conditions of the American system of higher education—decentralized and meeting diverse needs, with liberal admissions requirements and relatively low tuition, and subject to ordinary speech protections—it was assumed that students had a good deal of freedom.

That assumption has persisted through most of the century, as higher education has opened to an expanding body of students. However, over the past thirty years, students' freedom has been progressively curtailed—not in their immediate rights to speech but in their material circumstances. Now, two-thirds of American college students graduate with substantial debt, averaging nearly $30,000 (if one includes charge cards) in 2008 and rising, according to data from the National Center for Education Statistics and other sources.

In my view, the growth in debt has ushered in a system of bondage similar in practical terms, as well as in principle, to indentured servitude. The analogy to indenture might seem exaggerated but actually has a great deal of resonance. Student debt binds individuals for a significant part of their future work lives. It encumbers job and life choices, and it permeates everyday experience with concern over the monthly chit. It also takes a page from indenture in the extensive brokerage system it has bred, from which more than four thousand banks take profit (even when the loans originate with the federal government, they are still serviced by banks, and banks service an escalating number of private loans). At its core, student debt is a labor issue, just as colonial indenture was, subsisting off the desire of those less privileged to gain better opportunities in exchange for their future labor. One of the goals of the planners of the US university system after World War II was to displace what they saw as an aristocracy; instead, they promoted equal opportunity in order to build America through its best talent. The new tide of student debt reinforces rather than dissolves the discriminations of class. Finally, it violates the spirit of American freedom in leading those less wealthy to bind their futures.

Here are some ways that college student loan debt revives indentured servitude.

Prevalence. Contrary to the usual image of freedom-seeking Puritans in New England, between one-half and two-thirds of all white immigrants to the British colonies arrived under indenture, according to the economic historian David W. Galenson, totaling 300,000 to 400,000 people. Similarly, college student loan debt is now a prevalent mode of financing higher education, resorted to by two-thirds of students who attend. If upwards of 70 percent of Americans attend college at some point, it thus shackles not an unfortunate few but half the rising population.

Amounts. Indenture was a common practice in seventeenth-century England, but its terms were relatively short, typically a year, and closely regulated by law. The innovation of the Virginia Company, to garner cheap labor in the colonies, extended the practice of indenture to America, but at a much higher obligation of four to seven years, because of the added cost of passage and boarding immigrants, and also the added cost of the brokerage system that arose around it.

Student debt has similarly morphed from relatively small amounts to sizeable ones. The average federal loan debt of a graduating senior in 2008 was $24,000. That was a marked rise from ten years before, but even more tellingly, it was an astronomical rise from twenty-five years ago, when average federal loan debt was less than $2,000. Also consider that many people have significantly more than the average debt—25 percent of federal borrowers had more than $30,000 in student loans, and 14 percent owed more than $40,000 in 2008. Added to federal loans are charge cards, which averaged $4,100 for graduating seniors in 2008, and private loans, which by 2008 were taken by 14 percent of students (up from 1 percent in 1996) and totaled $17.1 billion, a disturbingly large amount in addition to the $68.6 billion for federal loans. Finally, for more than 60 percent of those continuing their education, graduate student debt more than doubled in the past decade, to a 2008 median of about $25,000 for master's degrees, $52,000 for doctorates, and $80,000 for professional degrees. That is on top of undergraduate debt.

Length of term. Student debt is a long-term commitment— standard Stafford Loans amortize over fifteen years. With consolidation or refinancing, the term frequently extends to thirty years—in other words, for many returning students or graduate students, until retirement age. It is not a brief, transitory bond, say, of a year for those indentured in England, or of 1980s student debtors, who might have owed $2,000.

Transport to work. Student indebtedness is premised on the idea of transport to a job—now the figurative transport over the seas of higher education to attain the shores of credentials deemed necessary for a middle-class job. The cost of transport is borne by the laborer, so, in effect, an individual has to pay for the opportunity to work. If you add the daunting number of hours that students work, one twist of the current system is that servitude begins on ship. Undergraduates at state universities work more than twenty hours a week, according to Marc Bousquet's work. Tom Mortenson, an education policy analyst, provides a telling comparison of hours a week required at minimum wage to pay tuition, which have grown roughly from twenty hours a week before 1980 to more than fifty hours a week now at public universities and colleges, and from about forty hours to a stunning 130 at private institutions.

Personal contracts. "Indenture" designates a practice of making contracts before signatures were common (they were torn, the tear analogous to the unique shape of a person's bite, and each party held half, so they could be verified by their match); student debt reinstitutes a system of contracts that bind a rising majority of Americans. Like indenture, the debt is secured not by property, as most loans such as those for cars or houses are, but by the person. Student loan debt "financializes" the person, in the phrase of social critic Randy Martin, who diagnoses this strategy as a central one of contemporary venture capital, displacing risk to individuals rather than employers or society. It was also a strategy of colonial indenture.

Limited recourse. Contracts for federal student loans stipulate severe penalties and are virtually unbreakable, forgiven not in bankruptcy but only in death, and they are enforced by severe measures, such as garnishing wages and other legal sanctions, with little recourse. In England, indenture was regulated by law and servants had recourse in court, but one of the pernicious aspects of colonial indenture was that there was little recourse in the new colonies. Alan Collinge, founder of the grassroots organization Student Loan Justice and author of *The Student Loan Scam*, has proposed that student debt be forgiven in bankruptcy as any other personal loan would be.

Class. Student debt primarily bears on those with less family wealth, just as indenture drew on the less-privileged classes. That this would be a practice in early modern Britain, before modern democracy, is not entirely surprising; it is more disturbing in the United States, where we eschew the determining force of class. The one-third of students without student debt face much different futures, and are far more likely to pursue graduate and professional degrees (for example, three-quarters of those receiving doctorates in 2004 had no undergraduate debt, and, according to a 2002 Nellie Mae survey, 40 percent of those not pursuing graduate school attributed their choice to debt).

Youth. Student debt applies primarily to younger people, as indenture did. One of the more troubling aspects of student debt is that it is not an isolated hurdle but often the first step down a slope of debt and difficulty, as Tamara

Draut, vice president of policy and programs at Demos, shows in *Strapped: Why America's 20- and 30-Somethings Can't Get Ahead*. Added to that burden are shrinking job prospects and historically higher housing payments. The American dream, and specifically the post–World War II dream of equal opportunity opened by higher education, has been curtailed for many of the rising generation.

Brokers. Colonial indenture prompted a system in which merchants or brokers in England's ports signed prospective workers, then sold the contracts to shippers or colonial landowners, who in turn could resell the contracts. Student debt similarly has fueled an extensive financial services system. The lender pays the fare to the college, and thereafter the contracts are circulated among Sallie Mae, Nellie Mae, and others. Sallie Mae was created as a federal nonprofit corporation, but it became an entirely private (and highly profitable) corporation in 2004.

State policy. The British Crown gave authority to the Virginia Company; the US federal government authorizes current lending enterprises and, even more lucratively for banks, underwrites their risk in guaranteeing the loans (the Virginia Company received no such largesse and went bankrupt). Since the 1990s, federal aid has funneled more to student loans than any other form of aid. Loans might be helpful, but they are a rather ambivalent form of "aid."

These points show the troubling overlap of indentured servitude and student indebtedness. While indenture was more direct and severe, akin to placing someone in stocks, it was the product of a rigidly classed, semifeudal world that predated modern democracies. Student debt is more flexible, varied in application, and amorphous in effects—a product of the postmodern world—but it revives the spirit of indenture in promulgating class privilege and class subservience. What is most troubling is that it represents a shift in basic political principle. It turns away from the democratic impetus of modern American society, which promoted equality through higher education, especially after World War II. The 1947 *Report of the President's Commission on Education*, which ushered in the vast expansion of our colleges and universities, emphasized that "free and universal access to education must be a major goal in American education." Otherwise, the commission warned, "if the ladder of educational opportunity rises high at the doors of some youth and scarcely rises at the doors of others, while at the same time formal education is made a prerequisite to occupational and social advance, then education may become the means, not of eliminating race and class distinctions, but of deepening them."

The commission's goal was not only to promote equality but also to strengthen the United States—and, by all accounts, American society prospered. Current student debt, encumbering so many of the rising generation, has built a roadblock to the American ideal, squanders the resource of those impeded from pursuing degrees who otherwise would make excellent doctors or professors or engineers, and creates a culture of debt and constraint.

The arguments for the rightness of student loan debt are similar to the arguments for the benefits of indenture. One holds that it is a question of supply and demand—many people want higher education, thus driving up the price. This view doesn't hold water because the demand for higher education in the years following World War II through the 1970s was proportionately the highest of any time, as student enrollments doubled and tripled, but the supply was cheap and largely state funded. Then, higher education was much more substantially funded through public sources, both state and federal; now the expense has been privatized, transferred to students and their families.

University of Chicago economist David Galenson argues in his work on colonial servitude that "long terms did not imply exploitation" because those terms were only fitting for the high cost of transport; because more productive servants, or those placed in undesirable areas, could lessen their terms; and because some servants went on to prosper. He does not mention the high rate of death, the many cases of abuse, the draconian extension of contracts by unethical planters, or simply what term would be an appropriate maximum for any person in a free society to be bound, even if he or she agreed to the contract. Galenson also ignores the underlying political questions: Is it appropriate that people, especially those entering the adult world, might take on such a longterm constraint? Can people make a rational choice for a term they might not realistically imagine? Even if one doesn't question the principle of indenture, what is an appropriate cap for its amounts and term? One of the more haunting findings of the 2002 Nellie Mae survey was that 54 percent said that they would have borrowed less if they had to do it again, up from 31 percent ten years before, which is still substantial (and, one can extrapolate, increased from 1980). The percentage of borrowers making this informed judgment will surely climb as debt continues to rise.

Some economists justify college student loan debt in terms similar to Galenson's. One prominent argument holds that because college graduates have averaged roughly $1 million more in salary over the course of their careers than those with less education, it is rational and right that they accumulate substantial debt to start their careers. However, while many graduates make statistically high salaries, the experiences of those who have taken on debt vary a great deal: some accrue debt but don't graduate; some graduate but, with degrees in the humanities or education, for example, are unlikely to make a high salary; more and more students are having difficulty finding a high-paying job; and the amount that people who have a college degree make over a lifetime has been declining. A degree is no longer the guaranteed ticket to wealth that it once was. An economic balance sheet also ignores the fundamental question of the ethics of requiring debt of those who desire higher education, as well as the fairness of its distribution to those often younger and less privileged.

Over the past few years, there has been more attention to the problem of student loan debt, but most of the solutions, such as income-based repayment, or IBR, are stopgaps that don't impinge on the basic terms of the system. The system needs wholesale change.

College student loan debt perverts the aims of higher education, whether those aims are to grant freedom of intellectual exploration, to cultivate merit and thereby mitigate the inequitable effects of class, or, in the most utilitarian scheme, to provide students with a head start into the adult work world. In practice, debt shackles students with long-term loan payments, constraining their freedom of choice of jobs and career. It also constrains their everyday lives after graduating, as they bear the weight of the monthly tab that stays with them long after their college days. The AAUP should consider student debt a major threat to academic freedom and make the abolition of student debt one of its major policy platforms.

A Note on Sources

The major source of data on student debt is the *Digest of Education Statistics* for postsecondary education published by the National Center for Education Statistics of the US Department of Education. The center conducts the National Postsecondary Student Aid Study every four years; the most recent data are from 2007–08. The Project on Student Debt publishes useful reports digesting and processing information related to key aspects of student debt. The loan industry also collects a good deal of information—for example, Sallie Mae's *How Undergraduates Use Credit Cards* (2009)—about the contiguous issue of charge-card debt.

The Hard Truth about Defaulting on Student Loans

By *WJSU*, January 21, 2014

CELESTE HEADLEE, HOST: I'm Celeste Headlee and this is *Tell Me More* from NPR News. Michel Martin is away. It's time for Money Coach. That's the part of the program where we talk about personal finance issues. And today, we focus on student loan debt. Americans reportedly owe $1 trillion in student loans. But what happens when so many can't pay or won't pay? Joining us to talk about that is Sandy Baum. She's a senior fellow at the Urban Institute. Sandy, welcome to the program.

SANDY BAUM: Hi. It's nice to be here.

HEADLEE: How big is this problem? How many people default on student loans every year?

BAUM: Well, the first issue is that the trillion dollar number can be somewhat misleading because what really matters is how much individual students owe. And it also really matters whether they owe the federal government or whether they have private student loans. More students have been defaulting in this bad economy, just as more people are defaulting on all of their loans.

HEADLEE: All right. Well, let's kind of pick apart your answer there. Let's talk first about the difference between somebody who owns—gets student loans from the government and those who get a private loan from, say, a bank. What's the difference?

BAUM: If you have a federal student loan, then you are borrowing from the federal government. And if you can't pay, there are provisions. You could be in an income-based repayment plan that guarantees that your payments will not be bigger than you can afford. There are also provisions for deferments, so you don't have to pay if you're in school and you don't have to pay if you can't afford it under forbearance.

If you have a private student loan, it's between you and the bank or Sallie Mae. It's between you and the lender, and they may or may not be cooperative in helping you to defer those payments when you're unemployed or your wages are low.

HEADLEE: I have to assume, Sandy—and I'm a person who is still paying my student loan in my forties—I have to assume that were the restrictions governing student loans not so very tight, that we wouldn't have so many people defaulting. And what I mean by that is you can't get rid of your student loan once you have it, even if you go bankrupt, right? You can't get rid of your student loan.

BAUM: It is possible to get rid of your student loans in bankruptcy, but very, very difficult. And that applies to both federal student loans and private student loans. And you're right that there would be fewer people defaulting if they were dischargeable in bankruptcy. But again, for federal student loans, people really should not have to default if they can figure out—and there are some bureaucratic hurdles—how to get into the appropriate repayment plan.

People with private student loans—and many people borrowed private student loans five or six years ago. Fewer people are doing that now. But those are a bigger problem, and those, if they were dischargeable in bankruptcy, that would make a big difference.

HEADLEE: And the other thing that you can't do, especially for a private loan, is refinance it.

BAUM: Well, some private lenders do allow you to refinance. And the federal government, the Consumer Financial Protection Bureau, is pressuring private lenders to allow students to refinance. But it is very difficult. Students should really think hard before they take those private student loans. And if they already have them, they should negotiate with their lenders. They should seek help from some consumer protection organization if they are struggling with their lenders.

HEADLEE: Let me give you a hypothetical situation. Let's say you have a student who's a few years out of college, lost their job, can't repay their student loan. They are now in long-term unemployment. Maybe they got a deferment without interest for, you know, a year. And that year has been exhausted. They can't pay. What happens to them if they don't pay that student loan?

BAUM: Not paying your student loan is a really bad idea. If you have a federal student loan, they will get that money out of you eventually. They could take it out of your Social Security payments when you get older. You really need to contact the government. You need to figure out how to get into a program that will postpone your payments if you have federal student loans. So defaulting is something that has really long-term consequences for students. It's not easy to get it to go away.

HEADLEE: You just talked about somebody with a federal loan. What if somebody's with a private lender and that private lender is not cooperating?

BAUM: Well, again, the private lender, that's when you need the consumer organizations.

HEADLEE: I see.

BAUM: The federal government, you really can—you just need to know that there are options. You could also go back to the institution where you were enrolled when you took the loans and ask the financial aid office for help. Not paying is really going to hurt you more than it's going to hurt anybody else. And that's true, even if you didn't graduate and even if you feel like your school didn't help you very much. Still, you owe money, if you have a federal student loan, to the taxpayers. And if you have a bank loan, you owe it to the bank. And they don't forget about these things.

HEADLEE: Yeah, I don't think they do. So we know—I mean, you say how bad it is for the students themselves to default. What about the parent or relative who cosigned on that loan?

BAUM: So cosigning a student loan refers only to private student loans because federal student loans don't require either a credit rating or a cosigner. But private student loans usually do require a cosigner. And everyone should know that cosigning a loan is like taking a loan because if you cosign and the student doesn't pay, you are responsible for that loan as though you had borrowed the money yourself. So parents should not cosign loans unless they are in a position to repay because they will have exactly the same problems that a student who can't repay would have.

HEADLEE: So when you saying exactly the same problems, if you're a parent, they could be garnishing your tax refund or your Social Security benefits?

BAUM: The garnishing is easier for the federal government to do than for private lenders to do. But you cannot discharge a student loan in bankruptcy. So whether you're the parent or the student, that's going to apply to you. One of the things that happens to people is that they've borrowed $10,000, and then they don't pay. And there is interest that accrues, and there are penalties imposed for nonpayment. And then they find that they owe 20 or $30,000. And that can happen to the cosigner, as well as to the original borrower.

HEADLEE: What groups tend to default more? I mean, my assumption—purely uneducated—is that it's probably young people who are having trouble finding a job. Is that correct?

BAUM: Actually, the people who default the most are people who dropped out of college without a credential. And part of that is because they have more trouble getting jobs. And part of that is because they don't really see why they should pay. And, you know, one thing that happens is, if you have a car loan, you know they're going to take your car away from you if you don't pay. So, many people pay their car loans first, and then they don't pay their student loans. So people who have accumulated other forms of debt also are likely to struggle with their student loan payments.

HEADLEE: How did we end up in a situation where student loan debt is treated so differently than any other kind of debt?

BAUM: The issue is why student loan debt is not dischargeable in bankruptcy. And one thing that's important to realize is that while it would be better if student loan debt were dischargeable in bankruptcy, you really don't want to get to that point. It's not a good thing to declare bankruptcy. So the question is really, why do people struggle to repay their loans? And one answer to that is that, first of all, most people don't. Some of the headlines would make you think that everybody borrows to go to college and that everybody who borrow struggles.

The reality is that a lot of people actually graduate from college without debt, and most of those who borrow, borrow reasonable amounts that don't cause them trouble. But too many students do borrow more than they can afford to repay. And there's a lot of lobbying that goes on. So why are private student loans not dischargeable in bankruptcy? Because the lenders have a lot of power in Congress, and they lobbied for that.

HEADLEE: To go a little further into this, I know a personal friend of mine who had no idea the difference between a private and a federal loan. When she was signing her paperwork, nobody was really clear on that. And she ended up with an 8 percent rate which she cannot refinance, and there's no way to get rid of that debt. I mean, I would imagine that, for many people, that becomes—I mean, that's more than a car payment. You're getting up towards your mortgage payment when you start paying that off.

BAUM: Well, of course, if there were other kinds of loans available at lower interest rates, you could take another kind of loan and use the money to pay off your student loans. So no one . . .

HEADLEE: You mean like a personal loan . . .

BAUM: Yeah, no one can . . .

HEADLEE: . . . Or a second mortgage.

BAUM: You can always prepay your loan. So that's really not that much of a problem. Although it would be better if you could refinance. In terms of whether people are confused, it used to be that you could get a federal student loan through a bank or through Sallie Mae and also a private student loan from them. And so it was much more confusing.

Now all of the federal student loans are direct loans from the federal government. So if there's a bank name on it, if there's a Sallie Mae name on it, then you know that is a private student loan and you want to be extra careful. It is much better to finance your education without taking those loans. But it's fine to take federal student loans.

HEADLEE: OK, so for the people that were already grandfathered in, they're kind of out of luck.

BAUM: Well, yes. If you've already taken a loan and you didn't know what you were getting, then you're already in that situation. And it's really good to get some personal advice about how to organize your finances, which loans you want to repay when. Maybe you have another kind of debt that you could refinance, and that would make it easier for you to repay your federal or your private student loans.

HEADLEE: Sandy Baum is a senior fellow at the Urban Institute, and she joined us from NPR's New York bureau. Sandy, thank you so much.

BAUM: Thank you.

Transcript provided by NPR.

Vocations Delayed by High Student Debt

By Peter Jesserer Smith
National Catholic Register, January 16, 2014

Catholic colleges are taking steps to reduce costs for students, whose lives after gradua-tion are often hindered by their accumulated financial burdens.

The increasing burden of student debt on Catholics has turned into a major road-block for young people trying to fulfill their vocations: whether it be for marriage, priesthood or religious life.

Cardinal Seán O'Malley of Boston raised the alarm in November about student debt, saying that "people are postponing marriage—are postponing a decision to go into the seminary or religious life—because they're saddled under these tremen-dous debts which former generations didn't have.

"If you have a $150,000 debt when you graduate law school, are you going to marry a girl who has a $130,000 debt and start off your marriage with over a quarter-million dollars' debt?"

Just last year, Georgetown's Center for Applied Research in the Apostolate (CARA) discovered that one out of three inquirers for religious life had an average student-debt load of $28,000. CARA's 2012 study reports that many institutes had to turn away applicants, and "slightly under half" of applicants with student debt were accepted into candidacy or postulancy with a religious order.

American families' student-debt burden totals more than one trillion dollars. *The Wall Street Journal* reported that the average student debt was $29,400, up 25% from four years ago, and that 10% of borrowers who started paying back their loans in 2011 had defaulted within two years. A survey by the Boston nonprofit American Student Assistance showed 29% of respondents reported putting off marriage as a result of their student loans, and 43% said that student debt factored in their deci-sion to delay having children.

"It's contributing to the destruction of a culture of marriage and the decline of the marital birth rate," said Allan Carlson, president of the Howard Center for Fam-ily, Religion and Society, who has researched extensively the challenges of student debt.

Carlson said healthy societies traditionally provided young people with start-up capital for marriage, such as dowries, wedding gifts of cash, land or property and help with housing, in order to encourage them to form families and have children.

"What we're doing is burdening young people with vast amounts of debt, and the result is they're delaying marriage, not getting married at all or having fewer children," he said.

Catholic Colleges Respond

Michael Galligan-Stierle, president of the Association of Catholic Colleges and Universities (ACCU), said Catholic institutions of higher learning are making strides to bend the cost curve down for their students.

"We are really looking to pass along value and affordability and transparency to our students and launch them in a good way," he said. "We really don't want to hamper them, because having financial debt down the road has severe consequences for everybody."

Galligan-Stierle pointed out that almost half the students at Catholic universities and colleges graduate in four years: a higher rate than non-Catholic private counterparts, where 38% graduate in four years, and public universities, where 21% graduate in four years. Fewer years generally translate into less accumulated debt.

He added that Catholic colleges have stepped up to make college more affordable, as government financial-aid grants decline, with close to nine out of 10 students receiving institutional aid that averages $12,000 per year.

Some ACCU-affiliated colleges have opted to freeze tuition rates or increase them by less than the growth of inflation. Galligan-Stierle said these combined efforts of the nation's 200 Catholic colleges have "flatlined what it costs to go to Catholic colleges in the last five years."

Ohio Dominican University in Columbus, Ohio, is one of the Catholic universities cited by the ACCU as among the 20 member institutions that have increased student aid by 80% over the past five years to offset tuition increases.

"We put together pretty good packages for our students, and so as long as they remain in good academic standing with the university, they can continue to receive that aid," said Laura Meek, director of financial aid for Ohio Dominican.

Managing Debt

Meek said Ohio Dominican focuses on pro-active financial counseling with students, both before and after they make the decision to spend four years at the university. Ohio Dominican students on average leave with approximately $25,000 in debt. But their student default rate in 2011 was 5.1%, or 60 borrowers out of 1,200, in 2011, which is lower than the average default rate of 7% for Catholic institutions and the 14% national average default rate reported by ACCU data.

"It's really important for schools to do as much proactive counseling as they can with students and families," she said. "We've really tried to beef up our own efforts at orientation about financial literacy topics, so students can really be looking toward budgeting, managing credit and looking at borrowing by assessing needs versus wants."

The University of Notre Dame in South Bend, Ind., is one of 70 Catholic and non-Catholic institutions nationally that bases its student financial aid on "demonstrated need," according to Tom Bear, Notre Dame's executive director for student financial strategy.

"We do a thorough assessment of what that need is," he said, "and then we meet 100% of that demonstrated need."

The university has an online tool that helps students and their families estimate their potential financial assistance, which Bear recommended should become standard for all universities.

Bear said the demonstrated need is met partly by self-help means, such as work-study programs and loans. He said the rest is met by Notre Dame's generous "gift assistance," which makes up the rest of the cost and never has to be repaid.

As of the 2012–2013 school year, Notre Dame students graduate with an average $29,000 of debt ($21,000 being federal loans), according to Bear. This debt amounts to approximately 12% of the total cost of Notre Dame undergraduate tuition, but he said it should be seen in the context of a reasonable investment, like a car purchase.

"We manage that loan amount for students, so that, over the last several years, the amount of loans our students have has actually been going down," he said.

Ave Maria: Tuition Cut

Ave Maria University in Naples, Fla., has opted to slash its tuition by 20% for 2014–2015 from $23,000 per year to just under $18,000. Jim Towey, president of Ave Maria, said the reduction was manageable because the university has kept a lean administration, has low maintenance costs (since the buildings are all new) and donors will provide $8 million in scholarships next year.

Towey said the average debt for an Ave Maria graduate is under $20,000. The new tuition reduction starting in 2014–2015 may help reduce that cost even further.

"Part of our mission is to keep quality Catholic education within reach of as many families as possible," he said. "Many of our families are home-school families or very large families. These families don't have a lot of money to begin with."

Carlson of the Howard Center said two systemic reforms need to occur to reverse the damage being done to young graduates: First, reform bankruptcy law to allow people to discharge student loans that they are unable to repay; and, second, remove the federal government from the business of providing student loans, which would disincentivize universities to look at the federal government as a guaranteed credit card and force them to exercise rigorous financial discipline.

He added, "My modest proposal is relieve the debt for couples responsibly giving birth to children."

Carlson has proposed that the federal government forgive at least $5,000 of the principal of student debt for each child raised by debt holders. For a married mother and father with a family of four, this would reduce their principal debt by $40,000. He also suggests that the same incentive be applied to married couples who adopt.

"I see it as a way for compensating the damage that's been done by the program," he said. "The government has created this monstrosity. One way to deal with it is to reverse the incentives from negative to somewhat positive for children and marriage. That's what I would do."

How Should Graduate School Change?

A Dean Discusses the Future of Doctoral-Education Reform

By Leonard Cassuto
The Chronicle of Higher Education, January 13, 2014

I talk a lot in this column about how graduate programs might be run differently. The graduate enterprise faces a lot of problems, so there's plenty to talk about. But I don't run a graduate program, and we don't hear enough from the people who do.

There's a reason for that. Administrators can't dissociate themselves from their institutions when they speak. As any administrator will tell you, even the most casual remark can become the object of Kremlinological scrutiny and speculation.

With that concern in mind, I recently conducted an email interview with a dean who works with graduate education in the arts and sciences at a well-endowed private institution—let's call it Very Good University. He's a full professor who came up through the faculty ranks and was named a dean less than a decade ago. Because I've shielded his identity here, he was able to offer some bracing observations and sound prescriptions. Here is our exchange.

What sorts of changes would you like to see in American graduate study?

The biggest one is that our doctoral curricula need to be changed to acknowledge what has been true for a long time, which is that most of our Ph.D. students do not end up in tenure-track (or even full-time faculty) positions—and that many of those who do will be at institutions that are very, very different from the places where these Ph.D.'s are trained.

The changes will differ from program to program but might include different kinds of coursework, exams, and even dissertation structures. Right now we train students for the professoriate, and if something else works out, that's fine. We can serve our students and our society better by realizing their diverse futures and changing the training we offer accordingly.

The other necessary change: We need to think seriously about the cost of graduate education. There is a perception that graduate students are simply a cheap labor force for the university, and that universities are interested in graduate students only because they perform work as teachers and laboratory assistants cheaper than anyone else.

At elite universities—or at least at elite private ones—that is simply not true, and I am glad that it is not. It is absolutely true that graduate students perform labor necessary for the university in a number of ways, but it is not cheap labor, nor should it be.

The cost of graduate education has repercussions for the humanities and social sciences, which is one reason you are seeing smaller admissions numbers and some program closings. It also has repercussions for the laboratory sciences, where I am seeing too many faculty members shift from taking on graduate students to hiring postdocs. Unfortunately, they regard postdocs as a less expensive and more stable alternative to graduate students, and postdocs come without the same burdens of education or job placement that otherwise fall on the faculty member who hires doctoral students.

I want to underline that I don't think that graduate programs should be cheaper, but we can't have an honest conversation about their future unless we acknowledge their cost.

What might those changes look like at your medium-size private university?

I am not sure. If I were, I'd be writing a white paper for the dean of our graduate school rather than talking with you. They would probably include coursework designed to prepare doctoral students for nonacademic careers, internship options, and even multiple dissertation options.

I have a sense of what this could look like in my own discipline, but this needs to be a collective conversation. Anyone can chart out a "vision" and write it up for *The Chronicle*. It's another thing altogether to make it work, starting from the ground up, at one's own university with the enthusiastic support of everyone involved. For that to happen, there needs to be sustained, open dialogue about the real challenges. And most administrators and faculty are unwilling to engage in that work in a serious way until they see examples of similar changes in the very top programs in their fields.

Why does this kind of change have to start from the top?

Both faculty and administrators are extremely sensitive to the hierarchies of prestige that drive the academy. In most fields, the majority of faculty members who populate research universities have graduated from a handful of top programs—and they spend the rest of their careers trying to replicate those programs, get back to them, or both. They are worried about doing anything that diverges from what those top programs do, and will argue strongly that divergences place them at a competitive disadvantage in both recruiting and placing graduate students.

Administrators are just as much to blame as faculty for that state of collective anxiety. No matter what deans, provosts, and presidents say, we all rely too heavily on rankings and other comparative metrics that play directly into these conservative dynamics.

Is this a version of the "mini-me syndrome," in which advisers try to mold their graduate students in their own image, writ large?

That is certainly part of it. The desire to see your own scholarly passions continue through students you have trained is truly powerful, and administrators underestimate that desire at their peril. Of course we all want our faculty members to be passionate about their research, and graduate training is one way that faculty research makes an impact on the profession. But there are moments when the desire for scholarly replication can be troubling. The training of graduate students should fill a greater need than our personal desire for a legacy.

Graduate school is where we all become socialized into the academic profession. It sets the template for our expectations of what it means to be an academic. No matter how many years go by, most of us hold certain ideals in our mind and think graduate training should be based on those experiences.

And we build and run our programs accordingly?

Right. Faculty members often try to either recreate a graduate program that they attended or carve out their own institutional training ground by creating a new center. Even as the number of academic positions has receded over the past five years, the administration here has been bombarded with requests for new graduate programs.

Administrators, again, are not blameless in that dynamic. We overvalue new programs, centers, and so on, as a way of being able to tell a progressive story of institutional growth. Every research university trumpets "the new" loudly. No press release ever comes out and says, "We're doing things the same way as last year, because it is all working so well!"

The focus on vaguely defined "excellence" contributes to that behavior, because there is nothing to define "excellence" beyond the hierarchies that are already in place.

Administrators are worried about looking too different from their peers or from the institutions with which they would like to compare themselves. As much as they might talk about innovation or disruption, they are worried that if they look too different, they won't be playing the right game. Of course, that also means that they will never actually leapfrog into the top, because we are all trying to do the same thing.

That makes you more conservative in your own job?

Let's just say I wish I were more creative and ambitious. On the other hand, I share my faculty's skepticism of wide-eyed visionaries who don't appreciate the real complexities and challenges that we are facing.

You say that professors are too defensive and afraid of innovation. What do you mean? Can you give an example or two?

Faculty members are too quick to experience any proposed change as a loss. That is especially true in humanities fields, where the "crisis of the humanities" has made faculty nervous and defensive. This temperament has made it difficult to take seriously proposals that could actually help sustain the programs they care about.

For instance, as cohorts get smaller in certain doctoral programs, it makes sense to think about combining them—to create both a broader intellectual community and better administrative support. But most faculty fear that kind of move—even if it could result in a newly defined and exciting intellectual community. They think it would erode the particular discipline to which they have devoted themselves.

Two other examples: First, nearly every private-university administrator I talk with says that the current state of language instruction is not sustainable. Most campuses think that they cannot continue to teach the languages they are teaching at their current levels while meeting expanding student demands in new fields (including languages that are more recently arrived in the curriculum). This is going to require some innovative and integrative solutions if we are going to provide graduate training in many fields, but the same administrators will tell you that it is hard to work with professors to resolve those problems, because they are so afraid of losing what they have now.

Second, we all know that we should change our graduate curricula across the board—from the laboratory sciences to the humanities—to reflect the fact that a diminishing number of our Ph.D.'s will work in tenure-track jobs. But how many departments have changed their requirements, introduced new classes, or rethought the structure of their dissertations?

Everyone is afraid that they will lose something by doing so, either because it will mean less time for their students in the lab or library, or because it will make their students less competitive, or because it will be interpreted by prospective recruits as an admission of weakness.

The long and short of what you say is that the conservatism of tenured faculty—which they learn from their tenured advisers before them—is hurting graduate students badly. It locks them into curricula and expectations that ill suit their prospects in today's world. How can we break out of this cycle?

It's not a cycle that we can break, but a structure that has limitations. We certainly can serve both our graduate students and our society better. Experimentation and innovation could have a significant effect, and small groups of tenured faculty members and administrators have the power to make these changes. The biggest barrier is our own collective fears and self-imposed conservatism.

But I see reasons for optimism. For example, the discussion of tracking Ph.D. placement in *The Chronicle* (and elsewhere) will have very healthy effects, and I think it is possible that we can, and should, create a future with a greater diversity of graduate programs, even if there are slightly fewer of them.

I also believe that the majority of faculty members who received their Ph.D.'s in the past 10 years are likely to take for granted that these changes are inevitable, and even desirable. For all of the challenges we've discussed, graduate education will be a necessary and vital component of the research university for at least, say, the next half-century. And I'm stopping there only because to go farther out than that is science fiction.

As we focus on the challenges, let's not forget that our current model of graduate training has been the source of tremendous creativity and innovation. For all the pessimism running through our conversation, the research university is still the most interesting, productive institution in American contemporary life—and what we have built in the American academy is truly remarkable. There's no other place I'd rather be.

Occupying the Future by Rejecting the Burden of Student Loan Debt

By Philip Mattera
Social Policy, Winter 2011

The most encouraging thing about the Occupy movement is the extensive involvement of young people. Previously, the news was full of reports on the hopelessness felt by recent college graduates (not to mention those without degrees) who see no place for themselves in the new labor market.

With the arrival of Occupy, the economic situation of twenty-somethings hasn't improved, but that feeling of despair has for many been replaced by a determination to seize control of the future. In doing so, a key issue is the burden of student loan debt. For young Occupiers, who haven't had a chance to take out a home mortgage on which to be foreclosed, their main relationship to Wall Street is through what they owe banks on education loans.

Occupiers are starting to move from simply bemoaning their student loans to rejecting the idea that those obligations have to be met. We're seeing the emergence of a movement for student loan debt abolition.

To put this movement in context, it's helpful to recall the history of higher education in the United States. Once the province of the upper class, colleges were transformed in the postwar era into a system for preparing a workforce that was becoming increasingly white-collar. The GI Bill and later the candidly named National Defense Student Loans were not social programs as much as they were indirect training subsidies for the private sector. The Pell Grants created in the 1970s brought young people from the poorest families into the training system.

It was this sense that they were being processed for an industrial machine that motivated many of the student protesters of the 1960s. As with many of today's Occupiers, they ended up questioning the entire way of life that had been programmed for them. After those challenges ebbed, the powers that be pulled a cruel trick. Now that college education had become all but essential for survival in society, students were forced to shoulder much more of its cost. The Reagan Administration slashed federal grant programs, compelling students to make up the difference through borrowing. As early as 1986, a congressional report was warning that student loans were "overburdening a generation."

Over the past 25 years, that burden has become increasingly onerous. Both Republican and Democratic administrations exacerbated the problem by giving the private sector greater control over the system. That was intensified by the privatization of the Student Loan Marketing Association (Sallie Mae) and by the refusal of Congress for years to heed calls to get private banks out of the student loan business.

It was not until 2010 that Congress, at the urging of the Obama Administration, eliminated the parasites and diverted billions in bank subsidies to an expansion of Pell Grants. This will reduce future burdens, but a great deal of damage has already been done. During the past two decades, student debt has skyrocketed. Last year new loans surpassed $100 billion for the first time, and total loans outstanding will soon exceed $1 trillion. The typical recipient of a bachelor's degree now owes $22,000 upon graduation.

Given this history and their gloomy job prospects, young people are justified in viewing student debts as akin to the unsustainable mortgages foisted on low-income homebuyers by predatory lenders. In October President Obama announced adjustments to student loan obligations, but they will make only a small dent in the problem.

Even before the Occupy movement, there was talk of a student loan debt abolition movement. It was inspired by the writings of George Caffentzis, including a widely circulated article in the journal *Reclamations*, in which he says: "Student loans are time bombs, constructed to detonate when the debtor is away from campus and the collectivity college provides is left behind."

The Occupy movement is creating a new collectivity and a new way of thinking that addresses the call by Caffentzis for a "political house cleaning to dispel the smell of sanctity and rationality surrounding debt repayment regardless of the conditions in which it has been contracted and the ability of the debtor to do so." Occupiers are also more receptive to Caffentzis's argument that student loans should be seen not as consumer debt but in the context of education as an adjunct to the labor market.

A decade ago, many U.S. activists were building a Jubilee campaign for third world debt cancellation. We now need a similar effort here at home to liberate young people from the consequences of an educational financing system that has gone terribly wrong and thereby free them to reshape society as a whole.

The American Dream Is
Alive and Well—Overseas

By Lane Anderson
The Deseret News National Edition, January 31, 2014

It's a common scene from an American household: Kristy Williams is plying her young son, Thomas, with Oreos and marshmallows to finish his studies. The difference is that Thomas is working with a tutor learning Mandarin Chinese, and the Williamses are living in Hangzhou, China, two hours from Shanghai.

Kristy and Joel Williams moved their four children from Houston to China a month ago after Joel's employer, Bray, a valves manufacturer, announced that they were looking for someone to work in their Hangzhou offices. Joel texted Kristy from work and said, "Would you want to move to China?" Kristy chuckled at first, but after thinking about it for a bit she thought, "Yeah, why not?"

The Williamses are part of a growing trend of Americans who are finding that some of the most exciting opportunities lie overseas, not in the U.S. Up to 6 million American citizens are now living overseas, according to the Migration Policy Institute, and a Gallup poll shows that those numbers have leaped in recent years; between 2009 and 2011, the number of American ex-pats between the ages of 25 and 34 surged from barely 1 percent to more than 5 percent.

While the U.S. economy continues to lag, with a deficit of nearly 9 million jobs, economies like China, India and Dubai are flush with jobs and possibilities for advancement. New college grads and ambitious career people like the Williamses are increasingly looking abroad in search of the next opportunity and the "American Dream."

Go East Young Man—Way East

U.S. college grads are coming out of school with more debt than ever, and the debt keeps climbing. According to the Project on Student Debt, the average debt load for American grads leaped from $26,600 in 2011 to $29,400 in 2012.

Even as college grads are taking on more loans, they face unemployment and poverty-level wages of $16.60 an hour, reports the Economic Policy Institute. The combination of soaring student debt and a sagging economy puts U.S. graduates in a tight spot.

Yet there are plentiful jobs overseas for American grads, according to Bruce Jones, president and founder of International Tefl Academy, which helped place

1,500 people in English-teaching jobs overseas last year. In China alone, there are at least 100,000 jobs for native speakers to teach English, Jones says.

"Think about it," says Jones, "there are more people in China learning and speaking English than the entire population of the U.S." Jones sees a lot of recent college graduates and soon-to-be college graduates coming through his doors looking for their next gig and trying to figure out how to make their student loan payments, but he's also started seeing retirees.

In Europe, English teachers will usually break even after living expenses, he says. But there is opportunity to make cold hard cash: the people who are banking money go to South Korea and China, where they can stash $1,500-$2,000 a month after living expenses, and housing and airfare are often paid for. The same goes for Dubai and Kuwait. Jones now has 25 offices around the world and has helped more than 10,000 native English speakers find work, and the demand shows no sign of slowing.

Making the Leap

Teaching English is a popular way to get work in a foreign country, but it's not exactly a career. Most people Jones works with teach for three years at most. Teachers can transition to other work in their adopted homes, he says. Americans go to Asia and China to make business connections and network while they are there, and some eventually end up at Samsung or LG.

Casey Clemence is vice president of human resources for India and the Middle East of a large American engineering company, and he says he is contacted by seven to 10 Americans every day that are looking to get into a career overseas—about half of whom are new college grads. "I think that a lot of Americans are looking for a viable job market," says Clemence, who moved to Saudi Arabia when he was laid off by Bank of America in 2009 and found the U.S. job market had dried up.

"There is high unemployment in the U.S., and people figure if they can find a gig overseas, pay the bills and pay down their student loans and get some adventure under their belt—bring it on," says Clemence.

A common route he recommends for job seekers is large accounting firms that have offices from Australia to Switzerland and need everything from auditors to administrators. The foreign service is another route that many people don't think about, but it's a great possibility for people who are "culturally alive, good with languages and smart," says Clemence.

Americans who already have work in the U.S. find that there are opportunities abroad, or that their employers expect them to do an international tour. When Goldman Sachs announced that it would finally be adding 1,000 jobs after the recession, for example, all of those jobs were available only in Singapore.

The Williamses' move to China was voluntary, but it seemed like a smart move to get ahead. "China and Asia are important to the company's long-term growth, and companies like executives with international experience," says Kristy Williams. The couple spoke to families who had done tours in China and Europe before making the move. "Everyone was of the opinion that this will only help you," she says.

Matt Mullens, a recruiting manager who moved to Kuwait in 1997 shortly after he graduated from college, warns that it's not easy to break into the global job market: "You're competing against educated English-speakers from India and Pakistan who are willing to work for less than Americans are," he says. Ex-pats should also be careful about where they take work—foreign workers often don't have the same rights as native residents, and a company can quickly terminate them without severance and cancel their sponsorship.

The Pay-Off Beyond Yen and Euros

Some companies offer generous ex-pat packages to entice workers, including perks like nannies, drivers and tuition for private international schools. Mullen followed his then-girlfriend to Kuwait where she took a school teaching job there in the late 1990s. Her travel and housing were paid for, and the couple realized that they could get ahead much faster than on her teaching salary in the states.

"One of the things people in the international community look at is what's my take-home pay versus if I stayed in the states," says Mullen. After tax breaks, housing and transportation stipends, and cost-of-living adjustments, that number can be significant. "If you make $35,000 as a schoolteacher in the states you can maybe save $5,000 if you scrimp," says Mullen. "Teaching overseas, you might save $20,000." The couple, now married with three children and in their late thirties, has used that savings to travel from Bahrain to the Philippines to Mount Kilimanjaro and to buy real estate investments in Arizona.

Another perk of the international lifestyle, says Clemence, is the people: "Tonight, we had Jordanians and Russians at our dinner table—and one of them was in the Soviet Union when it fell apart—those are conversations that are tough to find over a burger in Whittier, Calif.," he says.

The Williamses see their stint as an opportunity for their kids as much as for themselves and plan to enter their children in Mandarin-speaking schools so that they will be close to fluent by the time they leave. "Being so far away from everything forces you to rely on each other and strengthen relationships," Kristy Williams says.

She also acknowledges that there are hardships that come with living far away from home. Williams doesn't mind a regular diet of rice and vegetables that she finds at the local market, and hot dumplings that she buys from street vendors. Her kids, on the other hand, often long for pizza and chicken nuggets.

She has to travel miles away to a specialty store to get cheese and American-style milk. Washing machines are tiny, and dryers almost non-existent, so doing laundry for a family of six is a major time drain. Joel's company provides a nanny for a few hours every day, "but it ends up compensating for the difficulties more than being a luxury," she says.

Mullens also acknowledges that there is a downside to living far from home. He has missed funerals for two of his grandparents, and while he loves international travel, he's not crazy about the 26 hours of travel to see family back home in Arizona. So far, the trade-offs have been worth it, he says.

Clemence sees far-reaching benefits for his kids in a globalized world. His daughter goes to an international school with Tunisians, Koreans and Jordanians. Last month, she went to Istanbul to compete in the Model United Nations and was voted best delegate from 500 kids from 40 other countries. "How do I measure the benefit to that daughter in her future life?" he says. "No amount of money buys that."

4

E-Learning: Are We Learning Better?

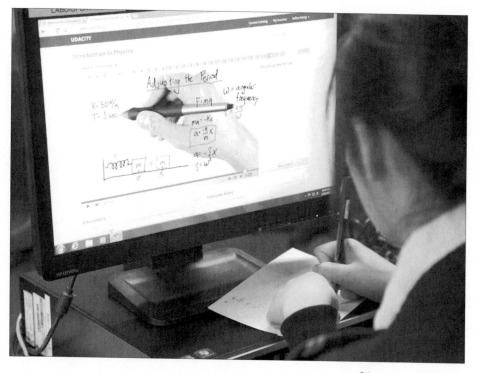

© Laura A. Oda/MCT Landov

Oakland Military Institute junior Selina Wang goes through an online lesson in physics on the Udacity website as she prepares for her final exam in the computer lab at her school in Oakland, California.

Classroom Technology in the Twenty-First Century

The introduction of new, innovative technologies has ushered in some of the most significant social changes in history. The steam engine, radio, airplane, television, and nuclear reactor all serve as evidence of this. In most cases, the innovators who made these advances possible benefited tremendously from the information and education they received in school. Ironically, the very place that fostered such innovative thinking—the classroom—has undergone relatively few corresponding changes. For centuries, the classroom has been structured in the same manner: student desks face the teacher, who in turn uses a chalkboard, dry-erase board, or overhead projector to outline the day's lessons.

In recent years, however, another set of major advances has made innovation in this long-standing approach to education possible. The Internet, social media, and their associated hardware have fostered "e-learning," or electronic learning. Using e-learning concepts, the traditional classroom, along with a number of traditional teaching approaches, have been enhanced, or in some cases replaced altogether. E-learning relies on the use of the Internet to facilitate the exchange of information outside the classroom. Students and teachers share lesson plans, background reading materials, and even lectures without setting foot in the same classroom. They can also conduct research, exchange ideas, discuss lessons, and ask questions of one another using this vehicle.

The goal of e-learning is to enhance the learning process in such a way that students in virtually any setting—urban, suburban, or rural—can maximize their potential. The various manifestations of e-learning are also being examined as vehicles for improving regional literacy rates (although the very concept of literacy in the information age is, according to some, in need of redefinition). The introduction of the concept of e-learning, however, has initiated a debate over whether it is actually enhancing or having an adverse impact on the learning process. In order to better understand this debate, it is important to analyze the various components of e-learning.

Central to e-learning is the Internet. Since its inception in the late twentieth century, the Internet has grown exponentially, both in substance and practicality, for users around the globe. A multitude of Web search engines enable users to gather information on virtually any conceivable topic. To be sure, within this myriad of relevant websites there are countless sites of questionable quality (including many that share illegal, fraudulent, or child-inappropriate material). Parents, educators, and children (among others) must therefore use vigilance when sifting through that which the Internet has to offer.

Despite the risks, the Internet undoubtedly makes easily available a wealth of information for those who seek it. It presents material from countless sources from around the world. The people and institutions who post this material share their knowledge, experiences, and points of view. From a scholastic perspective, this diversity is significant—students who come across this material in the course of their research gain access to thoughts and opinions that they might not otherwise glean by reading about an issue in their school or local library or learning about it through school curricula. Many experts refer to this supplemental learning as "connected learning."

The presence of connected learning via the Internet, according to some experts, underscores the rigidity and limitations of the traditional classroom setting. Advocates of connected learning argue that this concept lends a degree of volunteerism to learning—students step away from required educational processes and pursue this more comprehensive form of learning. The same experts, however, are not suggesting that the classroom should become extinct in light of the Internet's educational evolution. After all, as suggested earlier, a great deal of the information available on the Internet is biased, incorrect, inappropriate, or even illegal. Teachers and school curriculum designers are therefore needed to help guide students toward the best possible information, even if such material is decidedly different from that which is presented in course curricula.

There are many experts who argue that the ubiquity of the Internet and its use for educational purposes has thrust the World Wide Web into the classroom, whether or not educators are prepared for it. Educators, from K–12 teachers through university-level professors, are increasingly using the Internet to support their classroom activities, even if they retain the traditional lecture dynamic during the classroom period. This practice is referred to as "blended learning"—utilizing the Web, computer databases, and related hardware and software technologies to enhance the classroom experience as well as encourage further study after the bell rings. There are many degrees to which the traditional classroom dynamic is mixed with Internet-oriented resources, which lends an element of ambiguity and nebulousness to the overall concept of blended learning. Still, the increased occurrence of blended learning–related course changes underscores the value educators (some of whom, one study revealed, are not even aware they are engaging in the practice) place on such innovative technology in the modern classroom.

The above examples of connected and blended learning provide an illustration of the continuing evolution of education in the information age. Some proponents of e-learning embrace a more dramatic change in the classroom dynamic. One trend, for example, encourages a major shift away from the traditional model of in-class lectures supplemented by at-home exercises and homework. In "flipped" or "inverted" classrooms, students—via the Internet and other sources—watch or listen to lectures and research assigned concepts while at home, and then work on assignments in class, with teachers available to answer questions and discuss and share ideas with students about the assigned work. The guiding principle is that students will receive their first exposure to the material on their own. Upon returning to the classroom, the students, with the aid of their teachers and peers, process the information. Advocates of this model argue that flipped or inverted classrooms increase student engagement and, therefore, enhance the learning experience.

Some e-learning experts argue that the Internet was thrust into the classroom, and that educators have been forced to integrate it into their teaching environment with little guidance. The increased popularity of blended learning and connected learning concepts, however, demonstrate that there is increased attention being paid to how e-learning may best be applied in the classroom. Teaching institutions are increasingly adding courses on how to reconcile the relationships among knowledge, learning, teaching, and technological innovation. For some recipients of this training, the value of and methodologies for utilizing e-learning practices inspire new and more radical classroom designs.

One example is the "massive open online course" (MOOC). The MOOC completely eliminates the classroom, including the notion of teacher-student interaction. Instead, students are (often free of charge) given access to prerecorded lectures, libraries of relevant information, and other resources, as well as online assistance that is akin to a student advisor. The concept has gained increased popularity in recent years: approximately 4.5 million students enrolled in such programs by the end of 2013, with another 1.5 million expected to enroll by 2015. Harvard University, MIT, Stanford University, and Yale University (whose president resigned his post in 2014 to head a private MOOC) all offer such courses. Proponents of MOOCs point to their value for students who are interested in changing or enhancing their professional careers, giving these individuals a cost-effective alternative to enrolling in continuing education courses either online or at a traditional university setting. MOOCs will not, however, grant the student a degree and very rarely provide course credits. Critics also express concern about the undefined nature of some courses, as well as the quality of the material presented (as well as the teachers involved). Nevertheless, for individuals seeking to enhance their own realm of knowledge, scholars agree, MOOCs offer a reasonable resource, one that continues to evolve and gain popularity.

In addition to the utilization of online resources, e-learning employs another important element: hardware. An increasing number of educators, from the kindergarten through undergraduate and graduate levels, utilize different devices to complement their daily teaching exercises. Among these innovations are high-definition monitors and projectors, which can be used to present lecture materials as well as link to Internet resources such as videos and graphics. In fact, many available technologies can provide video links between the teacher's classroom and individuals and classrooms around the world, creating a "global classroom." Such innovations can, according to education scholars, transform the educational process by adding an experiential element to the traditional presentation of curriculum materials.

As the classroom layout continues to evolve, the role of the qualified educator remains vital. Educators must be knowledgeable and experienced not only in how to utilize such technology but how best to apply it. For example, an increasing number of school systems are implementing "iPad 1:1" programs, in which the school system requires the purchase of an Apple iPad for every student (how these devices are purchased depends on the financial conditions of the school district and the students). Students then download the necessary applications and software to collectively and independently pursue the curriculum materials. iPad 1:1, however, requires the educator leading the class to be fully versed not only in the technology, but also in how to use it effectively to encourage students to commit to and engage the learning process.

While there remains debate over the benefits of e-learning in modern American classrooms, there is little debate over the introduction of e-learning in areas previously underserved by quality educational programs. Understandably, for example, some of the world's lowest literacy rates are found in the developing world. In locales like rural sub-Saharan Africa, schools often provide students with outdated books and materials. Students in these regions frequently travel daily over great distances in order to go to and from school, carrying these heavy, damaged, and outdated books along with them. In an effort to change this dynamic, however, international development organizations have been introducing iPads and tablets in the classroom. Not only do such programs lessen the physical load these young students carry daily, studies show that the introduction of such technology has other benefits as well. First, students have up-to-date information from around the world at their fingertips when they use these devices at school. Additionally, students have this global library with them wherever they go, which expands the timeframe in which these young people are learning. Furthermore, because they carry such mobile technologies, young people living in rural, underdeveloped regions have access to online courses, including MOOCs and other innovative educational resources. Because of these benefits, international development organizations such as the United Nations Children's Fund (UNICEF) have endorsed tablet and iPad programs in impoverished regions.

E-learning technologies and their applications continue to evolve. As each innovation is introduced, however, entrepreneurs seize upon its success to produce even more advanced versions of them. Online classes, for example, have given rise to MOOCs. Software for devices such as the iPad is improving steadily as well, with enhanced graphics and memory storage capabilities. All of these developments are creating a more mobile and connected global community. With such success, particularly on the educational level, the use of this technology translates into major business. By the end of 2009, the e-learning industry was worth over $27 billion, according to a study by research firm Ambient Insight, and was expected to be double that in 2014.

Although the e-learning industry will continue to evolve and undoubtedly have an impact on the global society, there remains a debate over whether, over the long term, this impact will be positive or negative. Social scientists continue to study this impact as they also examine the very nature of educational advancement and literacy in the twenty-first century. Nevertheless, there is no denying that e-learning is changing the way Americans and other students are learning, both in and outside the classroom. The traditional classroom is, as a result of e-learning's evolution, undergoing a transformation of varying degrees, depending on the school system in which it is applied. Still, teachers and school administrators, as well as parents and other interested parties, who stay abreast of e-learning's applications will continue to play a role in how such innovation will be used to benefit the growth of their students.

Michael P. Auerbach

Bibliography

Bates, Tony, and Gary Poole. *Effective Teaching with Technology in Higher Education*. San Francisco: Jossey, 2003. Print.

Brame, Cynthia J. "Flipping the Classroom." *Center for Teaching*. Vanderbilt U, 2014. Web. 4 June 2014.

Chadwick, Kirsty. "E-Learning Trends for 2014." *BizCommunity.com*. BizCommunity.com, 21 Jan. 2014. Web. 4 June 2014.

Garrison, D. R., and Terry Anderson. *E-Learning in the 21st Century: A Framework for Research and Practice*. 2nd ed. New York: Routledge. Print.

Leu, Donald J., Jr. "Literacy and Technology: Deictic Consequences for Literacy Education in an Information Age." *Handbook of Reading Research*. Vol. 3. Ed. Michael L. Kamil et al. Mahwah: Erlbaum, 2000. Print.

Picciano, Anthony G., Charles D. Dziuban, and Charles R. Graham. *Blended Learning: Research Perspectives*. Vol. 2. New York: Routledge, 2014. Print.

Wasik, John F. "What Color Is Your Online Adult Course?" *New York Times*. New York Times, 17 Mar. 2014. Web. 4 June 2014.

Yowell, Connie. "Connected Learning: Reimagining the Experience of Education in the Information Age." *Huffington Post*. TheHuffingtonPost.com, 2 Mar. 2012. Web. 4 June 2014.

E-Learning Trends for 2014

By Kirsty Chadwick
Bizcommunity.com, January 21, 2014

E-learning has been around for quite some time now, and as its popularity continues to grow within the corporate and educational sectors, so does its capabilities. Computers are becoming increasingly essential as educational tools, while technologies are becoming more portable and cost-effective—mobile learning is a perfect example of this.

It has become imperative in recent years to look critically at the learning outcomes of training and to adapt those outcomes accordingly. Organizations no longer require an endless accumulation of general knowledge, but the focus is now rather on skills that help them to save money, decrease downtime and increase effectiveness.

According to research firm, Ambient Insight, the global market for self-paced e-learning products and services reached US$27.1 billion by 2009 and is likely to double by 2014. With that said, let's have a quick look at the e-learning trends for 2014.

1. From Textbook to Tablet

In March 2013, Sunward Park High School in Johannesburg, South Africa, successfully made the transition from physical textbook to tablet when the tablet project initiative was officially launched by the Basic Education Deputy Minister, in partnership with Modern Information Business (MIB).

Pupils at the school were overjoyed at no longer having to carry heavy suitcases around with them from classroom to classroom because they could now access their e-textbooks, a digital library and video tutorials via their tablets on the schools' open Wi-Fi Network. In 2014, 88,000 Huawei tablets will be distributed to 2200 public schools in Gauteng as part of a new e-learning initiative.

2. The Shift to Mobile

Mobile is thriving in Africa and local e-learning developers are increasingly focusing on apps as the most effective way to deliver learning content. According to UNICEF, South Africa houses the third-largest number of mobile subscribers on the continent, with around 20% of the population owning a smartphone. Smartphone growth in Africa has increased by 43% annually since 2000, and experts predict that 69% of mobiles in Africa will have internet access by 2014.

3. More Gaming

In recent years, gamification, the process of using game thinking and game dynamics in order to engage audiences and solve problems, has taken the world by storm. According to the analyst company, Gartner, more than 50% of businesses that manage innovation processes will gamify those processes by 2015 and more than 70% of the world's largest companies are expected to have at least one gamified app by the end of 2014.

4. MOOCs

Massive Open Online Courses (MOOCs) have become increasingly popular over the last two years, mainly due to their accessibility, as well as the fact that the courses are generally offered free of charge. While MOOCs currently don't have standardized quality assurance in place, this will likely change in the near future.

5. Social Media

Social media offers an array of opportunities to learn and interact. If used correctly, it can enhance the efficiency and standard of work that is produced by learners. The realization of the advantage of having these social networking tools at their fingertips is spreading amongst learners. Dr. Richard J. Light from the Harvard School of Education believes that students' success is very reliant on their ability to participate in study groups and that those who engage in these groups learn significantly more than students who don't.

6. Classes Online

The shift to online training, particularly within the corporate world, is happening rapidly, and 2014 is likely to see a large number of businesses moving over to online training. Since 2000, the global e-learning market has grown by 900%, and recent studies have projected that by 2019, 50% of all classes taught, will be delivered online.

7. Trading Desktop for Mobile

According to Comscore, a digital analytics company, 2014 will be the year in which the number of mobile users will exceed the number of desktop users. The technology for mobile phones and devices has become so advanced over the past couple of years that it only makes sense that desktops will eventually be used only by designers.

8. More Learning for Everyone

Recent statistics show that 47% of online learners are over the age of 26, compared to a significantly lower age group a few years ago. While older learners initially require more technical support than younger ones, they tend to perform on par or even better than their younger counterparts once they're up to speed.

9. HTML5

HTML5 supports scalable vector graphics, which means that e-learning content can be responsive to the learner. According to a recent 2014 prediction by Gartner, improved JavaScript performance will begin to push HTML5 and the browser as a mainstream enterprise application development environment.

10. Increase in Interactivity

Moving forward, courseware is likely to be more immersive and interactive as more companies begin to realize the importance thereof. The use of animations and games within learning environments keeps the tech-savvy generation engaged and entertained, leading to increased knowledge retention.

E-Learning: A Strong Alternative in Education?

By Maria Zain
OnIslam, March 17, 2014

When I first decided to home-educate a few years ago, one of the assurances I had was that the internet was there and readily available.

Not only was I able to source for lesson plans and craft ideas, print out worksheets and e-books for free, and compare and contrast my rants with the rants of the other bazillion home-educating mothers across the globe, I could safely say that whatever my children felt directed to learn, could and probably would be sourced from the internet.

I'm not saying that the net embodies the pre-dominant form of learning for home-educators but the resources that one can get from logging online is astonishing. Many years later, it doesn't play such a huge role as I thought it would, but certainly, online education can really be seen as an integral form of learning—and home-educators (even if they didn't subscribe to online programs for their children) would probably agree.

Generation Net

Societies across the globe are more dependent on the internet than ever before and this includes many young adults. Information passes instantaneously, correspondence is much easier, and in general, learning happens with a few clicks of the mouse or swipes at the touch screen. In fact, it can be said that this generation has more access to more information and resources than ever before—and because of that has real potential for greatness.

Unfortunately, on the flip-side, this same generation has real potential for abuse. It doesn't take a religious scholar or teacher to caution about the usage of the net as a means of education or entertainment. A rational mind would already process that the net itself is a tool that can be used for amazing plights to making poor choices.

So, why online learning? Simply because it plays into the profile of a progressive Muslim who uses the internet for the right reasons: to better one's self, to enable to help others, to build a platform for da'wah purposes, and to gain knowledge. Online education is a great choice.

Online learning has evolved so much that one can even complete a bachelor's degree with just a computer and high-speed internet connection. Taking advantage of online learning also encompasses taking advantage of a great blessing of this generation—the wide wings of education gliding into your own home.

The Muslim Rise to Online Learning

Everyone is probably familiar with Salman Khan and his infamous Khan Academy—an online school, which was actually born of Khan uploading math videos to help tutor his niece. Since then, the Academy has turned into one of the most prominent online learning programs on the net, covering more than just concepts taught in mathematics but also branching out to finance and economics, suited for adults as well.

Other Muslims have risen to the occasion as well. Dr. Bilal Philips runs Islamic Online University, offering the first of its kind bachelor of arts in Islamic studies and now is branching out for an online Islamic homeschooling program.

Nouman Ali Khan and his Bayyinah Institute for example, are also moving past podcasts and have established Bayyinah TV, with various courses that revolve around Qur'anic knowledge, including a running tafseer (interpretation) and themes in the Qur'an. In fact, Bayyinah TV was built on the premise of helping teach non-native Arabic speakers, the Arabic language.

All these are fantastic resources for Muslims.

However, education goes beyond knowledge of the deen. There are plenty of sites and programs with "secular" knowledge and information that also have been formulated in curriculum and programs.

Guidelines When Enrolling into Online Programs

Whether it is an adult or child entering into an online education, salient guidelines for effective use may surface as follows:

- Ensure the content of the program and the providers and research the general reputation of the same. Look up testimonials and reviews and even sit through some content with the children. If it involves a fee, is it worth the subscription?

- Ensure privacy settings at all times. Some online programs include a connectivity function where students across the world can connect real-time with lecturers/teachers and/or peers. How comfortable are you with this? Does this involve a camera function (because this can violate the comfort zone of some families)?

- There are online services (for example, tutoring Qur'an, hifdh [memorization], tafseer) that involve Skype—how much privacy are you comfortable with, with real time one-on-one learning, with probably the use of the camera function?

- What hardware, software and/or connection are needed to effectively use this program and what would they provide (books, print-outs)?

- What are the credentials that are procured at the end of this program? Can they be translated into a formal qualification that can be used in the job market, or is this "certification" going to only be used for personal growth and development, i.e., I have learned something new and that is all I really need?

There is obviously no right or wrong to these questions as every individual has different goals and objectives for learning.

Alternative or New?

Breaking education out of the "traditional" mold found mostly in brick and mortar schools reflects progress at many levels. Looking past these "traditional institutions," education and learning encompassed a lot more than subjects simply broken down into boxes, labels, textbooks, exercises and exams.

Education as a whole is more than really just going through an x amount of years in school, doing homework, taking exams, passing exams and moving up a grade. If one could do all of the same through an online school and cut down on the travelling and unnecessary socializing, there would be a lot more time to work on other endeavors and interests, outside the "school-box."

Online education on its own has great potential in reshaping the minds of teachers, students, their methodologies and skills, and even the job market—one that now requires a lot more than mere job loyalty and seniority to survive in the job arena.

I believe that online education is currently a great alternative to traditional schools and it has the potential to become the new way to procure an education and this may happen in the next few years. Perhaps even more collaboration with schools could take place.

Muslims and Online Education

Now nearly a fifth of the world, and a growing population in the West, Muslims should take full advantage of online resources for education. With the globe shrinking in size in terms of connectivity, taking advantage of such a great resource can be a great foundation and building block for Islamic education at large, da'wah work, as well as procuring other forms of knowledge through reputable sources.

With other problems that Muslims face as far as social problems are concerned, online learning can even help with curbing unnecessary mingling between genders (that could lead to other problems), gossiping, backbiting (and other activities) that happen intermittently at learning institutions.

But at the same time, it's granted that without proper monitoring, these things can also happen over the internet and the positive (and halal) side of social/physical interaction could also diminish, hence the reason to keep a balanced view as to how the internet should be used.

So, the proper use of the net with adequate accountability is also a driving force in making online education a success for the ummah. As Muslims, we are required to spend our time and the wonderful resources in this temporary world for the ultimate success in the Afterlife. And with the rise of online service education providers, the Muslim ummah have a horizon of opportunities to peruse such an option for personal development, as does the growing populace of Muslims as a whole.

Today's Learning Spaces

By Mike Kennedy
American School & University, March 2013

Advances in classroom tools come quickly, so schools and universities must make sure their facilities are flexible and welcoming to change.

It's a given in schools and universities that technology is a critical element in providing students with a high-quality education relevant to the 21st-century world. Designers and facility managers know that modern classrooms must be able to accommodate technological tools that enhance student learning. That's easy to state as a concept; it may be difficult to carry out in practice when the pace of technological advances outstrips the ability of administrators to adapt their facilities to keep up with the changes.

Consider: Less than three years ago, the general public had yet to lay eyes on the next big thing Apple was preparing to release. By February of this year, 4.5 million iPads have been sold to U.S.-based education institutions, according to Apple. (Worldwide, the figure is 8 million.) Combine Apple's tablet computers with other versions produced by competing companies, and the devices are transforming learning for millions of students.

Facility planners can't necessarily anticipate what technological changes are on the horizon that will send education in a new direction, but they should acknowledge technology's growing influence in making education more student-centered and individualized and they should create learning environments flexible enough to embrace new technological trends.

"The technology infrastructure of the 19th and 20th centuries is no longer keeping pace with the needs of the 21st-century learner," says the New Jersey Department of Education's Facility Guide for Technology. "New, flexible environments that encourage communication, collaboration, production and innovation are required to support student learning of core content knowledge."

Technology Trends

Educators have been saying for decades that technology had the potential to transform education—and it has happened time and again. Desktop computers in classrooms brought with them a new way for students to gain access to lessons and other education content. Classroom connections to the Internet removed limitations of distance and resources and enabled students to have access to virtually unlimited amounts of information. Laptop computers and wireless technologies made that information available beyond classrooms and school walls.

Not too long ago, seeing a landline telephone in a classroom was less likely than a UFO sighting. Now, nearly every teacher and teenage student has his or her own cell phone in the classroom, and tablet computers, smart phones and other mobile devices have become integral parts of the lives—and learning habits—of many students.

A survey for the Pew Research Center's Internet & American Life Project of 2,462 Advanced Placement and National Writing Project teachers found that 73 percent of the teachers say they or their students use cell phones in class as a learning device or to complete assignments. Forty-two percent of the teachers said students used cell phones to look up information in class; 38 percent said students used them to take photographs or record video for an assignment; and 18 percent said students used cell phones to upload school-related content to the Internet.

Forty-three percent of teachers say they or their students used tablet computers in class, and 45 percent used e-readers in class.

Flexibility for the Future

Those percentages may not be representative of classrooms and teachers in general, but the results show that technologies that barely made a blip on the public consciousness a few years ago can quickly become major factors in student learning. Classrooms should be able to welcome and incorporate these new trends without major disruption.

"Since no one can predict how educational technologies and teaching modalities will evolve, learning spaces must adapt to whatever changes the future may hold," states a white paper, 21st-Century Learning Environments, produced by the Partnership for 21st-Century Skills.

Classrooms with movable furniture and walls that can be reconfigured for different subjects or class sizes will help students provide the flexibility to adapt to future trends, the white paper says.

New Jersey's facility guide for technology identifies some of the tools that may be included to create a successful learning environment:

- Teacher workstations with the capacity to display information to an entire classroom.
- Individual networked classroom computing devices.
- Individual, portable computing devices for every child.
- Mobile laptop computer labs on recharging carts with wireless network connectivity.
- Instructional technology and vocational laboratories of 12 to 30 computer workstations.
- Information and technology resource centers with print and digital content and access to online subscription services.
- Distance/virtual e-learning resources for access to global curriculum.

The guide also recommends that instructional areas should have telephones with access to voicemail for each teacher; on-demand access to computing devices; high-speed network access to school, district and global resources; interactive whiteboards; access to digital cameras and discipline-specific peripheral devices such as digital microscopes; and networked black-and-white and color printers with scanning and faxing capacities.

As with most school-design processes, a plan that seeks to involve and get buy-in from a wide range of stakeholders is more likely to meet with success.

Achieving Success

"The design of technology-rich classrooms and schools has to be a collaborative process and the voice of a broad spectrum of stakeholders must be heard in all of the planning and design stages," the New Jersey guide says. "Teachers, students, technology staff, administrators, support personnel, board of education members and community members will provide valuable input when engaged properly."

Adapting classrooms and other learning spaces to incorporate new technology is unlikely to succeed unless schools make sure that the teachers and students using those tools have been shown how to use it effectively, according to the 21st-Century Learning Environments paper.

"Putting technology in place is just the starting point; like any tool, its effectiveness depends on the user's skill in handling it, and on the conditions in which it is employed," the paper asserts. "Technology can make a difference only when students, teachers, and administrators are provided the necessary supports to effectively integrate it into their daily routines."

Connected Learning Now

Embracing Our Students' Desire for a Different Kind of Teaching

By John Palfrey
Independent School, Summer 2013

A ninth-grader came into my office with a proposal. I am the head of a boarding school, founded in 1778, that is blessed with extremely bright students from around the world. This student had tracked down Apple Computer's sales representative for our region of the United States, and on his own initiated an extended conversation with the rep about buying iPads for all students and teachers at our school.

This student came to my office prepared to convince me of his iPad idea. He had thought it all through. He offered a set of pros and cons associated with changing from print-based textbooks, used by most teachers, and the digital alternatives that are beginning to emerge on the market. He recited chapter and verse about the benefits of iPad-based curricular materials over traditional printed texts: interactivity, better tailoring to student ability levels, better fit with contemporary student learning styles, less pressure on the back and arms from the backpacks worn by nearly all kids on campus. He nailed his case; it was seriously impressive.

Given his logic and enthusiasm, this student could not understand why I wouldn't immediately demand that all faculty begin teaching all courses from iPads. He found it amazing that we couldn't switch over immediately to electronic textbooks. It seemed to me a great teaching moment. I shared with him my views about change management, about the realities of technology and teaching, and about respectful student activism and its place in society. But I also learned from him about how he liked to engage with information—and why he cared so much about learning using an iPad.

I've been thinking about this student since he left my office. Perhaps the learning moment was not so much for this bright ninth-grader as it was for me, and for the school. Certainly his passion for experiencing a different kind of teaching was a good reminder that the demand side of the learning equation (the students)—not just the supply side (teachers and administrators)—matters most in the end. Teachers know best, in very many respects, and our authority and knowledge are plainly important. But we don't know everything, and student interest and passion can be the lifeblood of any great school.

Our institutions of learning, including schools and libraries in particular, risk falling out of step with the generation of people who are coming of age today. In the late 1990s, the same thing happened to the recording industry. A student at Northeastern University, Shawn Fanning, created a disruptive force—Napster—and in a matter of months had tipped the scales against an old distribution model for recorded entertainment in favor of a new, direct, digital model. The music industry (in)famously took years to embrace this change, initially fighting Fanning and all those who saw the world the way he did.

The analogy between recorded music and learning in a digital age is imprecise. But it is not irrelevant. Schools need to listen carefully to students and better understand the ways in which they are learning—and the ways in which they are failing to learn adequately.

We ignore our students and their preferred ways of learning at our peril. But we would be making an equally grave mistake by simply turning our great institutions into a field of computer-based correspondence schools, competing with each other to see who can provide the splashiest and most efficient distance learning.

The theory of "connected learning" offers a positive frame for thinking about how to take advantage of the best parts of the digital era while avoiding its pitfalls. Connected learning doesn't start with technology and ask how to apply it to education. Instead, it calls for educators to pull together all the various experiences, interests, communities, and contexts in which learners participate—in and out of school, online and offline—as potential learning opportunities. Connected learning is a way to think about how technology and other affordances of our age can improve student learning and our approaches to teaching.

Independent schools—both day and boarding—are environments in which connected learners can thrive. By design, students are connected to peers and adults not just in the classroom, but also in their clubs, artistic and musical endeavors, and sports teams. Learning goes on many more hours per day, in integrated fashion, than it does in most public schools. Some of our campuses have museums and laboratories; others have museums and laboratories a subway or bus ride away. Adults in independent schools have a bigger canvas to work with in order to connect these experiences for students. If the teachers I work with are any indication, independent schools are packed with devoted educators with active, curious minds and a hunger to teach as effectively as they can.

Of the many venues in which connected learning can take place in an independent school, three stand out as opportunities: at the margins of the curriculum, at the core of the curriculum, and as a form of public outreach.

At the Margins of the Curriculum

At the margins of the curriculum, connected learning means making available positive experiences for students that they would ordinarily not have in their core studies.

Imagine a group of students interested in learning about fashion design and design thinking who don't happen to attend an art school. Connected learning means finding ways to connect these students to one another, to experiences that would enable them to act on their passion for design thinking, and to adults involved in the fashion world. Perhaps it even means finding ways for them to lend their growing expertise to a broader learning community, online or offline.

Or imagine that a small group of students has an interest in studying Japanese in a school that doesn't have a Japanese teacher. A traditional way to meet this need might be to structure an independent project for the few students who want to pursue this course of study, and hire a teacher to support the students. A connected learning approach would call for teaming up with other independent schools to offer an online, partially peer-driven course in Japanese. The Global Online Academy exemplifies this latter approach, in which schools have formed a consortium to offer a series of networked courses that are otherwise not offered at those individual schools.

At the Core of the Curriculum

At the core of the curriculum, connected learning involves improvements to traditional, existing approaches to teaching.

In a math class, a teacher might use contests, puzzles, or games (online or offline) to excite students whose love of math has yet to show itself. In a chemistry class, a teacher might use an interactive tablet application to make the course materials and problem sets more effective, adjusting the rate of new material introduced and the mode of teaching it as data flow in about each student's performance.

A Russian teacher might find ways to give faster and better feedback to students, flipping the classroom in the process and using face-to-face time for higher ends. A course on computer science might include student-developed problems related to hacking systems in safe and lawful ways—and, thus, teach students how to make and remake code and develop a heightened sense of agency. A course in the humanities might benefit from relevant primary sources in the form of digitized texts or images offered by a library, archive, or museum located thousands of miles away.

For Public Outreach

As a form of public outreach, connected learning can enable an independent school to share its resources more widely with those who are not among its student body. Many independent schools see themselves as private schools with a public purpose. Schools struggling to reach their enrollment targets may deem this form of outreach to be strategically unwise or downright impossible. Yet it may be worth considering that an investment in outreach could result in higher visibility for a school, and potentially, more applicants over time.

Schools might take a functional approach: think not of "sharing" but of "building brand value" by offering materials to students who otherwise might never learn of their offerings. Independent schools might take a cue from what MIT did in launching OpenCourseware, a project that involves the sharing of teaching materials online, and build upon this tested model. A school might offer interactive experiences for younger students as part of its admissions process that would improve the school's reach and broaden the kinds of assessment that an admissions officer could draw upon.

A school might offer blended programs in which students come to the campus for a short period of time and rely upon distance-learning methods and social media to connect with peers and teachers for the rest of the year. A school with a library, archive, or museum might digitize some of its learning materials to share with the world via projects such as the Digital Public Library of America, which launched in April 2013.

Assess and Improve

Assessment of learning outcomes is an essential component of any educational change movement. A crucial aspect of connected learning is to assess carefully whether new approaches improve outcomes for students. Independent schools can and should be leaders in assessment of pedagogical innovation. This moment in history, with its rich and exciting set of opportunities for teaching and learning, is the right moment to rethink and recreate assessment methods and to put them to use in serving our students well.

This process of assessment and application of our ways of teaching is more fundamentally important than the specific modes of connected learning.

We have the raw materials—in our students and teachers—to make radical improvements in the learning outcomes for our students today, no matter how effective our schools have been in the past. Ambitious new pedagogical approaches do not need to, and should not, come with wholesale abandonment of what's worked before. Independent schools need to be actively engaged, with and for our students, in the experimentation and assessment business to avoid missing a major change in education.

Learning Together: The Evolution of a 1:1 iPad Program

By Carolyn Foote
Internet@Schools, January/February 2012

"Saying 'It's not about the technology' is like telling [Yo-Yo] Ma that 'It's not about the cello.'"
—Dean Shareski, educator

In November at Tech Forum Texas 2011 in Austin, keynote speaker Dean Shareski reminded us that "It's not about the technology. Except when it IS about the technology."

Westlake High School's iPad pilot initiative *is* perhaps one of those cases—intended to explore how a new portable technology, in the hands of teachers and students, can affect teaching and learning. Will the iPad's portability, ability to be personalized, and functionality impact its effectiveness in a school setting? In answering this question, so much depends on the purposes for which it is intended; the pedagogy accompanying its use; training afforded to teachers; the methods for implementing the new technology; and the tech support provided. By conducting 1:1 implementation in a pilot format, we are focused on these issues while we move through the process, keeping a close eye on what is working and what the impacts of the project are.

The iPad pilot began with just an idea. In the spring of 2011, Westlake principal Linda Rawlings and district technology coordinator Carl Hooker envisioned what could happen if Eanes ISD adopted iPads for teachers and some of the student body. Out of that and a fall 2010 iPad pilot conducted via our library was born the Westlake Initiative for Innovation (or WIFI), a pilot project for teachers interested in using iPads in their classrooms.

Getting Started

To participate in the pilot, teachers had to complete a Google form application, describing how they anticipated using iPads in the classroom. Since the majority of teachers submitting applications taught upperclassmen, a decision was made to issue iPads (using technology bonds funding) to all 11th and 12th graders, as well as a few other students. To prepare for the implementation, all teachers were issued iPads during the summer and attended in-service sessions to become more familiar with the tool's functionality. A trial rollout was done with a few students in the late

From *Internet@Schools* 19.1 (January/February 2012): 14–18. Copyright © 2012 by Information Today Inc. Reprinted with permission. All rights reserved.

summer to smooth out any kinks before actually "rolling out" the devices to the general student body as a whole. Also during the summer, a team of mentor teachers organized and planned fall in-service sessions around using various features of the iPad. And on Day 3 of school, in English classrooms across the building, iPads were issued to all of the students in the pilot. (Many of the details chronicling the common apps used, the method of distribution, and other technical details can be found on the blog for the pilot at http://eaneswifi.blogspot.com.)

To support the project from a hardware/software standpoint, an iPad help desk called the Juice Bar was set up in the library's pre-existing cafe space and staffed part time by student mentors and district technology staff. (Students selected the name for the Juice Bar through a poll conducted via QR codes read by their iPads. Juice Bar stands for getting creative juices flowing or getting a charge on the iPad.) We're redesigning the library cafe space to suit the creative purpose better, with more casual seating, bar seating at the window, and rolling mini-plexiglass idea boards. But it's far more than the library space that's being transformed, and one thing has quickly become obvious—the flexibility of the iPad as a tool has made it a go-to device for teachers and students.

The Impacts—Classroom

At the most basic level, schoolwide use of the iPad has improved productivity—primarily because teachers are finding ways to do things paperlessly more often—saving the district money and saving teachers time. Teachers scan an assignment or save packets and readings as PDFs, post them on their websites, and then students open the documents in a PDF reader on their iPads. Several apps, including Notarize and Neu.Annotate, allow students to write directly onto a PDF file, save it, and then email it back. Teachers are able to grade the document using the same apps and, again, email it to the student. Other methods of online transfer include the app WebDAV Navt, which the school can set up to access student and teacher network folders, shared network spaces, or tools such as eBackpack, Dropbox, etc.

More significantly from a learning standpoint, it has spurred creativity as well because of the camera, video camera, and the apps that can be used for creative storytelling, video production, etc. For example, our American Sign Language (ASL) teacher is finding the iPad an invaluable tool since so much of her curriculum is visual. Students can now film one another signing or practicing homework, film her signing a lesson to the class, and create projects using Keynote to embed video of signing. Teacher Barbara Vinson relates, "The movie apps, Keynote and iMovie, have made ASL projects come alive in the classroom. The use of the camera has allowed me to give immediate feedback to a student in the classroom. The students can videotape their presentations in the classroom and then critique themselves."

And because the camera is embedded in the device, projects that might have taken weeks in the past can be completed in a matter of days. Students in our French classes are using the iPad's camera to videotape skits, our Environmental Science class is using the camera and an app called LeafSnap to document plants, and our student announcements are being filmed once a week via the iPad. Music, band, and art students are finding it a creativity tool as well; in fact, the Westlake band performed a number strictly with iPad instruments at the first football game of the year. Many other apps afford creative opportunities, such as Zapd, which is a blogging app that the AP Human Geography students are using to write blogs on natural hazards. At our recent workshop, Dean Shareski shared with teachers how to use the Fotolr Studio HD app to edit photographs and add text to create one-word stories. iPads also afford a great deal of accessibility for students with special needs. There are a variety of apps that students can use, many free or inexpensive, such as Tap to Talk or Dragon Dictation. The iPad also allows students with special needs the equity of access that other, more difficult devices might not have.

Classroom use of the iPads can impact instructional pedagogy as well. Teachers have to learn to rethink their classrooms. Some are employing "flipped classrooms," and others are realizing, as Westlake collaborative education teacher Matt Zemo commented in a recent planning meeting, that it's important to examine how tight (or engaging) their lessons are from one moment to the next because if students have the opportunity to be distracted, they might be. There are also all sorts of intangibles that are of interest, as IESE Business School–Barcelona assistant professor Evgeny Kaganer has pointed out about the university's iPad pilot: "How does this [tablet device] affect team-based learning, social culture, collaboration. The critical thing is that it should go beyond delivering course materials".

Impacts in the Library

In the library specifically, there have been a variety of impacts as well. For one thing, since the library is a student hang-out we've been able to observe student use of the iPad in a more natural setting—seeing what uses they are naturally gravitating toward. As the project goes on, we've seen more and more purposeful use, naturally—as teachers use these tools more and more in their classrooms and as students discover new apps, download books, set up their study lists, create or edit movies, etc. With students working even more collaboratively, we've defined some areas of the library more for "play" and exploration and others more for traditional study, and we are trying to refurnish them accordingly. Part of observing the process is rethinking the form and function of a space when students are using more mobile devices. We can't think of the library as a storage space, but rather as an interactive creation center.

In terms of books, it's evident that some students are downloading their own books or accessing classics for free. So it's critical to add more ebook sources, roll out database apps, help students set up a "library" folder with all types of library sites on their own iPads, and constantly assess how the iPad pilot is affecting both our library space and our collection.

It'll be interesting to see how the ebook model plays out for our library. With the boom in YA literature, our print fiction collection still circulates heavily, but the non-fiction use varies more. We have some ebooks already embedded in our catalog that are used occasionally, but we are also getting ready to roll out OverDrive, which allows the library to build a downloadable ebook collection specifically for the school, with books that can be circulated via an iPad app (or downloaded to other devices) and then returned to the library electronically. (OverDrive, Inc. is one of the only players in this market, other than the free Project Gutenberg collection of out-of-copyright items, and the iPad app is a convenient way for us to provide books for students. However, OverDrive's pricing model is currently a little unwieldy for many schools, and its recent addition of Amazon titles for the Kindle platform has caused some privacy concerns. But like many ebook platforms, it is evolving frequently and may see changes that make it more affordable for schools.)

If ebooks can be embedded in the library catalog so students have one central location to access them, it makes for a more effective way to deliver them, whatever platform is used. For research purposes, databases such as EBSCO and Gale already have apps for the iPad, which makes these databases much more accessible to students. Students can also create a library folder on the iPad desktop, with the library's website and catalog as links, a move that allows them easy access to the library from wherever they are. Having 1:1 mobile devices in a school really challenges libraries to sort out their role in information literacy instruction. With these devices, libraries can embed themselves more into the curriculum and function as technical support as well.

Gathering More Info

In order to better understand how student use of the iPad is evolving, students, parents, and teachers on our Vision Committee are studying the pilot carefully. (Students from The University of Texas–Austin and Texas State University–San Marcos are conducting a study on the iPad pilot as well.) The first local survey results have just been collected and show very positive impacts thus far. Overall, 88% of the 854 students surveyed report that using the iPad has enhanced their learning experience, and 90% reported that the iPad had a somewhat positive or positive effect on their motivation to learn. Eighty-nine percent reported that the iPad had a positive or somewhat positive impact on their "desire to dig deeper into a subject."

Another thing our student survey is investigating is the distraction factor. Survey results are somewhat predictable—about half of students indicated they are somewhat distracted at school, but they are also indicating more distractions at home. But having a device with them in the classroom and at school every day is a teachable moment for our student body. Since we have a primarily college-bound population, many of our students will soon be sitting in college auditoriums filled with laptops and gadgets, and they will have to learn how to manage distractions. This pilot gives them an opportunity to learn to manage this kind of device as a learning tool in a somewhat smaller environment and with more guidance. As district technology coordinator Carl Hooker points out: "Students that have graduated from Westlake and move on to college say they felt prepared for the academia and the rigor by our system. However, they didn't feel prepared when it came to managing their digital lives. The technology becomes a distraction to them in college because we didn't really allow them to learn and focus within the same context. Giving students the ability to access information 24/7 is great, but giving them the ability to manage the distraction and utilize these tools for learning is even greater." As student Arnab Chatterjee pointed out at a recent meeting, "It's better students have this experience here rather than later affecting their opportunity to get or to keep a job."

While they do cost financially, iPads are proving to save the district money in a number of ways. Of course, paper costs have been substantially reduced. Hooker documents some of the savings in a recent blog post, noting savings on document cameras, video cameras, still cameras, and newer mobile laptop carts. Even apps themselves are much less expensive than software we might have purchased for the same function. They are also saving teacher time—valuable this year when our budgets have been reduced, and teachers are tasked with more responsibilities. Having a common device, and being able to access email, grades, student documents and create lessons all portably, has really improved the workflow for teachers across the campus.

One of the questions the district faced initially was regarding personalization. While the iPad can work somewhat effectively as part of a "cart" setup, the most powerful use of the tool is as a personal device. So as a district, we chose to allow both students and teachers to make the devices their own and rolled out a limited set of consistent agreed-upon apps across campus. (We are using Apple's Volume Purchase Program for additional apps that various departments or campuses need or want for their curriculum.) While this might pose a dilemma for some districts, it has created a tremendous sense of ownership as students and staff customize it for their own learning needs and classroom use.

Fostering a Climate of Exploration

Where is the pilot headed from here? We've been holding bimonthly after-school Appy hours in the Juice Bar to share apps with teachers (and students) and conducting biweekly "lunch 'n' learn" sessions for teachers to share. We've invited guest speaker Dean Shareski to conduct a workshop on digital storytelling that incorporated the iPad, and our Vision Committee is studying other schools that are also piloting iPads to see what we can learn from them. Decisions will be made this spring regarding extending the pilot to other grade levels, either at the high school or elsewhere in the district. Staff members at other district campuses are also starting to receive iPads, and some carts are being purchased at the elementary and middle school campuses. The district is assessing the need for parent workshops and more intensive teacher academies as well, as we begin to implement the devices on other campuses or grade levels.

One of the best things about the implementation of our particular pilot is how the teachers and students have been very much a part of the process—teachers planned and delivered the workshops before school; students, teachers, and parents who are members of the Vision Committee devised the survey and compiled it; students are serving alongside tech staff in the Juice Bar at the help desk; and there is a great deal of collaboration involved between staff and students in sharing apps. In general, the iPad lends itself to collaboration in ways that a laptop doesn't, which fosters a great deal of sharing. The pilot has also created an exploratory climate on campus—as teachers, students, and administrators learn at the same time how to use the iPad and what it will mean for their teaching and learning. Perhaps that is the best benefit of all. And we have to continue to ask, as Globally Connected Learning consultant Silvia Rosenthal Tolisano asks, what is the difference between uses of the iPad that just automate processes and those with more transformative uses, such as differentiating curriculum or allowing for new forms of creativity and communication (www.scoop.it/t/ipad-lessons/p/657884656/ipads-in-education-part-2). When we all, students and teachers alike, ask these questions and become learners, we become real partners in this thing called education.

iPads Promote and Enhance Education

By Lisa Kristoff
Boothbay Register, March 18, 2014

Last October, when the kindergarten through second grade teachers at Boothbay Region Elementary School returned from a one-on-one iPad program at the Leveraging Learning Institute in Auburn, they were jazzed.

"They came back with a tremendous amount of enthusiasm and excitement," Assistant Superintendent Shawn Carlson said at the February 26 CSD School Committee meeting. "I understood just how important it is for an initiative like technology in the classroom to be driven by teachers who are fired up about it."

Special Education teacher Charlinda Carlson led the presentation. The educators discussed the iPads apps they used and showed the board a half dozen iMovies that showed how the children used the iPads. The educators who created the videos included Donna Maxim, Lisa Andrews, Lisa Smith, Lucy Ann Spaulding, Lindsey Ingraham, Deb Mellor and Barb Crocker.

Charlinda Carlson said they returned aware of the potential that iPads offered to customize student learning, and that they were committed to applying what they learned in their daily teaching.

The iPads or iPad minis are being used to practice and reinforce math and language arts skills. Each student practices at his or her own pace and level.

For example, a math app will increase the level of difficulty based on the child's understanding.

While visiting a kindergarten classroom, AOS 98 Superintendent of Schools Eileen King observed some students were counting, some adding and subtracting, and some were doing double-digit subtracting.

"They were driving that on their own," King said. "The program recognized what level each child was at."

The kids, Charlinda Carlson said, and the other teachers, like getting the immediate feedback that the apps provide. Teachers also use the information to drive curricula and instruction.

"Providing feedback is so crucial to appropriate learning," King said. "If a student practices a concept incorrectly again and again and again, it becomes a learned concept. Having the ability to immediately put them on the right path enhances their learning."

Self-driven (thanks to the apps) students who are ready to move on to a new concept, do just that. Students who need more time to grasp a concept get it—and do not move on until they do.

"The iPads provide a way for us to customize each student's needs, and at varying degrees of difficulty," Mellor said.

Another iMovie, this one created by Charlinda Carlson, showed how an app called Book Creator changed a student's life. Due to fine motor skill issues, the young man disliked drawing and writing in class.

Thanks to the app, in just one day, he could successfully write a paragraph and import photos. His teachers were struck by his newfound enthusiasm about writing.

As Charlinda Carlson said at the end of the iMovie, "The iPad has leveled the playing field for him. He is a writer."

BRES Principal Mark Tess told the group, "This isn't an isolated incident. It happens with many students."

This child's success with Book Creator has also boosted his confidence when he does have to work on his handwriting skills in class.

"Now he knows that all I want is handwriting, that I want to see him forming letters, which is so important for brain development," Charlinda Carlson said. "Then, when he reflects on a book he's read, or is going to do a report, he gets to use the app.

"I could literally make an iMovie for every one of my kids using a different app that has changed their lives."

Each day the students have a little free time on the iPads. But the teachers always know what they will be doing with them—it's all on the signup sheet of approved areas.

Teaching Videos

Each iPad is equipped with a camera, microphone and speaker, enabling students to make videos of themselves as they learn.

A third iMovie of the presentation showed a first grade student working on math problems while recording his voice as they work through the problem. Using teaching videos, educators can listen to a student's video and know exactly where he is at with the concept being taught.

A link to the videos can be sent to parents, which keeps them involved and connected with their child's learning.

"Making teaching videos, they learn to become effective communicators," Mellor said.

When looking for apps, teachers look at how many levels are available within one app for reading and math; multiple grade levels allows teachers to individualize each student's learning. Many apps are free.

Charlinda Carlson said all of the young learners picked up on how to use the iPads very quickly.

Smith noted that there had been many occasions, as the technology had been rolled out, that teachers had been "more apprehensive because they were not as familiar" with the devices and because they thought they would need to teach the kids how to use it.

"Usually the kids will be there to help the teachers out, and it doesn't matter if they are 3 or 6 years old," Smith said. "Today, teachers from Bath were in my classroom and were absolutely amazed at how self-directed the kids were with the reading program being used, and how they got around places and could see the info (on how they were doing). The kids taught them (visiting teachers) how to use the iPads. I think the kids have even moved on from using iPads, to teaching others how to use them."

Board Chairman Larry Colcord asked about feedback from parents.

Mellor said it had all been positive and had come with some suggestions on how she could do it. Mellor has been uploading her students' books on YouTube. Parents get the link and then can send it to other family members across the country.

Charlinda Carlson said her kids' parents are proud of their kids and what they are accomplishing.

"We're constantly learning, too," Maxim said.

What Makes a MOOC?

By Tricia Bisoux
BizEd, July 2013

Three business professors discuss what they learned from teaching their first massive open online courses—and why they think MOOCs are here to stay.

While many educators have been wondering whether massive open online courses represent revolution or ruin for higher education, a relatively small number of professors have been testing the format's potential for teaching and learning. The first business professors began experimenting with MOOCs just over a year ago.

BizEd recently spoke to three professors who have delivered MOOCs through the Coursera platform. Hank Lucas, professor of information at the Smith School of Business at the University of Maryland in College Park, taught his first MOOC, "Surviving Disruptive Technologies," this past spring. Edward Hess is a professor of business administration and executive-in-residence at the Darden Graduate School of Business at the University of Virginia in Charlottesville. He has taught two rounds of a MOOC called "Grow to Greatness: Smart Growth for Private Businesses," based on his book by the same name. Finally, Christian Terwiesch is a professor of operations and information management at the Wharton School at the University of Pennsylvania in Philadelphia. He has taught two Coursera offerings of "An Introduction to Operations Management."

BizEd asked Hess, Lucas, and Terwiesch to share what they liked, what they learned, and why they think MOOCs have such tremendous potential for education.

What has been the biggest challenge of teaching a MOOC?

Lucas: I've taught a fully online course for our part-time MBA, for which I've created videos. But Coursera offers its own recommendations for producing online videos. It suggests making sure you're doing other things while you're talking, such as using a special table computer so you can annotate your slides—circle elements and underline words—as you record the lecture. I think that's very effective. As a result of this, I rerecorded all my videos for my regular online course.

Terwiesch: In the classroom, you can think on the fly and make up your lecture as you go along, but that doesn't work in a MOOC. This format forces you to think much more deeply about the topic, so you can teach it effectively in a series of brief ten-minute videos. That has been a very helpful exercise for me.

Have you had any bad experiences?

Hess: No, my MOOC has far exceeded my expectations. The quality and quantity of student engagement on the discussion forums, and the quality of their submitted work, has been in some cases as high as I've seen with my MBAs. In a single MOOC, I taught more people than Darden has graduated in its history.

Lucas: The most frustrating part was the tests, which were peer graded. Once students submitted their papers, three or four of them would grade each other's work according to a rubric I provided. Many emailed me about their concerns with the grading process. But I looked at some of the exams, and by and large the grading was good.

Terwiesch: I had a few students email me to ask if I could go over the material with them personally—I had 87,000 students, so email is not a good way of contact. But I actually had a very small fraction of students contact me directly. And many of them sent me wonderful messages to share how they used the tools they learned in class at work and to let me know how much more they understand.

How do you manage your MOOC?

Hess: I use the case method, and it works. Could I replicate the same classroom discussion that happens in my physical classroom in my MOOC? No. But can I deliver high engagement learning, promote critical thinking, and enable students to converse, debate, and learn from each other? Yes! In the discussion forums, students learned from each other and formed affinity groups that lasted beyond the course.

Lucas: Each week, my assistant Danielle and I use Google Hangouts to invite up to nine people to join us for an online conversation about that week's lecture. Each person appears in a window on the screen. Danielle monitors the discussion boards and sends me the email addresses of students who have been particularly active. I then invite those students to participate, and the entire class can watch the discussion. We post a Twitter hashtag, so the entire class can tweet comments and questions, which we monitor and respond to during the conversation. I record the hangout session, upload it to YouTube, and post an announcement about the video on Coursera's website.

I know that sounds complicated, but it has really worked. For example, one week we compared the models of FedEx and UPS to the problems the U.S. Postal Service is facing. I asked how postal services in other countries were handling these problems, and we got a range of views, including comments from students in Germany and Australia.

Terwiesch: I have to give credit to the Coursera platform. Many questions that students would typically ask the professor are answered by the community. I oversee the discussion forums each week, and if there's something the community can't resolve, I intervene. But the community is remarkably responsive.

Also, I ask students to create projects based on the material that they completed in their workplaces and share their experiences. We had close to 2,000 projects in the first round of the course, and I think we're going to get about 1,000 in the second. If we post those projects online, we will have created an amazing library of projects that document how people used operations management to change their businesses.

Many criticize MOOCs because of their high dropout rates. What do you say to that criticism?

Hess: I think too many people are focusing on the wrong numbers. The key questions are, how many students who attended the first class finish the course, and is that number meaningful to the school? [*Of more than 31,000 students in Hess's first class, 10,260 finished the course.*]

Lucas: If we were offering MOOCs for credit, it would be a different story. But right now, students who came to even one of my lectures took something away from it, and I know that many mastered the material. For instance, I had just over 16,000 students enroll in my course. At one point, Coursera's statistics showed that 8,000 were active. About 900 students took the midterm. How many years would it take for me to reach 900 students? Or talk to 8,000?

Terwiesch: Measuring graduation rates for students paying US$200,000 for their educations is important. But measuring completion rates when they can sign up for free? That's an irrelevant number. We shouldn't take a measure from the old industry and apply it to the new. [*Of 87,000 students who initially enrolled in Terwiesch's first class, 7,000 users were active in the discussion forums and took the final exam.*]

What impact will MOOCs have on higher education?

Hess: I expect we'll see more partnerships between four-year institutions and community colleges to bring more content to community colleges in a cost-efficient manner. One also could argue that the sector most disrupted by MOOCs will be for-profit education, which will be up against completely different competitors. Many business schools already use online learning combined with residencies in their executive MBA programs, so MOOCs most likely will drive improvements for those programs.

Lucas: Obviously, we can't keep giving away our product, and Coursera is working on a revenue model. For instance, Coursera now offers certificates, where students can pay a fee to show they've completed the course, as well as a model in which it licenses a MOOC to a school for use in a course and pays a royalty to the university that created it.

I also think we'll find ways for MOOCs to add value to the traditional classroom. So, say, five Nobel Prize-winning professors create MOOCs in economics. If a professor selects the parts of those MOOCs that are the most exciting, and brings those parts into class for discussion, that adds value. It would be rare that a professor could bring five Nobel-winning professors to class any other way.

Terwiesch: I think we'll develop a model where students can take the course for free but pay for extra support, extra lectures, and test taking monitoring if they're taking the course for credit. In places such as Africa and Asia, this model can reach thousands and thousands of students who otherwise would not be able to attend school.

In the 1990s, I once had a conversation with Jeff Bezos of Amazon.com, and we wondered whether bookstores would die out one day. A couple of years later, we knew that was exactly what was happening, but no one was willing to admit it because it sounded too evil. As business professors, we see innovation happen in industries all the time. This time it's happening in our own. I think we know exactly where this is heading, but we don't want to say it right now. This is a disruptive technology, and some people are going to lose.

But when the automobile came around, we didn't cry for the horse cart. If professors continue to reinvent what they teach and stay experiential, there will always be work. It would be incredibly naive to believe that we can continue to do business as usual, as if MOOCs hadn't come along. This is not a crazy trend that will stick around for a year and then go away. It's here to stay.

5 Reasons Flipped Classrooms Work

By Elizabeth Millard
University Business, December 2012

By now, most of us have heard the term "flipped classroom" and learned that the concept is not as aerodynamic as its name. But it is becoming a movement. In this type of learning space, lectures and other traditional classroom elements are swapped out in favor of more in-person interaction, like small group problem solving and discussion.

Instead of being a central feature of a course, lectures are delivered outside class via some type of streaming video, and students are expected to watch them on their own time. The model may well be paired with student response devices ("clickers") from companies such as i>clicker and Turning Technologies—or a web-based system with student response capabilities like Echo360's LectureTools—that allow instructors to get real-time answers to test questions or to drive discussions in a certain direction.

A professor might start a session with a five-question quiz on the lecture students were asked to watch before class, gathering responses through clickers. If most of the students indicate not understanding a specific aspect of the lecture— for example, correct responses on one of the quiz questions could be very low even though students ace the rest of the quiz—the professor could gear class time toward increasing comprehension of that aspect of the material.

Instructors use flipped classrooms in myriad combinations; one professor might integrate reading material and online chats into the nonclassroom work, while another could offer only a block of video without any supporting materials. No matter what the elements include, though, there are several advantages to the larger model itself. Here are five reasons to consider doing a flip.

1. Increases Student Engagement

Currently, there are no hard numbers to track the level of student engagement in a flipped classroom versus a traditional, lecture-based classroom. But there's plenty of anecdotal evidence to suggest that students respond well to using classroom time in a way that's more geared toward discussion.

"The difference between my classroom before flipping and after is dramatic," shares Michael Garver, who teaches marketing at Central Michigan University. "The students are fired up now. They're just devoted to active learning during the entire class period. It's wonderful." Like many professors using the flipped strategy, Garver breaks his lecture into short podcasts that accompany written or online materials. He begins every class with a brief quiz to make sure everyone is at the same level of comprehension with the material, and then, as he says, "the real learning begins."

Students use clickers as part of competitions, which Garver finds to be hugely popular. He might give them a real-world marketing scenario and ask them to make a decision based on 10 possible options. Given a short amount of time to "click in," students work in teams to come up with the best answers, and Garver tends to hear very lively debates during the process. "When I hear some good, solid arguments, that's when I know they're learning, and they'll retain the information," he says.

About 70 percent of his classes use these types of competitions on a regular basis, and often during class, the level of emotion and intensity is compelling. "When there's emotion, there's lesson retention," Garver says. "Students love this system because they're not listening to some old lecture. They're interacting and debating, and that makes them feel involved."

2. Strengthens Team-Based Skills

The group dynamic that Garver creates is an important part of many flipped classrooms. Although lectures are watched individually and tests still measure each student's comprehension level, teamwork is an integral part of in-class discussion.

As the Millennial generation and those that follow work their way through K–12, team-based approaches are likely to be even more important for higher education. The increasing use of technology in K–12 classrooms is also prompting more collaboration-based projects, according to James Ponce, superintendent for the McAllen Independent School District in Texas, in which Ponce recently gained attention for developing a major mobile technology initiative.

"Classroom technology isn't about teaching students how to use mobile devices," he says. "It's all about interaction—with teachers, with content, and with each other. We're creating a collaborative generation, and using technology for that effort." Ponce's students, and those across the country who participate in similar K–12 initiatives, will likely expect higher education to deliver the same type of team-based, interactive approaches they experienced throughout their school lives. Flipped classrooms tend to give them that environment, believes Sean Brown, vice president of education at Sonic Foundry.

"The Millennials are asynchronous kids when it comes to education," he says. "They've been raised in a world of interaction and communication, so asking them to sit and listen to a lecture, and then do homework on their own somewhere, is foreign to many of them. That's why higher education is succeeding with flipped classrooms, because it adjusts the delivery style to the students."

With the access that today's students have to information, making class time more effective through team-based activities also tends to make students feel like showing up is worth the effort.

"People are much more sensitive about this issue than they have been in the past," Brown notes. "There's kind of the question of 'Why should I haul myself to campus?' But if they know their team is depending on them, they're more likely to be participatory."

3. Offers Personalized Student Guidance

According to Roger Freedman, a physics professor at the University of California, Santa Barbara, professors are at their best when they can provide students with an active learning experience. "That means giving students personalized guidance about what they do and do not understand and personalized assistance with improving their understanding," he explains.

Freedman asks students to watch a video lecture the night before class, as well as complete two or three simple homework-type questions based on assigned reading and the video lecture. Each student can also submit a question to Freedman about something from the lecture or reading that they don't understand; he gives them homework points for submitting the question. Before heading to class, Freedman looks them over and chooses two or three of the most common queries to answer in person.

"Class begins with me giving the answers to the student questions I selected," he says. "You can hear a pin drop during this part of the class, because the students are so interested in knowing the answers to their own questions."

In large classes, it can be challenging for professors to keep track of individual student progress in terms of comprehension. But because data in a flipped model is collected and presented in a straightforward way, instructors are able to provide personalized instruction to some degree. "Clickers shine in the classroom because they offer students instant feedback about their understanding, and give instructors insight into the often surprising kinds of misunderstandings that students harbor," Freedman says.

4. Focuses Classroom Discussion

Students expect a higher level of discussion and technology usage than they did in the past, and it's likely that those expectations will only increase, believes Tina Rooks, vice president and chief instructional officer at Turning Technologies. "Kids don't want to power down their devices just because they're walking into a classroom," she says. "They know they have access to knowledge because of technology, so now they're looking for teachers who can coach them, and help them understand that information."

That prompts more focused discussions, she notes, and the delivery of immediate feedback through the clickers helps to provide a track for each class. The clickers can collect responses from quizzes, for example, and display the results (anonymized or not) on a screen in front of the class. Professors can also create multiple choice discussion topics and poll the students to see what type of direction they'd like to take.

Marsha Orr, the distance education faculty liaison in the School of Nursing at California State University, Fullerton, notes that clickers create a Socratic environment that allows students to think more deeply about the material, or to address the material from a particular viewpoint. Since some of her classes have students already in the nursing field, discussions might veer toward real-world experiences, for example, as opposed to more theoretical discussions among those who haven't worked with patients before.

Utilizing a variety of tools in this way—including not just clickers but also online video and discussion boards, printed materials, discussion groups, and peer review of written assignments—fosters more comprehension across multiple learning styles.

"We're not just presenting information and then testing them on it," she says. "Flipped classrooms and interactive materials let us increase the complexity of what we're teaching, because we have a stronger understanding of what they're learning and what they're not."

5. Provides Faculty Freedom

For courses taught by multiple professors, having an online lecture series can be valuable for delivering information in a standardized way, believes Bob Brookover, director of the Clemson International Institute for Tourism Research and Development at Clemson University (S.C.). In his department, he's found that professors often cover the same material in unique ways, especially for introductory courses.

Rather than have each professor record lectures that cover the same material, Brookover creates the lectures, allowing the professors to concentrate on in-class rich learning activities. The system provides flexibility, because comprehension might be higher in one class than in another, and the professor can hone in on specific areas where there's confusion.

Brookover's team meets on a weekly basis to decide on in-class activities, but there's freedom to be creative for each instructor, based on the discussions that come up in class. That structure of providing standardized lecture materials and more collaborative environments in class works well, Brookover notes.

"Professors appreciate the way they can take one topic and lead the students in a productive discussion for that particular group, in a way that's not based on lectures that take up class time," he says. "Students and faculty find the flipped approach to be very rewarding."

Ready to Flip?

Although flipped classrooms have numerous advantages, they're not for everyone yet. As Roberto Torreggiani, director of sales for i>clicker, has seen, adoption tends to be on a professor or a departmental level, rather than as a strategy for an entire institution. Also, professors who have limited time and technology resources may not be ready to create the type of online lecture materials that are necessary for a flipped classroom.

But as success stories keep accumulating, it's likely that more classes will get flipped. "We're seeing very enthusiastic professors and extremely motivated departments," Torreggiani says. "This is an area where the technology development is very rapid, and the adoption is very much on the upswing."

Blended Learning: A Disruption That Has Found Its Time

By Lisa Gonzales and Devin Vodicka
Leadership, November/December 2012

Combining different modes of delivery, models of teaching and styles of learning, blended learning offers the possibility for educators to reinvent teaching and learning.

Clay Christensen said it best in his book, *Disrupting Class.* Education needs an immediate, abrupt infusion of technology in public education that will do just that— disrupt the system (2008). Disruptive innovation is that which brings about non-traditional changes to improve a system. And some may say that system improvements are needed in public education and in teaching and learning.

In the pre-digital age, combinations of differing learning contexts were used for teaching. In today's classrooms, learning environments more frequently incorporate "e-elements" into varied instructional contexts. We are immersed in a paradigm shift in learning whereby blended learning has emerged as a flexible, differentiated, updated approach to learning.

Simply put, "blended learning" is learning facilitated by the effective combination of different modes of delivery, models of teaching and styles of learning, and applying them in an interactively meaningful learning environment. Think of it like this:

Mobile learning + eLearning + classroom learning = blended learning

The Innosight Institute released a report, "Classifying K–12 Blended Learning," in 2012 that outlined the different models of blended learning. They define blended learning as, "Any time a student learns at least in part at a supervised brick-and-mortar location away from home and at least in part through online delivery with some element of student control over time, place, path and/or pace."

However, there are four standard modes of blended learning that have proven to meet student academic needs and provide flexibility with instructional settings. The four blended learning approaches include:

The rotation model, where students rotate between teacher-led instruction and online learning.

A flexible approach, where students experience most learning online, while teachers provide a personal approach and touch.

The self-blend model, in which students choose their courses from a menu to supplement their regular, non-technical school offerings.

The enriched-virtual model, a whole-school experience in which students divide their time between attending a brick-and-mortar campus and learning remotely, using online delivery of content and instruction.

Fortunately, it does not require a massive investment to take steps in the direction of blended learning. The following resources are free, relatively easy to use, and very beneficial in terms of increasing options for student learning.

Content

In terms of content, the most notable free provider of instructional resources is **Khan Academy** (www.khanacademy.org), a website with more than 3,300 academic and real-world videos from basic arithmetic to quantum physics, introductory science to art history, and American civics to the basics of computer programming. These low-tech conversational tutorials last a few minutes and provide an introduction or a reinforcement of concepts and topics for students.

Khan Academy also has an exercise system that generates problems based on a student's grade and skill level, all of which can be monitored by the teacher. What makes Khan Academy the poster-child for blended learning is its ability to assist with the delivery of small chunks of content that can assist students needing reinforcement from a differing perspective, or those interested in higher-level skills.

- **Honorable mention:** www.knowmia.com. **Knowmia** boasts more than 7,000 teacher- and student-created videos in topics ranging from math to science, world languages to English, social studies and technology.

Conversation

During classroom learning, technology resources can be used to promote higher levels of engagement and interaction. One such approach is the use of a backchannel, which provides opportunities for students to use devices such as their own mobile phones, laptops or iPads to ask questions, provide input and share reflections about what is happening around them.

TodaysMeet (todaysmeet.com) is a free, simple option that works with just about anything that can get to the web. TodaysMeet allows for real-time conversations and connections with a live stream to make comments, ask questions and provide clarification. Even without web access. Twitter integration allows participants to use text messaging and interact with one another through this resource.

In a classroom, a ninth-grade teacher might pose a prompt such as, "What is your interpretation of 'walking in someone else's shoes' from *To Kill A Mockingbird*?" Students can then respond to the question during a classroom discussion, with the backchannel becoming the discussion platform. Students respond to the prompt, to the comments of others, and reflect on other applications of the concept or topic.

Want more information on the use of backchannels? Check out http://derekbruff. org/teachingwithcrs/?p=472.

Social Hubs

The link for students among the content, conversations and productivity tools can be a social hub such as **Edmodo** or a Learning Management System (LMS) such as **Haiku**. Edmodo boasts more than 7 million users and has been described as the "Facebook of education." Edmodo now has apps for iOS and Android platforms that promote mobile access as well.

Katie Angelone, social studies teacher in the Roseville Joint Union High School District, regularly uses Edmodo with her students: "I use Edmodo to engage my digital-native students, to teach them good digital citizenship and to post assignments and videos. Recently, students posted avatars (using the free program Voki) to describe what enlightenment philosopher they thought had the best and worst ideas and why. They had to view and comment on at least one other student's Voki.

"I have had students submit work digitally as well. Students have been asked to preview material before coming into class so they may be better equipped to participate in that day's activities (flipping the classroom). Students also are involved in discussions (kind of like a blog) and have sent me private messages asking for clarification on an assignment as well. Students and parents are enjoying Edmodo very much, as do I."

A Learning Management System can empower students and also be very useful from the standpoint of the instructor who is facilitating all of this activity. Haiku (www.haikulearning.com) is a popular option with both free and paid versions. The free version includes features such as a gradebook, attendance book, assignment list, and discussion forums.

The paid version, like many competing platforms, offers integration with student information systems and expanded customization options. Most LMS options also allow for importing and exporting of Common Cartridges, such as University of California Online Academy content (www.ucoa.org).

- **Honorable mention:** www.schoology.com. **Schoology** is a free LMS that incorporates online sharing, connecting, gradebooks, attendance management and more.

Productivity

In addition to providing access to content and conversation, students need ways to produce and share their work. Our favorite, free web-based resource for this purpose is **Google Docs**. This ever-expanding suite of tools includes word processing, presentations, spreadsheets, forms, and drawings. Additionally, sharing options allow for groups of students to collaborate and work as teams in real time or asynchronously.

Importantly, that collaboration does not require students to be in the same place as they work with one another. This article, for example, was co-authored in Google docs with relative ease, in spite of the fact that the two authors live hundreds of miles apart.

In the world of conventional K–12 education, we now have enormous opportunities to connect our students and emphasize collaboration through online/blended learning.

For example, Craig Miller, ninth-grade computer literacy teacher in the Pajaro Valley Unified School District, regularly uses Google docs with his students. Miller said, "When my students are placed into project teams by their teachers, the first question they ask each other is, 'What is your gmail address?' After sharing a document, presentation, spreadsheet or drawing online through the address, they are able to work collaboratively from their respective houses in real time. Keystrokes are literally displayed on each student's screen as the characters are typed. The team is truly looking at the same document as if they are all in the same room."

The Next Steps

Greg Ottinger, director of blended and online learning at the San Diego County Office of Education, says that "Leaders are wise to thoroughly evaluate LMS options before making a selection" because not all options work in every environment. As with all of these blended learning resources, Ottinger points out that "the transformative aspect can be realized when the LMS is coupled with professional development, a reliable Internet connection, and overall program vision and management."

For those interested in moving in the direction of blended learning, our recommendation is to start small—pick one of the suggested resources and engage in a small-scale pilot to identify issues, opportunities and challenges. To accelerate the learning curve, connect with others who are engaging in this work—colleagues both within your organization and outside the organization can provide valuable insights that will help you make progress.

For example, you can use the ACSA Community (http://community.acsa.org), LinkedIn's 21st Century Education, the International Society for Technology in Education or Technology Integration in Education groups to ask questions and cultivate relationships with those who have similar interests or experiences.

The process can also be assisted by using research and resources from agencies such as the International Association for K–12 Online Learning (www.inacol.org). Emerging forms of professional development such as Leading Edge Certification (http://leadingedgecertification.org) can also be powerful accelerators in the learning process.

Continuous Learning

Girlie Ebuen, math teacher and BTSA support provider at Murrieta Mesa High School in the Murrieta Unified School District, blogged about her experience with the LEC certification: "I had never blogged before, but now I see a blog as a tool for reflection both as a learner and instructor. Working with more web 2.0 tools such as VoiceThread and several Google apps, I realized how much I can vary assessment in an online course. The LEC course confirms my belief that in order to teach, I need to continue to learn."

Most importantly, take the time to step back and realize that our educational system is at an inflection point. The broad changes in society, coupled with rapid advances in technology, are creating possibilities for transformation that simply were not feasible just a few years ago. Enjoy the process and appreciate the opportunities to be a part of the reinvention of teaching and learning. This is an amazing time to be an educator.

Bibliography

Christensen, Clayton. (2008). *Disrupting Class: How Disruption Innovation Will Change the Way the World Learns*. New York, NY: McGraw Hill.

Staker, Heather & Horn, Michael. (2012). "Classifying K–12 Blended Learning." San Mateo, CA: Innosight Institute.

6 Ways Tech Will Change Education Forever

By Issie Lapowsky
Inc., November 21, 2013

Want to know what college will look like in 10, 20, 30 years? Here are six predictions from some of the brightest minds in academia and business.

Tensions were high Wednesday at New York University's Stern School of Business, as a group of academics, venture capitalists, and entrepreneurs faced off during a panel discussion on the future of higher education.

The panelists, including NYU President John Sexton, Harvard Business School professor Clayton Christensen, and Codecademy CEO Zach Sims, among others, were charged with predicting the future of the traditional university. Will emerging technology and online learning dismantle the notion of "college" as we know it?

Predictably, the academics took a markedly more conservative view than their start-up counterparts, but there was one thing everyone in the room could agree on. As Sexton put it, "The status quo is not an option. We're in for what I call a radical restructuring of higher education today."

Here are six big ideas about how tech incumbents are about to drastically change the face of education:

1. Technology Can Help Universities Discover Talent.

NYU President Sexton heads up the third most expensive university in the country (and, yes, my alma mater), but even he admits that this model is far from perfect and that there are too many universities charging students too much for too weak an education. In the future, he said, there will be a major consolidation of colleges across the country. That doesn't mean, however, that he thinks the traditional university will disappear.

"I want to resist being cast as a dinosaur here, but the fact that opera doesn't have the same broad-based appeal as Jay Z doesn't mean society would be better off without it," he said. "There will still be room for a dinosaur or two."

But those universities that are left standing, he says, will have to do a much better job at identifying talented students, who can't afford to pay $61,000 a year for school. "We're doing a horrible job right now," he said. "If we use it correctly, technology will become a talent identifier."

Sexton pointed to NYU's own partnership with University of the People, a non-profit that offers tuition-free online education to students in the developing world, as a prime example of technology's ability to unearth talent. Promising students identified at University of the People are eligible for admission at NYU's Abu Dhabi campus.

2. Low Cost Education Technology Will Eventually Rob Universities of Students.

As a scholar of innovation, Christensen approached the future of higher education through the prism of past industries that have been disrupted. He said there are two concentric circles of potential customers for any innovation: the inner circle consists of the wealthy, and the outer circle, of the masses. When a new industry arises, he says, it almost always begins in the innermost circle.

"Initially, products and services are so costly and complicated that only the wealthy have access," he said.

It was the case with the mainframe computers of the 1950s and early televisions in the 1960s. The problem is, the companies that tend to start in those inner circles have a tough time disrupting their own technology with a more affordable and accessible option. Their business models don't allow for it. So, an incumbent comes in with the more affordable, more accessible technology and begins selling it to the outer circle of people, who have no other option. Slowly, but surely, customers from the inner circle begin gravitating to the new innovation. That's how the transistor radio disrupted the television and how the personal computer rendered the mainframe computer obsolete. And so it will go with education, Christensen said.

"The people who jumped on first to online learning were the ones who couldn't come to NYU. It was better than nothing," he said. "But the technology will get better and better and then the customers get sucked out. The question is not whether this will occur, but what role universities will play."

3. Loans Will Be Paid Back Later.

Fear of debt is one of the biggest barriers for people who want to pursue higher education, particularly these days, when a degree does not necessarily equate to a job after college. That's why Andre Dua, who counsels local governments and schools in his role as a director at McKinsey & Company, says there's plenty of opportunity for disruption in education finance. By 2025, Dua predicts, we may begin to see organizations offering loans that don't need to be paid back until a graduate has attained a certain income of, say, $50,000 or more.

4. Students Will Demand Practical Skills Training over Soft Skills.

Zach Sims founded Codecademy two years ago, after dropping out of Columbia University, where he was studying political science. The education he was receiving, even at this elite institution, he said, wasn't preparing him for life in the real world. In fact, he said, two thirds of college graduates say they will need further training after graduation. In the future, Sims predicts that companies like Codecademy, which teaches people how to code online, will become a more viable alternative to the traditional liberal arts education. Unlike many undergraduate programs, students will walk away from these decentralized online courses with a portfolio of work they can show to potential employers.

"We're still focusing on two- to four-year degree programs that aren't coupled with what people need to know to find a job," he says. "At Codecademy, we're doing one part of something much larger to fix the system."

5. The University Will Become Unbundled.

When universities first took form, if you wanted to hear someone speak, you had to be in the room with them, and if you wanted to read a book, you had to go to the library. Obviously, said Albert Wenger, of Union Square Ventures, that's no longer the case. "We wound up with a hugely bundled model," he said, and now is the time to unbundle it.

According to Wenger, more start-ups will arise that offer some element of the university experience. Science Exchange, for instance, is a Union Square Ventures-backed company that enables researchers to borrow lab space anywhere around the world.

6. The University of Tomorrow Will Not Look Like a University (or a MOOC).

"I think Coursera and Udacity will be as bad for higher education as the University of Phoenix," said Clay Shirky, a writer-in-residence at NYU's Journalism Institute. "Even though the leaders of those companies right now seem to be true believers, they're one management change away from the scummy business practices that Kaplan and Kapella have adopted."

That doesn't mean Shirky is content with the current model of education, either. "If universities went away today, tomorrow, no one would say, 'Hey, you know what we need?' And come up with something that looks exactly like a university," he said.

Instead, Shirky expects to see more specialized schools like Rockefeller University, which focuses on biomedical research. Others might not look like a university at all. Instead, he suggested, they might look like Polymath University, an online university that's focused on educating students to complete a project, not a major.

"If you think about our stock keeping inside the university, there are seven big constructs: class, course, grade, credit, degree, department, major. Not one of them is real. They're all just how we do it," he says. "Here's what's real: Students are real. Knowing things is real. Being able to do things is real. People will find alternate ways to teach those things. That's where the really disruptive stuff comes from."

5

Politics of the Good Teacher

© Tammy Ljungblad/MCT/ Landov

Audrey Pribnow, with Teach for America, reads *Musk Ox Counts* to her class of first-graders at University Academy in Kansas City, Missouri.

Grading the Graders

Throughout United States history, teachers have played an integral role in the shaping and development of the country's future leaders. Teachers are responsible for giving children the knowledge and skills they will need to succeed in life. Additionally, it is anticipated that they will inspire their students, giving them the desire as well as the tools necessary to advance. The sphere of a teacher's influence, therefore, extends beyond the classroom—the lessons taught and examples set often return home with the student.

Because of their high social consequence, teachers, as well as the school systems that employ them, are frequently placed under extraordinary scrutiny. School systems with low standardized test scores, high dropout numbers, and low college acceptance rates are seen as underperforming and often face funding cuts for not doing enough to provide a quality education. Such a critical focus on the public school system has long been manifest in the United States—in a scathing 1983 report titled *A Nation at Risk*, President Ronald Reagan's National Commission on Excellence in Education criticized the country's public school system for producing students with substandard skills, especially when compared to the school systems of other nations.

Since that commission's report, advocates for comprehensive education reform have examined a wide range of issue areas. In addition to the imposition of standardized testing, modified curricula, and other, student-focused policy changes, critics have also called for tenure reform for teachers and improved teacher training and professional development programs. Teachers—through their unions and, in turn, the collective bargaining process—have accepted some proposed changes and rejected others. Many education professionals and outsiders have expressed concern, however, that the seemingly benign initiative of pursuing the best possible educational system has become a politically charged issue. Furthermore, as the political storm surrounding education reform intensifies, teachers—the involved party that most directly engages with students on a daily basis—continue to serve as lightning rods.

Depending on the grade level, subject area, and geographic location, a teacher receives a comprehensive education and training regimen prior to obtaining a job. Teachers must typically hold a bachelor's degree at minimum, although an increasing number of employers require educators to obtain a master's degree or a PhD in their respective areas of expertise. Throughout the course of their education, would-be teachers often participate in internship and student teaching programs that help to familiarize them with the subject matter they seek to teach, as well as with school curricula and protocols.

Such classroom and on-the-job training helps aspiring teachers develop certain traits and skills that will enable them to manage effectively a diverse group of students. In addition to an ability to speak publicly, assign work, and properly apply grades, teachers must demonstrate a number of desirable personal qualities. Among these traits are creativity, compassion, optimism, and a sense of humor. Teachers in the modern classroom are asked not to act simply as lecturers or disciplinarians. They are called upon to foster within their students an interest in not only the subject at hand but also in the overall learning process. In the ideal educational environment, experts argue, students feel a sense of inclusion, largely thanks to a fair-handed, respectful, and personal approach demonstrated by their teachers.

As the nation's economy, social norms, and population continue to change in the twenty-first century, the United States school system and the educators working therein must adapt. Students in most communities come from a diverse set of backgrounds. Many represent different ethnicities, religious backgrounds, family compositions, and economic strata. Teachers are called upon to not only recognize this cultural, social, and economic diversity but also to embrace it—and encourage students to embrace it as well—as part of the learning process. Educators are instructed to "know their audiences" in the classroom and even use the diversity of the students to the benefit of the educational mission.

Furthermore, teachers in the twenty-first century must be knowledgeable of, and able to utilize, the best available technologies in their daily lessons. This aspect of teaching—particularly at the higher education level—can be challenging for some. Hardware and software such as overhead laptop projectors and Microsoft's PowerPoint are used for in-class presentations, while other devices are used to connect students and teachers who are geographically distant from one another, creating a virtual classroom. Many teachers rely on the Internet to share information with their students via educational websites, social media, and other online utilities that allow students to connect with their teachers even after class has adjourned. Technology, when used effectively, can add new dimensions to the learning process. However, when misused or abused, the very same innovations can be detrimental to students' development. Teachers must be discerning in their application of available technologies and make informed decisions on how to use them to positive ends.

But a changing nation calls for changing standards. In addition to pursuing the diverse set of professional qualifications and characteristics discussed above, teachers are falling under increased scrutiny for how they are demonstrating said qualities and adapting to the evolving academic environment. The politically charged outcry over education reform commonly includes calls for more accurate assessments of teacher efficacy. Such evaluations are seen as a joint operation—teachers must conduct their own evaluations of student performance, while an increasing number of parent- and even student-generated teacher evaluations are being introduced in systems across the country. For example, in 2013, in response to legislation establishing new teacher evaluation standards, the Colorado Department of Education began to offer the Colorado State Model Evaluation System, an optional resource that includes a structured spreadsheet assessment that gauges teacher qualifications and the level of achievement attained by a given teacher's students. In the Northeast, public schools in Boston have given students a bigger hand in the educator assessments, collecting feedback from students on teacher performance; teachers in Connecticut must log their accomplishments, qualifications, and student achievement rates in a formalized evaluation.

The Connecticut teacher evaluation law and the system it established have sparked a debate, both among educational leaders in the state and across the country. Teachers have complained about the amount of time they must spend managing and logging the required data. Other reform advocates express concern that the assessments are too rigid and that these evaluations focus solely on empirical student achievement, and not enough on other aspects of individual growth. Still others suggest that the evaluations are too focused on science and mathematics, to the detriment of other areas of study. At the same time, however, some leaders welcome what they see as a constantly improving system that empowers teachers to set their own classroom goals for improvement rather than imposing general achievement goals upon educators.

The Connecticut, Colorado, and other state teacher evaluation models have generated discussion over whether teachers should be the only ones to analyze student achievement. Teachers working under these systems have complained that they spend too much of their day completing their evaluations and not enough time focusing on teaching the curriculum. The Bill and Melinda Gates Foundation—an education-oriented nonprofit—has echoed this concern. The foundation suggested, as an alternative, a system combining student surveys, independent classroom observers, and analyses of student achievement gains that would alleviate some of the assessment responsibilities teachers endure. The foundation has also expressed disapproval of publicly releasing the results of teacher evaluations, claiming it deters promising talent from the profession and does nothing to improve teacher performance.

The political strife surrounding teacher evaluations is often fomented by a disconnect between broader national standards and the unique needs of specific schools. Typically, teachers are given periodic evaluations throughout their career—from their first years as student and probationary teachers through the point at which they are offered tenure. A school principal, assistant principal, or department head may perform these evaluations and keep assessment results within the school—although in order to comply with state and federal requirements, schools will release general statements on their teachers' proficiency, including ratings from "Exemplary" to "Below Standard." In this setting, the principals, teachers, department heads, and other administrators work as a unit toward building and maintaining the optimal educational environment for their students.

Conducting evaluations and addressing assessment findings in-house allows for a more tailored approach to improving student achievement and teacher efficacy. Every school's staff and student body has unique strengths and weaknesses, and participants in the school system who are familiar with the local community and a given school's unique academic environment can often take a more nuanced approach to improving the quality of education provided. When evaluations are conducted by external parties (such as state or federal agencies) for the purposes of assessing a school district's overall performance, there exists a risk that the evaluators will focus on negative numbers without considering the variety of factors that might be behind a school's shortcomings. For this reason, during collective bargaining negotiations between teachers and school administrations, teachers are often asked to approve some form of evaluation as part of the new contract—administrators, in a good faith effort, ask their teachers to help create an open evaluation system that addresses their specific needs.

Whatever the manner in which teacher evaluations are conducted, there are political as well as professional issues surrounding documented teacher performance. A perceived poor performance by a school district's faculty can jeopardize state and federal funds and create friction. School districts are therefore expected to take a critical eye when it comes to their teachers. Teachers, in many evaluations, should not just have the proper training and understanding of the curricula and subject matters at hand—many evaluations test whether teachers demonstrate positive personal characteristics, such as organization, patience, and a dedicated work ethic.

Another problematic aspect of government-mandated teacher assessment is the lack of uniformity in the evaluations. Often, federal laws will be implemented with general guidelines for states, which in turn defer to municipal governments for further interpretation. As long as municipalities comply with the intent of the legislation, they are frequently allowed a considerable degree of latitude. Such practices empower local communities, but there are risks. As shown here, for example, Connecticut, Massachusetts, and Colorado all recently passed laws that require school systems to perform and report the results of teacher evaluations as a component of comprehensive education reform initiatives. However, in many ways, each of these programs differs from one another in style and substance, even though they satisfy the same federal requirements. In fact, evaluation systems may differ considerably even from district to district.

One of the persistent concerns about this diversity in evaluation systems is that, based on different assessments, a teacher's proficiency may be greater or less than that of another educator in a different district. For example, a teacher who is given a rating of "Proficient" in one district might find that rating different using the criteria of another district—he or she might be seen as "Exemplary," or perhaps even "Developing," in this alternative district. This lack of uniformity across evaluation systems, experts say, establishes vague standards and could even lead to legal issues among educators, unions, and administrations.

The teacher in modern American schools is more than just a lecturer. The ideal teacher is also a mentor and role model for students. These expectations are lofty, to be sure, yet understandable considering these professionals are charged with educating the nation's children. Teachers by and large accept these responsibilities upon entering the field. Still, there is a political undercurrent to education in the United States, one that has been in existence for decades. It has placed teachers under a microscope in the form of evaluations and assessments. How such documentation is used in a positive, apolitical manner remains an important issue in the overall pursuit of reforming the American public school system.

—Michael Auerbach

Bibliography

Adams Jr., Jacob E., and Rick Ginsberg. "Education Reform—Overview, Reports of Historical Significance." *StateUniversity.com*. Net Industries, 2014. Web. 2 June 2014.

Bates, Tony, and Gary Poole. *Effective Teaching with Technology in Higher Education*. San Francisco: Jossey, 2003. Print.

Chu, Dan M. "Another Revolution Starts in Boston." *Phi Delta Kappan*. PDK Intl., 2013. Web. 2 June 2014.

Darling-Hammond, Linda, and Joan C. Baratz-Snowden. *A Good Teacher in Every Classroom: Preparing the Highly Qualified Teachers Our Children Deserve*. San Francisco: Jossey, 2005. Print.

Frahm, Robert A. "Teacher Evaluations: Too Much Science, Not Enough Art?" *Connecticut Mirror*. Connecticut News Project, 2014. Web. 2 June 2014.

Loveless, Tom. *Conflicting Missions? Teachers Unions and Educational Reform*. Washington: Brookings, 2011. Print.

"Teacher Evaluations: The Role of State Laws and Collective Bargaining". *US Chamber of Commerce*. US Chamber of Commerce Foundation, 20 Jan. 2011. Web. 2 June 2014.

Van Driel, Jan H., Douwe Beijaard, and Nico Verloop. "Professional Development and Reform in Science Education: The Role of Teachers' Practical Knowledge". *Journal of Research in Science Teaching* 38.2 (2001): 137–58. Print.

Walker, Robert J. *12 Characteristics of an Effective Teacher*. 2nd ed. Morrisville: Lulu, 2013. Print.

Ten Characteristics of a Good Teacher

By Patricia Miller
English Teaching Forum, 2012

This article was first published in Volume 25, No. 1 (1987).

From time to time during the 15 years I have been working in the field of English language teaching and training, I have put myself in the position of language learner rather than teacher. In addition to enjoying language study and finding the process fascinating, I find it beneficial to view the process through the eyes of a student. Even though I have felt at odds with some teachers and their methods, I have learned something from every teacher I have ever had, even the worst of them.

The Ten Characteristics

There is a line in Saint-Exupery's *The Little Prince* that applies to any endeavor, but especially teaching. It reads: "That which is essential cannot be seen with the eye. Only with the heart can one know it rightly." The essence of teaching is difficult to qualify, but that line leads directly into my most essential criterion.

    1. *I want a teacher who has a contagious enthusiasm for his teaching*—one who, as Richard Via says, loves his students and his work. Mr. Via is an educational specialist in using drama techniques to teach EFL at the East-West Center in Hawaii. I was fortunate enough to attend his teacher-training seminar in Korea in 1976. It was a pleasure to be in his audience. His enjoyment in transmitting knowledge and participating in the seminar was apparent and infectious. His passion for teaching instilled a passion for learning in all the participants. For me, the most crucial factors in effective teaching are who the teacher is and how he acts in the classroom. This influences the way the students react toward the target language and, therefore, their success in learning it.

    2. *I want a teacher who is creative.* Teaching must be more than simply opening a book, doing exercises, and following an outline written by someone else. In the tedium of repetition, the student can go through the motions of doing the exercises without his mind being engaged. What can a teacher do to engage the student's mind? There are a myriad of techniques that the creative teacher can employ—information-gap exercises, games, songs, jazz chants, problem solving,

and other techniques that allow the student to utilize the skills he has already developed in his first language.

3. *I want a teacher who can add pace and humor to the class.* The humor of one of my teachers had the effect of alleviating my nervousness—of reducing my affective filter. There was a rapport among the students and the teacher because we were all laughing together. We had a good time learning, and we made a lot of progress because we were not afraid to make mistakes; we could take chances. As Krashen would say, the affective filters of the students were low, facilitating acquisition.

Another teacher that I had maintained an excellent pace in the class. She never lost an instant consulting a list or thinking about what to do next; she had prepared—that was evident—and she was going to capitalize on every second. I was somewhat nervous in her class, but I didn't have time to worry about it because events moved so quickly. I was literally sitting on the edge of my seat so that I wouldn't miss anything, and my adrenalin was a positive force.

I should add that humor is a double-edged sword: it can backfire, for what is funny to one person may not be funny to another. Humor across cultures can add a layer of difficulty to communication.

4. *I want a teacher who challenges me.* I had several teachers who always spoke to me in Spanish, both in and out of class. I felt they were showing confidence in me and challenging me to speak Spanish. The student's passive knowledge of the target language is always greater than his active knowledge. There is no reason why a teacher should use any language other than the target language except possibly for purposes of expediency. When a teacher reverts to the native language, he is showing a lack of patience with the students' struggles in the target language. In addition, switching codes is confusing. I was given a test in which all the instructions were read to me in English, so that I would be sure to understand everything. Then I had to answer in Spanish. But the test had three parts and I had to continue switching codes back and forth from English to Spanish; I found this very confusing. It is like going off a diet—once you cheat a little, then you want to cheat a little more. If someone speaks to me in English, this activates my English channel and I am prepared to think in English. Speaking in the target language to the learner prepares and challenges him to speak in that language.

In addition, I want a teacher who can maintain a level of difficulty high enough to challenge me, but not so high as to discourage me.

5. *I want a teacher who is encouraging and patient, and who will not give up on me.* Some of the teachers that I have had demonstrated incredible patience with all of their students, never allowing even a shadow of displeasure to cross their faces in reaction to continued incorrect speaking after endless correction (which may say something about the policy of correction). When the teacher is positive—encouraging initial and repeated attempts—the students will apply themselves more diligently. Motivation thrives on success.

One teacher I had appeared on several occasions to give up on me. She would struggle to have the other members of the class repeat the combination of an indirect object pronoun followed by a direct object pronoun—the nemesis of the Spanish-language student. They would have numerous chances to supply the correct combination in various tenses, but I often was given only one opportunity. For the life of me, I do not know why the teacher gave me only one chance. Was it because I was struggling and she wanted to spare me any unpleasantness? Or was it because in her mind I didn't need the practice? I felt that I needed the practice and wanted at least a chance to try. I felt that the teacher was discouraged and had lost confidence in my ability to progress. As a result, I lost my incentive and became unsure of myself.

6. *I want a teacher who will take an interest in me as a person*—one who will try to discover discussion topics that interest me. When I was teaching, one of the first things I did was to try to find out what my students' interests were: hobbies, past employment, family, travel, etc. The easiest, most accessible area of conversation is oneself. The initial and intermediate stages of development for the language student do not abound with opportunities for coherent self-expression. Most of the time, we language students feel fairly incompetent because we cannot express ourselves adequately, as we are accustomed to doing in our native language. Thus, if we can discuss some little accomplishment we've had, or something that we take pleasure in or are proud of, so much the better.

7. *I want a teacher who knows grammar well and who can explain something on the spot[1] if necessary.* I also want a teacher who is realistic and has the simple courage to admit that he doesn't know an answer if indeed he doesn't. I have had some teachers who, probably as the result of the de-emphasis on grammar explanation in the structuralist tradition, did not provide enough explanations. It seems to me that a more eclectic approach would take into consideration the needs of the adult learner, who should be given some insight into the intricacies of grammar.

8. *I want a teacher who will take a minute or two to answer a question after class,* or who will take five minutes to correct something that I have done on my own. I had several teachers who did this willingly and who encouraged the students to do extra work on their own. I also had a teacher who made some corrections for me at my request, but somehow I felt as if I had encroached on her time. Is teaching to be exactly 50 minutes of the hour and no more? First, we as teachers need to encourage students not only to study what is required, but to pursue on their own areas in which they are interested. Acquisition is facilitated when it concerns information that we need or are interested in. And second, we need to appreciate our students' efforts.

9. *I want a teacher who will treat me as a person, on an equal basis with all the members of the class,* regardless of sex, marital status, race, or my future need for the language. In some of my classes women were given discussion topics relating only to the home and family, and men were rarely asked to talk about their

families. Men were also given more "talk" time than the women. This can be discouraging to the student, and that is not conducive to progress. As teachers, we must look carefully at our classes to be certain that we are including everyone equally. I know that I have probably been guilty of bias toward the brighter and more energetic students—they're more challenging for the teacher and more interesting for the class. But now that I have been a victim of bias myself, I will certainly be more aware of treating my students equally.

10. Finally, I want a teacher who will leave his emotional baggage outside the classroom. The classroom is a stage, and to be effective the teacher must in some cases be an actor. I do not want to interrupt my concentration by worrying about what might be bothering the teacher. Nor do I want a teacher who sustains himself through ridicule or sarcasm, playing havoc with the emotions of his students and thereby blocking any learning/acquisition that might take place.

Conclusion

The qualities that I have discussed can be separated into four areas—(1) affective characteristics, (2) skills, (3) classroom management techniques, and (4) academic knowledge:

Affective Characteristics

- enthusiasm
- encouragement
- humor
- interest in the student
- availability
- mental health

Skills

- creativity
- challenge

Classroom Management

- pace
- fairness

Academic Knowledge

- grammar

A teacher's effectiveness depends on his demonstration of the affective characteristics. These are inborn in some of us, but they are also within the grasp of most teachers. Most of us want to be encouraging, enthusiastic, and available, but we just have to be reminded once in a while. The classroom management techniques of peace and fairness are often overlooked, but they can be crucial to effective teaching. These are not techniques that require training, but again, simply awareness. The specific teaching skills of creativity and challenge are associated more with the types of materials and activities, and their level and appropriateness. Ease and facility in these two areas come with experience and familiarity with the syllabus and materials. Lastly, a teacher who knows his grammar gives himself credibility and stature in the eyes of his students. With a little training in how to explain grammar and how to teach it, teachers have an indispensable tool.

Note

1. Editor's Note: on the spot = without further consideration; at once; immediately.

Born or Made: What Makes a Great Teacher?

By Stacy Williams, James Wolgamott, Deborah Anthony,
Kathleen Nawrocki, Allan Olchowski, and Joshua Smith
Loyola, September 11, 2013

We've all heard it said, "great teachers are born, not made." The statement insinuates that young people always knew they would become teachers, inherently love children, and are lifelong learners.

As former teachers and current teacher educators, we know there is much more to great teaching than destiny.

It is true that many people enter the profession of teaching with a passion for children and learning. Some arrive committed to providing quality education to all, regardless of race, ability, or socio-economic status. Others intuitively uncover strengths and nurture what students bring to the classroom. Still others possess a calm, deliberate, and patient approach, even under the most challenging circumstances.

However, to find individuals with all of these dispositions and attributes is rare. Even if an individual possesses all of these attributes, it is not nearly enough. Great teachers must strive to improve their dispositions and also be able to digest research on effective practice, interpret learning theory, and advocate for their students and families.

Preparation of a Great Teacher

Learning how to teach effectively, to say nothing of being great, requires a massive commitment of time and energy. In addition to obtaining a well-rounded background in several disciplinary areas, becoming a great teacher requires foundational coursework in educational theories and evidence-based practice.

At first, all students struggle with challenge to connect theory and practice. We train them to resist the temptation to rely on their experience as a student or a gut reaction to solve a problem.

Course assignments require students to consistently and critically consider what it means to become a reflective teacher. They provide candid and constructive feedback to peers and are encouraged to be open to feedback themselves. They learn how to write plans, implement, and revise lesson plans multiple times based on guidance from others.

Additionally, the teacher candidates become well-versed in a variety of cutting-edge, pedagogical practices and authentic assessment practices. They learn to review data from multiple assessments, modify practice, and offer individualized support to students who are struggling, as well as to those who excel.

This attention to differentiated instruction is a challenge for new and veteran teachers alike. However, great teachers hold high expectations for all students and consistently think of ways to make learning accessible to all.

Learning through Consistent Field Experience

As undergraduates, elementary education teacher candidates at Loyola participate actively in field experiences in local schools every semester. Secondary education minors and Master of Arts in Teaching (MAT) students participate in two field experiences before their internships. These schools are our partners in teacher preparation.

Each semester education students return to campus well before their peers in other majors to begin internships when local school system teachers return to work. In addition to working with Loyola Professional Development Schools (PDS) faculty members who possess extensive experience as teachers and school leaders, students are paired with carefully selected, highly qualified teachers who support them throughout the year.

Our PDS faculty work closely with 15–18 students and their mentors at three school sites. The faculty spend at least one full day at each school supporting teacher candidates, offering advice to mentor teachers, and serve on the school-wide planning teams and committees. During the first semester of internship, students spend one day every week in that same classroom getting to know their students, observing their mentor teachers, and reflecting on what is working and what could be done differently.

Throughout this experience, the teacher candidates have opportunities to teach lessons, receive feedback, and reflect on practices. The second semester of internship is a full-time teaching program, following the school system schedule. The student moves toward independent teaching as the mentor teacher observes and assists.

This gradual release process is intentional and provides a sense of confidence and an appreciation for difficulties associated with the day-to-day work of a teacher.

Great Teaching Is More Than Classroom Management

Many people equate a quiet, orderly classroom with learning. While this can be true at times, chatter emanating from small-group discussion and even a bit of laughter is likely an indicator that students are learning. Great teachers create a learning community where children feel safe and see clear ways to be successful every day.

Creating a positive learning environment—often coined classroom management—is consistently cited as a challenge area for new teachers. Principals often ask faculty in Schools of Education to spend more time with our candidates in this area. Constructing a dynamic and balanced classroom requires applying theories on child and adolescent development, being open to learning from role models who value the learning community approach, and a willingness to try new approaches.

Great teachers master the content and carefully construct engaging activities that attend to multiple learning strategies. They adjust plans as needed and make seamless transitions among different components of the lesson. They are meticulously prepared and organized, but make it appear to their students that the lesson flows naturally as if they just thought of a cool idea or way to learn a complex concept.

Great teachers do not merely provide students with information and they do not exist simply to raise the test scores of their students. Rather, great teachers focus their energy on designing lessons that engage students and help them to acquire intellectual habits of mind. They ensure that students truly understand and connect what they are learning to their daily lives and the lives of their friends and families.

Great teachers are champions for democracy. They provide students with choices of what they learn and how they demonstrate mastery of content and expectations. They assess understanding, collect data, and use those data to design future lessons.

Great Teachers View Diversity as an Asset

The economic challenges confronting students and families in urban and rural schools are real and pervasive. Great teachers make a serious commitment to care about all of their students and to believe that a good education makes a difference in children's lives. They communicate with families in respectful and positive ways.

Great teachers value diversity as an enhancement to the learning environment and do not view it as a challenge or a problem to be solved. They are advocates for children and families and actively seek collaboration with other teachers and school administration.

All teachers are expected to implement the latest curricular standards and meet the ever-changing mandates from local, state, and federal interests. However, great teachers question the integrity of the proposed changes and critically examine potentially negative impacts on students, especially students who are marginalized by inequities in the system.

Great teachers are rightfully accountable for their students, but they question the reliability, utility, and privileging of standardized test scores as the most effective or sole measure of student learning or teacher effectiveness.

What Makes Loyola University Maryland Different?

Unlike most teacher preparation programs, the PDS faculty in Loyola's School of Education are full-time, clinical faculty members who spend countless hours supporting teacher candidates in our partner schools. Additionally, we provide a solid background in educational theory, research on innovative practice, and hold up Jesuit ideals of social justice, service, and, most importantly, cura personalis—care for the whole person.

Our conceptual framework insists on competence, conscience, and compassion. Our teacher candidates are encouraged to build on learners' strengths instead of looking for deficiencies. We firmly believe that our framework is a foundation for greatness.

How do we define greatness?

Great teachers are lifelong learners who start their careers by making a difference in classrooms.

Great teachers increase their spheres of influence to schools, school systems, and communities.

Great teachers take advantage of professional development and make time to grow and develop.

Great teachers change lives and create a better future.

There are countless good teachers who want to be great. Here at Loyola we are proud that our students strive to become great and are always striving to become even greater. After all, greatness is not just born, but made—through determination, commitment, and a hunger both to succeed and also serve.

Role of the Teacher in Higher Education

By Mallikarjun I. Minch
Golden Research Thoughts, October 2012

Abstract

A teacher can never truly teach unless he is still learning himself. A lamp can never light another lamp unless it continues to burn its own flame. The teacher who has come to the end of his subject, who has no living traffic with his knowledge but merely repeats his lessons to his students, can only load their minds. He cannot quicken them the aim of teaching is simple; it is to make student learning possible. To reach is to make an assumption about what and how the student learns; therefore, to teach well implies learning about students' learning. A good teacher can be defined as a teacher who helps the student to learn. He or she contributes to this in a number of ways.

Introduction

The task of the teacher in higher education has many dimensions; it involves the provision of a broad context of knowledge within which students can locate and understand the content of their more specific studies; it involves the creation of a learning environment in which students are encouraged to think carefully and critically and express their thoughts, and in which they wish to confront and resolve difficulties rather than gloss over them, it involves constantly monitoring and reflecting on the processes of teaching and student understanding and seeking to improve them. Most difficult of all perhaps, it involves helping students to achieve their own aims, and adopt the notion that underlies higher education; that students' learning requires from them commitment, work, responsibility for their own learning, and a willingness to take risks, and that this process has its rewards, not the least of which is that learning can be fun.

These are not easy tasks, and there is no simple way to achieve them. Still less are there any prescriptions that will hold well in all disciplines and for all students. How we teach must be carefully tailored to suit both that which is to be learned and those who are to learn it. To put it another way—and to add another ingredient— our teaching methods should be the outcome of our aims (that is, what we want the students to know, to understand, to be able to do, and to value), our informed conceptions of how students learn, and the institutional context—with all of its constraints and possibilities—within which the learning is to take place. Mostly faculty members serve on academic or administrative committees that deal with the policies of their institution, departmental matters, academic issues, curricula, budgets, equipment purchases, and hiring. Some work with student and community organizations. The proportion of time spent on research, teaching, administrative, and other duties varies by individual circumstances and type of institution.

At the university level, we hope that students will provide their own motivation and their own discipline, and bring their own, already developed cognitive abilities to bear on the subject matter. Nevertheless, the teacher still has a crucial and demanding role to play in the process of student learning, by creating a context in which the students' desire and ability to learn can work most effectively.

Teacher Is an Information Provider

A traditional responsibility of the teacher is to pass on to students the information; knowledge and understanding in a topic appropriate for the stage of their studies. This leads to the traditional role of the teacher as one of provider of information in the lecture context. Lecturing has always been a central role of higher education teachers. The lecture remains as one of the most widely used instructional methods. It can be a cost-effective method of providing new information not found in standard texts, of relating the information on to the local curriculum and context of actual practice and of providing the lecturer's personal overview or structure of the field of knowledge for the student.

The Role Model

The importance of the teacher as a role model is well documented. The teacher should model or exemplify what should be learned. Students learn not just from what their teachers say but from what they see in the practice and the knowledge, skills and attitudes they exhibit. Teachers serve as role model not only when they teach students and also fulfill their role as teachers in the classroom, whether it is in the lecture hall or the small discussion or tutorial group. The good teacher can describe in a lecture to a class of students, their approach to the problem being discussed in a way that captures the importance of the subject and the choices available. The teacher has a unique opportunity to share some of the magic of the subject with the students.

The Facilitator

The move to a more student-centered view of learning has required a fundamental shift in the role of the teacher. No longer is the teacher seen predominantly as a dispenser of information or walking tape recorder, but rather than as a facilitator or manager of the students' learning. The introduction of problem-based learning with a consequent fundamental change in the role of relationship has highlighted this change in the role of the teacher from one of information provider to one of facilitator.

The Mentor

The role of mentor is a further role for the teacher. The mentor is usually not the member of staff who is responsible for the teaching or assessment of the student and is therefore off-line in terms of a relationship with the student. Mentorship is less about reviewing the students' performance in a subject or an examination and more about a wider view of issues relating to the student.

The Assessor

The assessment of the students' competence is one of the most important tasks facing the teacher. Most teachers have something to contribute to the assessment process. Examining does represent a distinct and potentially separate role for the teacher. Thus it is possible for someone to be an expert teacher but not an expert examiner. All institutions now need on some of their teachers with a special knowledge and understanding of assessment issues. The teacher has a responsibility not only to plan and implement educational programs and to assess the students learning, but also to assess the course and curriculum delivered. Monitoring and evaluating the effectiveness of the teaching of courses and curricula is now recognized as an integral part of the educational process. Evaluation can also be interpreted as an integral part of the professional role of teachers, recognizing teachers' own responsibility for monitoring their own performance.

The Planner

Curriculum planning is an important role for the teacher. Most colleges and universities have education committees charged with curriculum within their institution. Teachers employed by the colleges and universities may be expected to make a contribution to curriculum planning. Curriculum planning presents a significant challenge for the teacher and both time and expertise is required if the job is to be undertaken properly. The best curriculum in the world will be ineffective if the courses which it comprises have little or no relationship to the curriculum that is in place. Once the principles that underpin the curriculum of the institution have been agreed on, detailed planning is then required at the level of the individual course or phase of the curriculum.

The Resource Developer

An increased need for learning resource materials is implicit in many of the developments in education. The new technologies have greatly expanded the formats of learning materials to which the student may have access and make it much easier for the student to take more responsibility for their own education. The role of the teacher as resource creator offers exciting possibilities. At least some teachers possess the array of skills necessary to select, adapt or produce materials for use within the institution. The production of study guides a further role for the teacher. Study guides suitably prepared in electronic or print form can be seen as the students' personal tutor available 24 hours a day and designed to assist the students with their learning. Study guides tell the student what they should learn—the expected learning outcomes for the course, how they might acquire the necessary competencies—the learning opportunities available, and whether they have learned it—the students assessing their own competence. The teacher's personality affects students' behavior, their relations with each other and their attitude towards learning. Students gradually adopt their teacher's ideas, whether they are desirable or not. If the teacher is friendly and courteous, he or she stimulates thoughtfulness, helpfulness and consideration in the students. A good learning situation depends largely upon satisfactory interpersonal relationships, and hence the teacher's personality is vital. Effective teaching involves thorough planning the organization of learning materials, interesting and challenging presentation, teaching methods that are suitable for the students in the class and good techniques of classroom management. Problems of motivating students, generating interests, seeing students participating in activities never arise in classrooms where there is wholesome students-teacher relationship.

Conclusion

One of the most important characteristics of a good teacher is the ability to identify students' problems and needs. When students are comfortable or at ease with the teacher, they can give their full attention to learning. The good teacher does not place emphasis wholly upon academic achievement but recognizes and appreciates many other types of abilities and leadership qualities in students.

When teachers are sensitive to the needs of students, they are quick to notice the ones who seem unable to excel in anything, who are afraid to talk in front of a group, who are too easily discouraged or who are consistently inattentive in class. So teachers need to know how students should grow and develop and be familiar with the typical behaviors of each age level. Teacher who knows something about the factors that have influenced the lives of students are better prepared to accept them without reaching adversely to their undesirable behavior. At least the teacher is expected to be more patient, sympathetic and understanding. It should be the teachers' primary duty to understand students, to be just, courteous, to promote a spirit of enquiry, fellowship and joy in them and not to do or say anything that would undermine their personality, not to exploit them for personal interests. We need to celebrate the important roles both male and female lecturers play in colleges and work to redress the gender balance to ensure the healthy development of students today. Lecturers can often be stable and reliable figures in the lives of the students that they teach. They inspire students to feel more confident, to work harder and to behave better. Thus, it has been rightly said that "students are the future of any country," and teachers play an important role in shaping their bright future

Bibliography

Abraham. Nain, College Autonomy-Policy Practice and prospects, Centre for Civil Society, New Delhi, 2004.

NCTE, National Curriculum Framework for Teacher Education, New Delhi,2009

Pandey K P, Modern concepts of Teaching Behaviour, Anamika Publishers, New Delhi, 1997.

Raza Moonis, Education , Development and Society, Vikas Publishing House pvt Ltd, New Delhi, 1990.

Sethi Priyanka and Sacharan S. K , Development Higher Education through Five Year Plans, University News. Vol. 48 (51).

Singh M K , Moral Dilemmas in the Era of Globalization University News, Vol, 48(39).

You've Got to Have Faith to Be a Great Teacher

By Ellie Herman
EdSource, January 30, 2014

For the last four months, as part of a yearlong search to understand what great teaching looks like by visiting 11th grade English classrooms across Los Angeles, I've had a chance to observe great teachers in schools across the socioeconomic spectrum, from a very low-income community in Watts to an elite private school in Sherman Oaks. Despite radical differences in approach, personality and philosophy, I've been struck by the realization that the teachers I'm following share five common practices. And in the end, these practices are rooted in the same state of being.

What they all have in common is faith—not religious faith but an unwavering belief in something or someone, even in the absence of material evidence. All great teachers have faith in their students, in the process of learning and in themselves. It is what underlies the five practices I've observed in great teachers:

1. Great teachers listen to their students.

Listening is more than just sitting around hearing about their students' problems, though many times these teachers do that. Instead of coming in with a prepackaged educational agenda, great teachers first listen closely to the educational and socio-emotional needs of their students. This listening can take the form of assessment tests, but also involves a deep awareness of and respect for the lives and home cultures of their students, whether they are at-risk students in a very low-income community or privileged students at a private school. "Ms. Castillo got to know me," says Genesis, a 16-year-old girl in Cynthia Castillo's 11th grade English class at Augustus Hawkins RISE Academy in South Los Angeles, a school centered on community involvement. At her previous school, Genesis says, the teachers were nice but never talked to the kids outside class. Here, Cynthia spent time talking to her outside class and encouraged her to take on leadership roles. Now she's president of the class—and she's turned her grades around. "Ms. Castillo doesn't just talk to me like a student," says Genesis. "She talks to me like a person."

2. Great teachers have an authentic vision for their students.

Some of the teachers I'm following are interested in standards-based education and some are not. But no matter what they think of standards, all have a personal, authentic vision of what they want for their students. Because they listen to their students, the vision they have is a response to what their students need, not to some need of their own. This vision does not have to be abstract; for some teachers, especially in skill-based subjects, their vision is mastery of a specific body of content, which they believe will be invaluable to their students. For others, though, the vision has to do with personal qualities: inculcating a lifelong curiosity or turning their students into lifelong readers. For an example of vision in action, read the extremely moving post in the Good Men Project by a student in Dennis Danziger's class at Venice High, who was astonished to find that he loved to read when Dennis "punished" him by sending him to the library for an hour every day. Ernesto Ponce would never have set out on this unconventional educational path if not for Dennis's vision of what he wanted for his students.

3. Great teachers have an unequivocal belief in all students' potential.

By "potential" I do not mean only that they believe that all of their students will go to college. In some communities, like the elite private school Harvard-Westlake, because of the extensive resources of the parent body, college is inevitable for most students before they're even born, so a "belief" in this "potential" would not be meaningful. In other settings, like the Special Ed classroom of the amazing Carlos Gordillo at the Roybal Learning Center in a low-income neighborhood near downtown L.A., college is highly unlikely for most of his students. What I mean instead by "potential" is that in all of the teachers I'm following, I see a belief, sometimes one that flies in the face of years of evidence to the contrary, that the student in front of them is capable of achievement beyond what anyone might think possible. The teachers I'm following understand that life can take astonishing and unpredictable turns. Because of that belief, they do not ever give up even on students who never appear to make progress.

4. Great teachers are calm, persistent pushers.

Remember the scene in "Mean Girls" when math teacher Tina Fey admits she's "a pusher"? The teachers I'm observing do not ever stop pushing their students no matter how low or high their level and without regard to their students' complaints or apparent lack of interest. And they remain amazingly calm. Even when aggravated, they seem able to take a breath and brush the moment off. They don't seem to take anything personally because they have faith in their vision and in their students' potential. Kristin Damo, who teaches English at Locke High School in Watts, often faces classes with several students who talk continually in class and often wander from their seats to chat with others—despite very clear class rules and Kristin's consistent enforcement of them. Despite the continual challenge of working with students who cannot or will not stay on task, Kristin never loses her temper, gently and repeatedly reminding off-track students what they need to be doing, leading them back to their seats, and complimenting them personally when they do succeed at focusing or completing work.

5. Great teachers practice non-attachment to short-term results.

"Non-attachment" is not a lack of interest. The teachers I'm observing are definitely *interested* in short-term results, reading student work closely and tracking their students' progress. But—and this is where they diverge radically from the current perceived wisdom about teaching—they do not invest emotionally in those results or take them as evidence of success or failure, either for their students or for themselves. The teachers I'm observing seem to take a much longer view of education. They see their classes, and what their students learn from their classes, as something they hope their students will carry with them for the rest of their lives. They understand that what their students carry with them may be quite unexpected or go beyond the narrow technical definition of the subject matter. They are aware that they may never know the impact their class has had on someone. "You wrestle with yourself," says Carlos Gordillo of the challenges of teaching students in Special Ed. "But I've seen kids turn it around. You think it's the end, but it's not." For Kristin Damo, it's about the hope that the practices they learn in class will translate to a lifetime of intellectual curiosity. "At the end of the day, they may not remember what I taught them," she says, philosophical after a particularly difficult class. "But they'll remember that I was a person who cared about them on a fundamental level."

Which leads me to faith. Because at heart, all of these practices are rooted in a *faith in the work itself*, in the daily practice of showing up and engaging in the struggle of learning with their students. People burn out when they lose this faith; that's what happened to me. Demoralized by a lack of the visible progress I wanted to see and sufficient evidence that I was making a difference, I became unable to keep going.

As we talk about the best way to attract and retain good teachers, what would happen if we talked about developing this faith—in our students, in the process of learning, and in ourselves?

Is Good Teaching Crippling Our Students?

By Lisa Torina
California English, November 2012

A few years ago when I was teaching a reading intervention class, I walked into the classroom on the first day of school and wrote on the overhead, "This year, you will learn to read as if your life depends on it." Then, without saying a word, I wrote specific directions for their first activity. I sat down at my desk and waited for the students to follow the directions. As I expected, the students read the overhead and then looked at me for clarification. I stared back at them. They looked back at the overhead, and then back at me. Finally, a student asked, "What are we supposed to do?"

Until that day, I had spent every waking moment of my teaching career trying to find new ways to engage students, to present material, to explain new concepts. I became an expert presenter of visual and sensory aids, a master of recitation, and the owner of an impressive film and music library. In time, I prided myself on so artfully developing my craft, that a student could scarce escape a lesson without accessing the curriculum one way or another. It was my mission to leave no child behind. But then one day, as I stared back at those expectant faces waiting for me to explain the simple directions on the overhead, I realized that something unavailing had happened. The students had become so accustomed to artful teaching that they could not read my simple directions and follow them without my visual cue, verbal reiteration, and gesticulation. I began to wonder if, in all my efforts to engage my students, I may be making students dangerously dependent on me. For now, it is no bad thing; without that dependency, I would be out of a job. However, one day, a student may be required to read something upon which her life or welfare depends, and I will not be there with a graphic organizer.

Experienced teachers can become so good at anticipating student pitfalls that they clarify items of potential confusion before students experience any kind of failure. We anticipate things students will fail to read, the directions students will fail to follow, the text students will fail to understand, and we point these out to students beforehand. But are students becoming dependent on teachers to do this for them at the cost of important literacy skills and autonomous thought? On a written assignment that instructs high school students to write their answers in complete sentences, often students will write simple one- or two-word answers and not even attempt complete sentences. A reasonable teacher might respond by accepting the student's answers, or giving partial credit, and then follow with a verbal reminder to all students to be sure to use complete sentences. An experienced teacher might even anticipate that students will fail to read and follow the directions and thus remind students beforehand to answer in complete sentences. In either case, does the student learn to read more carefully? No, the student has learned to rely on the teacher for important cues and reminders. I fear students have come to rely so heavily on teachers' written, visual and verbal cues that today's students are becoming incapable of engaging in a task if given one without the other. It is much like my own dependency on post-its to help me remember things that I have nearly forgotten how to remember without them.

I do not suggest that all innovative teaching practices are causing a problem. On the contrary, much researched pedagogy, including hands-on science exploration, real-life math application, service learning, simulated historical reenactments, and frequent checking for understanding deepens student learning and allows students to apply invaluable skills and knowledge to real-life situations. Rather, the problem of students' crippling dependence on well-meaning teachers is students' inability to access or engage in simple or complex text as a result of how text is currently presented in many classrooms. I am talking about the dangers of spoon-feeding text to students. Such spoon-feeding as annotated summaries, PowerPoint synopses, movies, audio recordings, graphic organizers, worksheets, and interactive Web sites fail to repeatedly require students actually to read written text. In many classes, this is not necessarily problematic. In fact, interactive learning and creative teaching strategies are vital to deepening students' understanding of the content in all subject areas. Indeed, even in a language arts classroom, this type of pedagogy is crucial to teaching important concepts and engaging students in literature and writing. However, it also creates a paradox unique to the language arts classroom in that it may cause students to become reluctant, if not incapable of engaging in sustained reading, writing or listening.

I encountered this problem recently when I confronted my class about their reticence during a discussion of Edgar Allan Poe's "Cask of Amontillado." Aside from assisting the students through the most difficult opening paragraph, I had uncharacteristically assigned the reading to be done almost entirely independently. The next day, it was clear that most had not read it. "It's boring!" they wailed.

"Really?" I said, "Did you know last night's reading is about how the narrator allegedly leads his drunken victim deep into an underground catacomb piled with bones, chains him to a granite wall, and buries him alive to get his revenge?"

"What? It is?" they cried.

"You mean you didn't know?" I asked

"No!"

"Then how did you know it's boring?"

I encounter this all the time. Students will read as much as I guide them through in class. I can frontload a text, engage students in reading, assist their comprehension, and check for understanding with a variety of assessments. But if I leave students to engage in reading on their own, be it in class or at home, they will not do it. There are many theories about reluctant readers, but I am reminded of a time a preschool teacher told me her group of four-year-olds were complaining about not wanting to finish their preschool lessons. Each day, she allotted a designated time for these activities that engaged the children in preschool writing such as letter tracing. In response to the students' reluctance, she intended to conduct fewer of these sit-down writing lessons and, instead, liven up the lessons with more fun, interactive learning activities. Have teachers become so good at engaging students that students no longer know how to engage themselves?

I realize that good teaching ensures that all students can access the literature. I also realize that good teaching engages all students in learning. I don't think teachers should stop supplementing literature with lessons that help students do these things. However, I think depriving students of daily independent reading practice is harmful to important literacy development. I think students should learn to read as if their lives depend on it. Students should be held accountable for carefully reading and deciphering written text independently of teacher cues. Students should have opportunities to organize information from a text without the aid of a teacher-produced worksheet. Only when students practice functional literacy independent of teachers, have good teachers attained their goal.

Measuring Good Teachers

By Kate Rix
Scholastic Administrator, Spring 2013

*It's the million-dollar question. How do you fairly evaluate your most valuable asset—
teachers?*

When the eight-day Chicago teachers' strike ended last fall, organized labor celebrated a big win, but not over salary raises. The new contract bumped teacher pay
by about 18 percent—far short of the 30 percent increase the union was seeking.

Instead, teachers claimed a victory over Mayor Rahm Emanuel on an issue not
directly tied to money. A major focus of the fight, it turned out, was evaluation—
specifically, how much of a teacher's evaluation should be based on student test
scores.

Like most districts across the country, Chicago was required under state law
to put a teacher evaluation system into place to qualify for Race to the Top funds.
Emanuel, and district leaders, wanted to see test scores count for as much as 45
percent of teacher evaluations. In the end, the new contract calls for test scores to
account for 30 percent of teacher assessments.

"Should we use tests to judge teachers? Yes, it's patently a good thing to do," says
W. James Popham, professor emeritus at UCLA's Graduate School of Education.
"But only the right tests."

How to measure good teaching has been a third-rail question since 2009, when
Race to the Top legislation offered federal funds to states that required "substantial" evaluation systems. Two years later, the incentives got bigger. Districts that
formally evaluated teachers stood to earn waivers from some No Child Left Behind penalties.

Since 2011, as many as 40 states have installed systems that try to measure good
teaching. Test scores are part of the picture. But which test scores should count and
how much? And what about the other measures of a teacher's worth?

Measuring Good Teaching

Just a few weeks after Chicago's strike, members of Newark's teachers union approved a contract that pointedly addressed the evaluation question. The new contract includes a system that assesses the district's 5,000 teachers every year based on
four measures, including student achievement, and it awards merit pay for teachers
who rank as "highly effective."

Like many districts, teacher evaluations in Newark used to be based on one annual classroom observation by an administrator. The new system, now in its first year, uses four equally weighted core indicators of effective teaching: lesson design, rigor and inclusiveness, culture of achievement, and student progress toward mastery.

Newark's approach is similar to systems that have been developed in other school districts, including Denver and New Haven. In each of those cities the evaluation process starts at the beginning of the school year, when teachers set goals for themselves. The goals can relate to classroom management or student achievement growth, or to other areas, including effectiveness with specific student populations or with certain content areas.

In Newark, every school formed an evaluation committee that includes two administrators and a peer teacher. Teachers meet with this committee during goal setting, at the midpoint, and again at the end of the year.

Most districts recommend at least two classroom observations for every teacher. In Newark, observers will watch to see how teachers rank in the identified areas of effective teaching, looking for evidence that teachers are giving students the tools they need to meet the standards.

"We shifted our focus more toward Common Core indicators," says assistant superintendent Mitch Center. "For example, there is an indicator called Precision in Evidence. How well are our teachers providing instruction about precision and providing evidence?"

The framework, Center says, is not a script but a rubric to help all teachers identify the elements necessary for student learning, and to help administrators go deeper during evaluations.

Observers are encouraged to pay attention to how teachers plan and execute a lesson over time, how well they maintain student focus, and how they build the overall arc of a lesson sequence.

"We are saying, 'Don't look at anything in isolation,'" says Center. "Everything is part of a broader story. We're trying to help administrators be in classrooms more and for teachers to think about curriculum maps."

As for the question of where student test scores fit into the equation, in Newark, the answer is nowhere and everywhere.

The idea of "mastery" is sprinkled throughout each of the district's core effective-teaching indicators, but none is based solely on test scores. In addition, the district's rubric doesn't designate any specific assessments for tracking student achievement.

"We are looking for a demonstration of learning, and similarly over time, at how teachers are monitoring growth," Center says. "But what does this mean? This is the challenge that every district and school and state department of education is grappling with. We have no clean, simple answer, but we're wading in and trying to gauge."

And the scrutiny is paying off for some teachers. "Highly effective" teachers are collecting merit pay, some of it coming from an unlikely source: Facebook founder Mark Zuckerberg gave the district $100 million to reward its effective teachers.

Evaluation Tied to Development

Some districts are quite specific about what percentage of a teacher's evaluation should come from student assessments, even as the debate over which test scores to use continues.

Unlike New Jersey, Colorado passed a state law requiring that a full 50 percent of district teacher evaluation systems be based upon student test outcomes. (The other half is based upon three factors: professionalism, student surveys, and observation.)

Three years ago, Denver launched a new district initiative, Leading Effective Academic Practice, to help develop the new evaluation system. One of LEAP's core mandates is to figure out which, if any, existing assessments can be used to measure teacher quality. A team of teachers and administrators meet every month to discuss the issue.

"We are trying to make sure that we have a good grasp on this so that it is not a mystical calculation that nobody really understands," says Theress Pidick, director of teacher effectiveness for Denver Public Schools.

The emphasis on test scores presents another major challenge for the district: how to create fair evaluations for the 70 percent of district teachers required to teach untested content areas or grades.

"We don't want to crank out assessments for the sole purpose of evaluating teachers," Pidick says. "We're still trying to figure out the distinct component that can fall within that 50 percent—for example, teacher- and team-created assessments or school-wide measures that give an indication of how schools are doing."

The second half of Denver's evaluation system uses three factors identified by the Measurements of Effective Teaching (MET) Project, a study funded by the Bill & Melinda Gates Foundation that looked at seven districts (Denver among them).

Observation: Schools select peer teachers to observe their colleagues, matched by grade level and content area. All non-tenured teachers are observed twice a year by their peers and once by a school leader.

Professionalism: Teachers are evaluated for their practices outside the classroom, including levels of collaboration with colleagues.

Student surveys: Teachers of students in grades 3–12 are given a score based on student perception surveys given every spring. Questions are yes/no and extend to areas over which the teacher has little or no control, such as general school climate and safety. Part of the value of the surveys, says Pidick, is that data can be disaggregated by gender and ethnicity.

"A teacher may get a high score overall, but perhaps Latino girls might respond differently than white girls," Pidick says. "The conversation then would be about how the teacher can be more culturally responsive."

Denver's program emphasizes professional development for their classroom instructors. Each indicator used to evaluate teacher performance is aligned with specific professional development materials, including exemplar videos and readings.

"This is about growth and providing information so teachers can get better at their craft," says Pidick. "Our primary intention is to give data and support to assist practitioners in their growth so we have an effective teacher in each of our classrooms and our students benefit. We need to keep students first and foremost in mind."

Every Teacher, Every Year

Many districts implementing more codified, systematic evaluation plans are doing so after years of very little evaluation. Before installing its new program, New Haven evaluated tenured teachers once every five years, using only classroom observation.

Like many districts, New Haven had been using Charlotte Danielson's Framework for Teaching Evaluation Instrument, but in practice, evaluations were based on a snapshot of classroom performance.

"I could have gone into a classroom and looked once. It could have been a good day or a bad day. That's not a true picture of what happens in a classroom," says Michele Sherban-Kline, director of teacher evaluation and development for New Haven Public Schools. "It wasn't that useful, and there was no rating associated with it. To see how [teachers] were doing, you'd have to read between the lines."

Under its new system, launched in 2010, New Haven requires teachers to set professional goals at the beginning of the school year. For teachers of grades 4–8, one of these goals must be directly tied to standardized test outcomes. The district does not use value-added data, but looks mainly at previous growth for each grade level. So the goal could relate to a grade level's vertical score in reading or math, looking at the data from year to year, with the aim of either maintaining or increasing growth by a certain number of points. Or the goal could look at bands of achievement, with the target to move a grade up from basic to proficient.

The system requires evaluators to observe teachers in the classroom at least once before the midyear meeting.

"Administrators wanted to get into the classrooms again," says Sherban-Kline. "Because it wasn't required, observation took a backseat. Now, principals are dedicating the time, delegating other responsibilities, so they can observe the teachers in their building."

In New Haven and Newark, there are new evaluation systems for administrators, too. Sherban-Kline says that principals are evaluated in part on how well they coach their teachers.

"We are developing training for administrators that focuses on their responsibility for teacher growth and development," Sherban-Kline says. "Everybody is held accountable for student learning growth."

The Fuzzy Scarlet Letter

By Aaron M. Pallas
Educational Leadership, November 2012

The public release of teacher evaluation scores is unfair and misleading—and it provides little useful information for parents.

Critics of the public release of teacher evaluation scores sometimes liken these ratings to the scarlet letter worn by Hester Prynne in Nathaniel Hawthorne's classic novel. The comparison is apt. But public school teachers who are subjected to public shaming because of their students' test scores can rarely expect the opportunities for redemption offered to Prynne, whose humility and good works over time changed the meaning of her scarlet A from "Adulteress" to "Able."

U.S. political and economic leaders tell us that serious problems require bold action. In the realm of public education, this has meant a rapid expansion of systems intended to hold schools and teachers accountable for student performance. Such accountability has been applied to schools for 10 years under No Child Left Behind. But there is still considerable debate over whether individual teachers should face public accountability for the results of their evaluations. After all, personnel evaluations in most sectors of the economy are viewed as a private matter between employer and employee. Should it be any different for teachers?

Teachers as a Commodity

The debate between transparency and privacy is framed by the multiple purposes that teacher evaluations are intended to serve—purposes that are often in tension with one another. Some policymakers and practitioners emphasize the use of teacher evaluations for *selection*—to weed out ineffective teachers and perhaps identify the best ones for rewards, such as merit pay. Others view teacher evaluation as a tool for *direction*, pointing teachers toward aspects of their classroom practice that they can improve.

But now we are witnessing the emergence of another, more insidious view of teacher evaluation—one that frames teacher quality as a commodity that can be exchanged in the marketplace. In this view, evaluations signal to parents that some teachers are better than others. Who wouldn't prefer their child to have a teacher judged "highly effective" over one judged "ineffective"?

Such ratings can kick off a market-based competition in which parents try to bargain to acquire the highest-quality teacher for their own children. Those who approve of such a use of teacher evaluations argue that parents have the right to information that will enable them to exercise choice in the marketplace of schools and teachers. This logic, casting parents as consumers in a free market, has been central to debates about the public release of teacher value-added scores as well as formal teacher evaluations.

So Far, Parents Aren't Biting

We don't have a great deal of evidence about the mischief that linking teachers' names to their evaluations might cause. To date, the most publicized disclosures of teacher rankings have been unofficial and partial rankings, not official and comprehensive ones. In 2010, the *Los Angeles Times* matched Los Angeles students' test scores to their teachers and published value-added scores produced by a respected economist using a complex statistical model. The newspaper conveyed some information about the margin of error in the scores and provided some technical material about the methods used, but it largely ignored its own caveats in describing particular teachers as more or less effective. The outcry from teachers and others was immediate (Gardner, 2010).

A year later, the *Los Angeles Times* updated its ratings, using the most recent year of test data available. Stung by the initial reaction and critiques, the *Times* revamped its online reports, conveying the uncertainty in the measures more successfully. The second time around, public reaction was muted. In both cases, few parents pressured principals to move their children to the higher-ranking teachers or clamored to escape from the lower-ranking ones.

In New York City, the Department of Education goaded the major media organizations into requesting its Teacher Data Reports—the school district's internal value-added scores produced for reading and math teachers in grades 4–8 (Hancock, 2011). The United Federation of Teachers, New York City's teachers union, sued to block their release; when the litigation subsided, with the courts ruling that the individually identifiable ratings could be released to the media, the department released ratings from 2007–08, 2008–09, and 2009–10. The local media publicized these ratings widely in the winter of 2012, with the tabloids publishing front-page stories, replete with ambush-style photos, about the teachers identified as the "worst" teachers in New York City (Chapman, Lesser, & Fanelli, 2012; Macintosh, 2012; Roberts, 2012).

There's little question that the published ratings subjected a great many New York City teachers to shame and ridicule. One of my own students, a teacher in Brooklyn, reported overhearing a student say to one of her colleagues, "I don't have to listen to you! You got a *D*!" And at least one outstanding middle school math teacher decided to leave teaching at least partly due to a Teacher Data Report that ranked her as the worst 8th grade math teacher in New York City (Pallas, 2012).

The political leaders who engineered the public release of the Teacher Data Reports may have misjudged the political fallout. The annual ratings were shown to be highly imprecise, with an average confidence interval of more than 50 percentiles (Corcoran, 2010). And many parents, as well as others in the school community, saw that the ratings didn't align with their own impressions of their children's teachers. As in Los Angeles, there is little evidence so far that New York's publication of unofficial teacher rankings has resulted in new pressures from parents to place their children in the classrooms of particular teachers.

How to Choose?

To illustrate the difficulty parents would have in identifying the "best" teachers on the basis of public ratings, I examined the value-added scores of 2,656 New York City 4th grade teachers who taught reading in the 2009–10 school year. These teachers were spread across 703 elementary schools, with an average of about four teachers per school; 33 schools had just one 4th grade teacher who taught reading, and three schools had 10 or more.

As researchers and scholars alike have noted, these value-added scores are not precise. I found that for more than half of the teachers, the range of plausible scores was so wide that it's unclear whether they were in the top 20 percent of teachers or the bottom 20 percent.

To take this one step further, I compared the scores of the 4th grade reading teachers who were teaching in the same school. This comparison is presumably what many proponents of the public release of teacher evaluations have in mind: empowering parents to choose the best teacher in the school for their child.

First, let's admit that there are several problematic assumptions weighing down the free-market concept here. For example, a value-added measure might purport to describe Ms. Walters's contribution to the achievement of her average student, but if your child isn't average, the value-added measure may not indicate how your child would fare in her classroom.

Second, a value-added score for Ms. Walters will almost certainly pertain to her performance in a prior year, not to the current year or a future year in which your child might be in her classroom. Given what we know about how unstable value-added measures are from one year to the next, perhaps the fine print should mimic that in automobile ads: "Your mileage may vary."

And finally, there's the peculiar notion that parents are actually allowed to choose their child's teacher within a school. In most schools, the mechanisms for assigning students to teachers' classrooms don't provide much room for parental choice because allowing parents to pick the most popular teacher in the school for their child would be neither equitable nor efficient.

With these caveats in mind, how might a parent go about using value-added rankings to pick a teacher for his or her child? Of course, in the 44 elementary schools in New York City with only a single 4th grade reading teacher, there would be no choice involved. In 2009–10, there were 146 elementary schools with two 4th grade reading teachers, and one of the teachers had a higher value-added score than the other in just 26 of them (18 percent). The percentage was similar for the 522 schools with three or more 4th grade reading teachers.

Overall, if we tabulate the nearly 4,800 comparisons among pairs of 4th grade reading teachers teaching in the same New York City elementary school, one teacher in a pair was demonstrably more successful in promoting performance on the state English language arts test *in only 12 percent of the comparisons*. And we would expect teachers to differ 5 percent of the time by chance alone.

Of course, many of these 4th grade teachers who were teaching reading were also teaching mathematics, and their value-added scores on the state mathematics test could be subjected to a similar analysis. When teachers teach multiple subjects in self-contained classrooms, parents don't have the luxury of mixing and matching teachers to optimize their children's achievement. A teacher who is systematically better than another on all of the dimensions that a parent might judge important would be a rarity.

Rigid Boxes

Public education is shifting from a system of perfunctory evaluations, with few consequences for teachers and schools, to evaluations that are used to support high-stakes decisions about teachers' employment prospects.

The problem with making such evaluations public is that virtually all methods of evaluating teachers have both random and nonrandom errors that may mask a teacher's true performance. Accurate classroom observations, for example, require extensive training of observers (more than most school districts now provide); and even assuming expert evaluators, how well a class session goes can vary substantially from day to day.

Student test scores are even more problematic: Even if we really believed that a state's 4th grade math tests covered all of the mathematics that students should learn in that grade (and does anyone really believe this?), any effort to use students' test scores to compare one teacher with another will be imprecise because the comparisons are based on small samples of students and curricular content.

The state of New York has now passed a law requiring its school districts to publicly report teachers' composite effectiveness scores ranging from 0 to 100 as well as their final rating of *highly effective, effective, developing,* or *ineffective* (New York State Education Department, 2012). Variations of this approach have been adopted in many other states and school districts. But a score of 75 out of 100 points on an annual evaluation, or a summary grade of *developing,* may not convey that that 75 could just as easily have been a 64 or an 89, or that the teacher classified as *developing* might actually be *effective.* We can always construct rules and algorithms that will assign someone an unequivocal rating, but without the appropriate context, this rating will appear to be much more precise than it actually is.

In spite of the inherent uncertainty in teacher evaluations, policymakers want to treat the evaluation measures as though they are infallible and use them to place teachers in rigid boxes, labeling them as good teachers or poor teachers. Policymakers and the media treat these labels as definitive, but the raw material being stuffed into the boxes will rarely fit in one box without spilling over into the adjacent ones.

If states and school districts insist on publicizing individual teachers' evaluation scores—slapping a metaphorical scarlet A on some teachers and a stamp of approval on others—the only fair thing to do is to admit that the scarlet letter is fuzzy, a bit out of focus. Anything else is bad fiction.

Bibliography

Chapman, B., Lesser, B., & Fanelli, J. (2012, February 24). More than a dozen teachers earned lowest scores on controversial rankings. *New York Daily News*. Retrieved from www.nydailynews.com/news/a-dozen-teachers-earned-lowest-scores-controversial-rankings-article-1.1028113

Corcoran, S. P. (2010). *Can teachers be evaluated by their students' test scores? Should they be? The use of value-added measures of teacher effectiveness in policy and practice.* Providence, RI: Annenberg Institute for School Reform at Brown University.

Gardner, W. (2010, October 1). Suicide of teacher and published rankings. [blog post]. Retrieved from *Walt Gardner's Reality Check* at http://blogs.edweek.org/edweek/walt_gardners_reality_check/2010/10/was_suicide_of_teacher_caused_by_published_rankings.html

Hancock, L. (2011, March/April). Tested: Covering schools in the age of micro-measurement. *Columbia Journalism Review*. Retrieved from www.cjr.org/cover_story/tested.php

Macintosh, J. (2012, February 25). Teachers who got zero ratings. *New York Post*. Retrieved from www.nypost.com/p/news/local/they_re_doing_zero_zilch_zippo_for_txwNreDd3vwBXoVXUuOLIP

New York State Education Department. (2012). *Guidance on New York State's Annual Professional Performance Review for teachers and principals to implement Education Law 3012-c and the commissioner's regulations.* Albany, NY: Author.

Pallas, A. (2012, May 15). The worst eighth-grade math teacher in New York City. [blog post]. Retrieved from *A sociological eye on education* at http://eyeoned.org/content/the-worst-eighth-grade-math-teacher-in-new-york-city_326

Roberts, G. (2012, February 26). Queens parents demand answers following teacher's low grades. *New York Post*. Retrieved from www.nypost.com/p/news/local/cursed_with_the_worst_in_queens_f5wLhEdDRN1Wl9h1GQgxAM

A Brief Overview of Teacher Evaluation Controversies

By Simone Pathe and Jaywon Choe
PBS.org, February 4, 2013

Why is it so hard to determine what makes a good teacher? The answer is both complicated and polarizing. In recent education reform history, judging teacher evaluations has become as much an issue as how to evaluate student achievement.

The NewsHour's American Graduate team recently traveled to Bridgeport, Conn., to document how one charter school's system of constant instructor feedback is incentivizing good performance and encouraging teachers to stay in the classroom.

Nationally, charters have experienced higher rates of teacher turnover than traditional public schools.

In contrast to charter schools, public school administrators are often in conflict with teacher unions over how to evaluate their professionals. At times, as in the recent case of the Chicago Teachers Union strike, negotiations have become so disruptive that thousands of students are left out of the classroom as the grownups try to reach a deal.

Below, we've outlined several key controversies over teacher evaluations in recent history:

Feb. 17, 2009: Game on with Race to the Top

President Barack Obama signs into law the American Recovery and Reinvestment Act, which, among other things, sets aside roughly $4.35 billion for states to improve their education systems.

The competition, known as Race to the Top, distributes funding to states that meet specific requirements and set up concrete plans to improve their schools. One key area of reform, as laid out by the law, is teacher evaluations. As such, the contest sparked a whole host of reforms, many of which have lead to a number of conflicts between unions and government officials.

2009: Michelle Rhee Launches IMPACT

Without union negotiations, District of Columbia Public Schools Chancellor Michelle Rhee launches IMPACT—an evaluation system best known for its prioritization of value-added assessments, representing 40-percent of a teacher's evaluation.

Observations conducted by "master educators," and teachers' commitment to professional development, also contribute to their final score. "Highly effective" teachers are eligible for bonuses, while "ineffective" teachers face dismissal. Critics of the program, particularly teachers' unions, charge that it removes experienced teachers, but many states—motivated by President Obama's Race to the Top program—have studied IMPACT while overhauling their own teacher evaluation systems.

Aug. 14, 2010: *Los Angeles Times* Publishes Teacher Scores

Despite resistance from teachers' unions, the *Los Angeles Times* publishes value-added scores derived from seven years of data looking at 6,000 elementary school teachers in the Los Angeles Unified School District.

The following month, Rigoberto Ruelas, who had taught fifth grade for 14 years, commits suicide. His family blames the publication of his "average" and "less effective" ratings for raising students' standardized test scores, and United Teachers Los Angeles urges the newspaper to remove the database from their website.

Feb. 28, 2012: *New York Post* Reveals NYC's "Worst Teacher"

New York Post publishes the name and salary of New York City's "worst teacher" with a link to a database of value-added scores for teachers across the city.

Sept. 10, 2012: Chicago Teacher Union Strikes for 7 Days

After months of heated negotiations with Chicago Mayor Rahm Emanuel, the city's teachers union and its 26,000 members vote to go on strike, preventing more than 350,000 children from going to school. While wage cuts played a large role in the decision to walk out, much of the teachers' discontent stems from newly imposed and significantly tightened teacher evaluation requirements.

The city's new REACH (Recognizing Educators Advancing Chicago's Students) initiative dictates that student growth, often based on test scores, will account for 40 percent of a teacher's evaluation score, which is 10 to 15 percent higher than the state's requirement. Chicago Teachers Union President Karen Lewis estimated that the new requirements could result in the firing of 6,000 teachers, though that number has been disputed. After seven days, the union reached an agreement and called off the strike, but broader education reform issues remain.

Jan. 8, 2013: Measures of Effective Teaching

A three-year Bill and Melinda Gates Foundation study of 3,000 teachers in seven school districts, known as the Measures of Effective Teaching (MET) project, concludes that value-added scores were an accurate assessment of teachers' impact on student performance.

But, noting that these assessments were even more accurate when combined with other performance measures, the study recommends that value-added scores only represent one-third to one-half of a teacher's evaluation.

Jan. 16, 2013: Florida Teachers Union Argues New Education Reform Law Is Unconstitutional

The teachers union in Florida brings a case before a circuit court in Tallahassee contesting the constitutionality of the state's new education reform legislation.

The union argues that the new law, which takes effect in the 2013-2014 school year, unilaterally imposes new salary restrictions and violates its right to collective bargaining.

Teachers are also upset over the new merit-pay system, which would compensate teachers based on how well their students perform on tests. Under the new law, teachers are graded based on math and reading results from the Florida Comprehensive Assessment Test. But for those who teach other subjects, evaluations are based largely on the performance of other teachers.

A Florida judge strikes down the new merit-pay provision, calling it "wholly invalid."

Jan. 17, 2013: New York City Misses Deadline

New York City misses its state-imposed deadline to reach an agreement on new teacher evaluation policies, jeopardizing the prospects of receiving $450 million in state and federal funding. Despite having had more than two years to approve the new measure, the teachers union and city government were unable to reach a compromise over changes to the city's evaluation methods. As was the case in Chicago, the union expressed concerns over making student test scores account for 40 percent of teacher evaluation grades, an increase of 20 percent.

The union also wants the agreement to include a sunset clause that would require a re-vote of the evaluation process in 2015. But because the dismissal process takes two years, including such a clause could mean that the city has almost no way of removing teachers.

The original legislation, passed in 2010, called for 20 percent of an evaluation to be based on test scores, while also shifting the rating system away from a binary structure.

Jan. 19, 2013: Los Angeles Teachers Union Reaches Agreement

United Teachers Los Angeles approves the use of students' standardized test scores in their evaluations. However, the agreement with Los Angeles Unified restricts the value-added model, known as Academic Growth Over Time, which had been coupled with intensified observations and student and parent feedback in performance reviews.

Under the agreement, teacher evaluations can be based, in part, on raw state test scores, school-wide value-added scores, and high school exit exams, as well as suspension, attendance, graduation and course completion rates. The deal was heralded as a victory for the teachers union.

Teacher Evaluations: Too Much Science, Not Enough Art?

By Robert A. Frahm
The Connecticut Mirror, March 19, 2014

"[A] strong body of evidence now confirms what parents, students, teachers and administrators have long known: effective teachers are among the most important school-level factor in student learning . . ."

—*State Department of Education handbook on teacher evaluation*

As teacher Alison Taylor conducts a poetry lesson for her third-graders, veteran principal Jason Bluestein watches and listens closely, scratching notes into a spiral notebook—a process he will repeat again and again this year, more often than ever before.

Here in Room 216 at Burr School, Bluestein's hour-long observation is just one step under a controversial, time-consuming new statewide evaluation system that requires schools to rate teachers like Taylor not only through classroom observations but on whether their students meet specific academic goals.

The system, required under state law, has gotten off to a rocky start, prompting complaints from educators across Connecticut. According to some, the system, which ranks teachers in four categories from "below standard" to "exemplary," has left educators worried about the complexity of the process, uncertain about its accuracy, and buried in paperwork.

It has also thrust Connecticut into a simmering national debate on whether schools, using student test scores, can develop a truly reliable formula to measure effective teaching—a job that many consider as much an art as a science.

"The whole system is just predicated on a number here, a number there that's going to tell you that a kid is learning . . . and learning is so much more complicated than that," said Bluestein, who, like principals across the state, has found himself mired in the details of the process. After visiting Taylor's classroom, he reviewed more than four pages of notes, typing his observations into one of a series of forms in a software program Fairfield is using to meet the requirements of the new law. It is one of 22 forms that must be completed by the end of the year for each of Burr's 29 teachers, he said.

"There is good work to be had in parts of this process, but it's just way too cumbersome," said Bluestein, who estimates he is doing three or four observations a week.

A University of Connecticut study of pilot evaluation systems in 14 districts last year found similar complaints, with some principals reporting working on evaluations "on a near-daily basis."

Teachers, too, reported spending more time on evaluations.

At Burr School, Taylor, like other teachers, spent hours outlining goals for her evaluation plan. Each teacher also is required to fill out reports both before and after formal classroom observations and must take part in midyear and end-of-year evaluation reviews.

"It's a lot of input into the computer," Taylor said. "That time has to be taken from something, and, unfortunately, it takes time from our instructional planning time."

The complaints from educators became so frequent that state officials, led by Gov. Dannel P. Malloy, in January agreed to grant schools more flexibility—allowing them, for example, to scale back the number of observations required for experienced teachers who maintain satisfactory performance records.

State Education Commissioner Stefan Pryor said the state expects to continue fine-tuning a program that is still in its first full year. "We're very proud of the fact . . . we have revised our system instead of simply defending it," he said.

The latest revisions could provide some relief next year for principals such as Bluestein, but Fairfield officials say there are no plans to reduce the number of observations scheduled for the remainder of this school year.

Setting Student Goals

Aside from the paperwork, a key area of concern has been the setting of student goals, including test score targets. According to the UConn pilot study, teachers and principals reported getting little or no training on the process. As a result, some "are selecting far too challenging targets while others are choosing far too easy," UConn reported.

Taylor said teachers feel more pressure and may be more conservative in setting targets for their students because those scores are directly connected to the evaluations. "If we don't meet the goals, it's kind of a negative," she said. "In the past, we kind of aimed high."

The setting of growth targets for students "is, in most cases, inherently arbitrary," the UConn study said. "Should 100 percent of students score a 70 percent on an exam or should 70 percent of students score at 100 percent? If half the students fall below a certain performance level at the beginning of the year, what percentage should reasonably be expected to meet it by the end of the year?" the report said.

To a large degree, the movement linking student test scores to teacher evaluations is rooted in the Obama administration's education policy, first as an element in the Race to the Top competition for federal funds and later as a requirement for states seeking waivers from the rigid mandates of the federal No Child Left Behind law.

"The whole idea of using student test scores . . . is really tricky," said David Title, Fairfield's superintendent of schools. "It's conceptually appealing, but it's very difficult to do technically. . . . There are so many different variables that impact student achievement. . . . What you're not able to do, in my view, is prove cause and effect."

Nevertheless, the idea has gained traction. Four years ago, New Haven schools won national attention when the district and the teachers' union developed an evaluation system that uses test results as a factor in rating teachers. Since then, dozens of teachers have resigned or been dismissed as a result of the evaluations. Last year, 20 teachers, about 1 percent of the workforce, left the district after receiving poor evaluations.

"I won't say [the system] is perfect, but it's light-years ahead of where we were," said New Haven Federation of Teachers President David Cicarella.

Most teachers support the idea of removing colleagues who are found to be obviously ineffective, Cicarella said. "We all use the same litmus test . . . . You hear teachers say, 'Would I want my kid in that teacher's room?' If the answer is no, we've got to do something about it."

He said that rigorous, multiple observations are key to the system. He agreed that the observations are time-consuming, and that principals can be overwhelmed if they have too large a caseload, but said, "Compared to what they used to do—go in there 15, 20 minutes, half an hour, write up three or four paragraphs and that's your evaluation—that's what got us in this boat to begin with. The [former] evaluations were so superficial."

In New Haven, officials eased the burden by computerizing the reporting process and training veteran teachers as "instructional managers" to assist in conducting evaluations, he said.

As for using student data in the evaluations, Cicarella said the New Haven system, like the state model, requires teachers to set their own individual targets for student growth based on the composition of their classes and factors such as previous academic performance. "At the end of the day, we have a responsibility for students to learn," he said.

In Connecticut, the movement to hold teachers more accountable for student growth gained momentum four years ago when lawmakers passed a sweeping school reform law calling for a new evaluation process. Today, 41 states have laws linking evaluations to student performance, according to the National Council on Teacher Quality, an advocacy group promoting the use of student performance as a measure of teacher quality. In 19 of those states, including Connecticut, student growth is the predominant factor in evaluations, the council reports.

"It's a huge policy shift," said Sandi Jacobs, a council official. "We think it's absolutely appropriate that evidence of student learning should be part of teacher evaluation . . . but it can't be the only thing."

A three-year study sponsored by the Bill & Melinda Gates Foundation concluded last year that it is possible to identify teacher quality by a combination of classroom observations, student surveys and student achievement growth. Officials who designed the Connecticut model—which includes a blend of observations, student growth and surveys of parents and students—cite the Gates study as part of the research supporting the new approach.

Nevertheless, the use of student testing gains in evaluating educators has drawn skeptics. Noted education historian Diane Ravitch called the practice "junk science" in a foreword to a recent special issue on high-stakes teacher evaluation in the academic journal *Teachers College Record*.

Ravitch, a professor at New York University, wrote that judging teachers largely on student test scores is an "untried theory . . . [that] wreaks havoc on our schools and our teachers . . . [and] will squander billions of dollars that should have been spent in classrooms, or in funding research that conceptualizes more fully the many and varied aspects of good teaching."

Teacher ratings can fluctuate because of changes in the composition of classes, she said. "This year's highly rated teacher is only average or worse than average next year. A district gives a teacher a bonus this year, then fires her the next," she wrote.

In Connecticut, the state is changing its annual statewide test and is seeking federal approval to allow schools to delay until the 2015–2016 school year the use of that test in evaluations. This year, teachers and their evaluators must decide individually which other standardized tests or classroom exams they will use to measure their students' academic growth. They also must predict how much progress they expect their students to make.

"How well are teachers really equipped to make these predictions?" asked Title, the Fairfield superintendent.

At Burr School, teachers are choosing among various standardized tests as part of their evaluations, but the school is changing some of its curriculum, and the tests "are not really caught up with that yet," said Lisa Sherman, a math and science specialist who has worked with teachers on setting their evaluation goals.

"It's really hard for teachers to write a goal based on a standardized assessment [that] . . . doesn't really match the curriculum," she said.

Nevertheless, Pryor, the education commissioner, said that allowing teachers to set individual classroom goals and student growth targets is the heart of the Connecticut model—unlike systems in other states that prescribe specific growth targets.

"What could be more important than the fact that teachers and supervisors are sitting down and giving appropriate time to the development of goals regarding the growth of youngsters' achievement?" Pryor said. "That's exactly what ought to be happening."

What Does "Proficient" Mean?

Some educators question the accuracy of the system or fear that schools will be so focused on complying with the many evaluation requirements that they will lose sight of the real purpose—to improve teaching. "If you have to have the very latest software program just to calculate teacher effectiveness, that's a signal right there you're over-engineered," said Title. "A false sense of precision comes with this."

The UConn report found wide variations in ratings of teacher quality among the 14 pilot districts studied last year. The small Columbia school system classified 76 percent of its teachers as "exemplary" and the rest as "proficient" but had no teachers in the categories "developing" or "below standard." Meanwhile, schools in Capitol Region Education Council (CREC) rated 15 percent of their teachers as exemplary, 76 percent as proficient, 9 percent developing and less than 1 percent below standard.

Matrix for determining summative teacher rating

The two major factors of a teacher's evaluation – student growth/development and teacher observation ratings – are combined using this matrix. A "4" means exemplary, a "3" means proficient, a "2" means developing and a "1" means below standard.

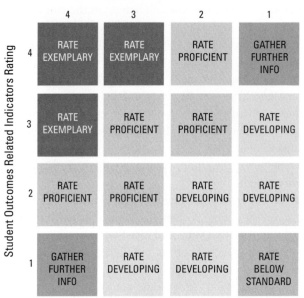

Teacher Practive Related Indicators Rating

	4	3	2	1
4	RATE EXEMPLARY	RATE EXEMPLARY	RATE PROFICIENT	GATHER FURTHER INFO
3	RATE EXEMPLARY	RATE PROFICIENT	RATE PROFICIENT	RATE DEVELOPING
2	RATE PROFICIENT	RATE PROFICIENT	RATE DEVELOPING	RATE DEVELOPING
1	GATHER FURTHER INFO	RATE DEVELOPING	RATE DEVELOPING	RATE BELOW STANDARD

Student Outcomes Related Indicators Rating

Source: The State Department of Education handbook on teacher evaluation

But does "proficient" mean the same thing in Columbia as it does in CREC schools? Or Norwalk? Or Bridgeport? Would a "developing" teacher in one district receive the same rating in another?

"There's a concern about consistency," said Columbia's superintendent, Lol Fearon, who noted that school systems use different tests and that some test data was not yet available when the pilot districts' results were reported to UConn.

With personnel decisions, including termination, on the line, the accuracy of evaluations could be crucial. One superintendent, New London's Nicholas Fischer, has told state officials that the guidelines are too vague and could lead to legal challenges.

"The distinguishing characteristics between the [rating] levels are often fuzzy," he said. "It would be very difficult for teachers to know what exactly it is you expect them to be showing you in the classroom."

Overall, the 14 pilot districts in the UConn study rated almost no teachers below standard and just 4 percent in the developing category—figures that were questioned by Robert Rader, executive director of the Connecticut Association of Boards of Education.

"It seems to me in any occupation, [to say] that only 4 percent are in need of development . . . would be very rare," Rader said. "I'm not looking to fire teachers—I think the vast majority are good—but I do think 4 percent is a very low number."

Rader, a member of a state committee that developed the evaluation guidelines, said, "I want to make sure what we're doing is really telling the true story of what's happening in our schools."

Looking for Failure?

Teachers' union officials on the same committee bristled at Rader's question.

"Evaluation systems should not look for failure," said Mark Waxenberg, executive director of the Connecticut Education Association, the state's largest teachers' union. "I don't want us to [create] a system that inhibits teachers from taking risks for fear of being tainted by an evaluation tool."

Among those who have fielded complaints from educators is state Rep. Andy Fleischmann, co-chairman of the legislature's Education Committee. Fleischmann said he understands the recent decision to ease some of the evaluation system's requirements, but he thinks teachers and administrators will become more comfortable with the process over time. He remains a supporter of rigorous evaluation.

"It makes sense to me over the long run that we'd make sure teachers are aware of their students' progress, and that some portion of their evaluation would be based on student academic growth," he said.

One of the biggest tasks for state officials, as the evaluation system unfolds, will be to convince educators that the new evaluations are, as Pryor says, "far better than many alternatives . . . [and] a big move in the right direction."

At Burr School, Bluestein did not hide his frustration with the process. He said he believes in school reform and does not want to return to the status quo, but he added, "I think the system is just not doing what it's intended to do."

The UConn report concluded that the state's evaluation model has the potential to improve schools but needs more work, including further examination of the relationship between evaluation and student achievement.

One obvious change has been the increased number of classroom observations by administrators. Lisa Sherman, the math and science specialist at Burr, said she hasn't undergone any observations since she became tenured eight years ago. Like other specialists in Fairfield, such as guidance counselors and school psychologists, she is exempt from the process this year but will undergo observations starting next fall.

Although the amount of time and paperwork associated with the system has ratcheted up the stress among colleagues, Sherman said, "I do think the process of being observed and getting feedback and having conversations . . . is good."

Younger teachers such as Taylor—who is in her third year of teaching and not yet tenured—have been accustomed to more frequent observations. After teaching her recent poetry lesson, Taylor met with Bluestein for a post-observation conference—something both she and Bluestein described as the most valuable part of the evaluation process.

In a friendly, collegial conversation in Bluestein's office, the two exchanged ideas about what worked and what strategies Taylor might try in her class of 25 children.

Taylor said she was pleased with how the class responded to the poetry lesson but would like to find a way to spur even more interaction and conversation among the children themselves.

"I've been trying for a long time to have it be more them and less me," she told Bluestein.

"It's an experimentation thing," Bluestein replied. "Every class is a little different," he said, suggesting that she might get children to work more independently by posing a problem directly to them and asking, "How do you want to solve this?"

By the end of the year, Bluestein must rate Taylor on each of 17 factors identified in a state handbook on the evaluation process—factors such as "Promoting student engagement and shared responsibility for learning" and "Selecting appropriate assessment strategies." Those ratings will be combined with ratings based on the progress of Taylor's third-graders as part of a complex formula to give Taylor a final score on a 200-point scale.

As he wrapped up the 20-minute conference with Taylor, Bluestein reassured her. "Nice job, as always," he said.

"I have to fill out my form . . ." he told her. "I would say for your paperwork, just keep it very brief."

❖

Two Factors for Evaluation

Under Connecticut's new teacher evaluation guidelines, teacher ratings are determined by a formula that weighs two major components: Teacher practice and student outcomes.

Teacher practice scores are based largely on classroom observations, with evaluators scoring teachers on a 1 to 4 scale on 17 separate elements, such as "Promoting student engagement and shared responsibility for learning" and "Planning instructional strategies to actively engage students in the content." Parent surveys may also account for a small portion of this score.

Scores on student outcomes are based on how much progress students make toward individual goals, such as test score targets, established by each teacher early in the school year. School-wide performance or student feedback also is factored in.

After averaging, combining and weighting the scores, evaluators rank teachers on each of the two components according to the following scale:

Range	Rank
50–80 points	Below Standard
81–126 points	Developing
127–174 points	Proficient
175–200 points	Exemplary

STATE DEPARTMENT OF EDUCATION EVALUATION HANDBOOK

Colorado Begins Controversial Teacher-Grading System

By Kristen Wyatt
The Denver Post, August 1, 2013

The video shows a 4th grade music teacher leading her pupils through four-beat patterns with a rest. Two dozen judges are watching, grading how well she's engaging students and leading the lesson.

None of the judges is a music teacher. They're school administrators learning how to evaluate educators in a discipline not their own. It's no easy task, and as Colorado prepares for statewide implementation of standardized educator effectiveness ratings, it's the kind of thing many schools are going to be doing in every classroom.

Colorado adopted a statewide teacher-grading system three years ago, a rating that sorts educators from "highly effective" to "ineffective." Teachers with too many consecutive low ratings could lose tenure, while new teachers and those on probationary status will need passing marks before achieving tenure, or non-probationary status.

After three years of development and pilot tests, the effectiveness ratings begin for all 178 Colorado school districts this fall. The stakes are high, and many teachers in Colorado aren't exactly sure how it will work.

"There's massive anxiety about it," said Stephanie Rossi, a social studies teacher at Wheat Ridge High School in Jefferson County, the state's largest school district. "Are we ready for it? No, because we don't know what it is."

The teacher and administrator ratings will be 50 percent based on student test scores. The rest of the rating is based on more subjective evaluations of how well teachers perform.

Denver is training administrators and teachers in peer evaluations, where teachers will be graded on everything from how they use technology in their lessons to how they respond to pupils who don't understand certain instructions or terminology. Student feedback is also a factor, with children getting to weigh in on how their teachers are doing.

The teacher evaluators were training recently in how to make sure they arrive at similar ratings, even in a subject area they've never taught. The evaluators reviewed guidelines after seeing the music video, then raised fingers to show how they would have rated the example lesson.

"What did you guys get? Fours? Fives? OK, let's look at the exact evidence," said Danielle Ongart, who is leading the training for Denver Public Schools.

The administrators reviewed the lesson. Did students learn the pattern, or just mimic the teacher? How did the teacher monitor student progress? Was the lesson adjusted based on how the pupils responded? The evaluators went through pages of detailed benchmarks to decide a final rating.

The goal of the exercise was to make sure observations result in similar scores for the teachers, regardless of who is observing them.

DPS started rating all teachers last year, but the ratings don't start counting toward tenure until this school year.

By the 2014–15 school year, the ratings can start damaging teachers rated "ineffective." Teachers with tenure face losing that status after two years of "ineffective" ratings. Struggling teachers are supposed to receive extra help to improve student outcomes.

State education officials say they're helping smaller districts adjust to the new teacher rating scheme. But resources are scarce, and schools are still climbing back to budget levels they had before the recession.

Denver has received several million dollars from the Bill and Melinda Gates Foundation and has its own rating system that complies with statewide requirements. However, many districts will be using state templates or writing their own to gauge teacher effectiveness.

Katy Anthes, who is leading implementation of the educator effectiveness evaluations for the Colorado Department of Education, said state districts will be ready. But she conceded the change won't be without headaches.

"We have the tools and templates and technical assistance to help schools make the change. But I will say, this is a big change," Anthes said.

State education officials are hoping that within a few years, teachers will embrace the ramped-up evaluation process as a chance to become better at their profession.

They have reason to hope. Denver physical education teacher David Weiss at Slavens K–8 School said the new evaluation process is a boon for electives teachers who don't have test scores to point to, or administrators who know his field.

"Since this all started, I've had conversations about my instruction that I haven't had before. The conversation was much easier to have, and it's nice to have a clear framework," Weiss said.

Rossi, the Jefferson County social studies teacher who hasn't gone through evaluations yet, said teachers are optimistic they'll have an experience like Weiss. Rossi was an outspoken critic of the evaluation law that was adopted in 2010, but she said she's optimistic it will result in better experiences for students.

"It was a poorly written law, but once it was law, teachers rose to the challenge and said, 'What are we going to do, how are we going to implement it?'" Rossi said. "So I've noticed a lot more intensive conversations about classroom teachers. Not that those conversations haven't been going on all along. But I've seen more commitment."

Gates Foundation against Releasing Results of Teacher Evaluation

By Rob Meiksins
Nonprofit Quarterly, March 5, 2014

The Bill and Melinda Gates Foundation is well known for its support of measurement and has invested heavily in promoting a system to evaluate the effectiveness of teachers in the classroom. This system is called the "Value-Added Method" of evaluation, or VAM. However, as the Gates Foundation describes it, VAM is intended as a tool to help identify which teachers are successful and effective, and which need some form of development to improve their efforts in the classroom. In other words, its use is intended to be private, between the teacher and the district.

In Florida, a judge ruled in a lawsuit by the Jacksonville *Florida Times-Union* that VAM results are public, and therefore must be disclosed. The newspaper had fought for release of the data for more than a year, arguing that parents have a right to know how teachers are doing, and the public should have a look at VAM to see whether and how it works. As quoted in the *Washington Post*, the Gates Foundation has come out against this:

> "We at the Bill & Melinda Gates Foundation oppose the public release of individual teacher information because there is no evidence to suggest it will lead to improvement in teacher performance. It will not attract new intelligent and passionate individuals to the profession, and it will not make our schools more effective."

VAM is a complex tool that measures the impact a teacher has on students against the achievements expected of those students. Based on standardized testing, a formula projects how the students in a given classroom are expected to improve over the course of a year. At the end of that year, if they have done better, it is assumed that the teacher has had a positive impact, and is evaluated accordingly. If the students have not improved to the anticipated level, the teacher is assumed to have had a problem, and a development strategy will be worked on with them to help them be more effective.

Florida wrote this kind of evaluation system into law with Section 1012.34(a)1 of its statutes, reading:

> "Performance of Students. At least 50% of a performance evaluation must be based upon data and indicators of student learning growth assessed annually and measured

by statewide assessments or, for subjects and grade levels not measured by statewide assessments, by district assessments as provided in § 1008.22(8), F.S."

Reactions to the release of VAM scores by the teachers in Florida and their union have been strong. The system itself has little support from the profession, who accuses it of reducing the act of teaching to an algorithm, and releasing the results could lead to misinterpretation by parents who do not completely understand it.

The Gates Foundation states, "If we want to truly help teachers improve, we must develop evaluation systems that give personalized feedback collated from multiple sources, and we must then give teachers the time, support and resources they need to use that feedback to improve their practice."

Now that scores intended to be private have been released, will parents demand new teachers for their child based on poor VAM scores? It sounds like it; one reader of the *Washington Post* article comments, "I also believe teacher evaluations should be available for parents to look at. We as parents should be able to within reason choose teachers that teach our children."

Another Revolution Starts in Boston

By Dan M. Chu
Phi Delta Kappan, March 2013

High school students in Boston transform conversations on teacher evaluation and succeed in having their voices heard.

Seven years. A lot can happen in seven years: The first African-American president was elected in the wake of the worst recession since the Great Depression; *Avatar* shattered box office records, ousting *Titanic*, the Arab spring brought down decades-long monarchies, and somewhere in Boston, students found a glaring issue within their own education system. Seven years. That is how much time has passed since students began the ongoing battle for student feedback in teacher evaluation. There were struggles, there were triumphs, and it has been a long battle that has yet to finish.

Beginning with Homework

Student feedback in teacher evaluation was not the initial idea envisioned by many Boston Student Advisory Council (BSAC) members. BSAC is a citywide body of student leaders representing most high schools in the Boston Public Schools. One Monday afternoon in 2006, BSAC members gathered to discuss various issues plaguing their schools—everything from school safety and racism to lunches and sanitation. Because BSAC represents the entire district, students had to be strategic and find a common goal that each member would be willing and eager to work on. A similar concern shared by everyone was the abysmal quality of homework.

There are two types of homework: good homework and bad homework. Good homework enriches students' educations. It not only reinforces what they learned for the day, but also builds on the groundwork laid by the day's lesson. Bad homework, on the other hand, does nothing more than force students to grind through more of the same thing they already spent hours on in school. Although there is a saying that practice makes perfect, there is a limit to how much practice one can do. Twenty to 30 algebra problems a night is manageable; assigning 100 of them does not help the student. Busy work only forces students to divert valuable time from more productive endeavors, such as sports and extracurricular activities.

BSAC members agreed the quality of homework was not as good as it could be, but they needed more evidence. So, BSAC surveyed 777 high school students and found that students believed that homework too often failed to enhance their education.

Constructive Feedback

One more question had to be answered: Why were teachers assigning bad homework? After flipping through contract books and student manuals, BSAC concluded that teachers were not being held accountable for quality homework, among other things. Administrators evaluated teachers infrequently, and rarely did the reviewers see the true side of the classroom since they came in for only one period per year at best. Students agreed that they could contribute to evaluations because they were in the classrooms longer than administrators and, as a result, they had more information about the student-teacher relationship. With many students contributing to teachers' evaluations, there was also a greater chance of ensuring that teachers would receive more accurate feedback than those who relied on a single evaluator's visit. With students contributing to evaluations, teachers can only benefit from multiple perspectives. Thus BSAC decided to work on two issues: a policy that advocated for better homework and student involvement in teacher evaluations.

Thus began a long, fierce battle. At the center of our teacher evaluation campaign were the concepts of building relationships and student voice in the classroom.

A decade ago, the idea of students evaluating teachers was revolutionary, even radical. In 2006, BSAC members met with the president of the Boston Teachers Union (BTU) and the superintendent of the Boston Public Schools (BPS). The BTU opposed the initial proposal but the BTU had always been supportive of student voice. This was our opportunity to work together and develop a holistic system. The superintendent suggested BSAC first work on a more modest form of student input in teacher evaluation. This tool would have no weight in a teacher's performance evaluation, but would allow students to provide feedback on classroom management and instruction. Dubbed constructive feedback, BSAC agreed on this course of action.

BSAC worked with students, teachers, administrators, and a Pennsylvania State University professor to develop a tool for students to give teachers feedback. BSAC's tool allows a student to give teachers feedback on areas from homework to classroom management. One of the most noteworthy components of the survey is a section that allowed students to assess their own learning. The student self reflection part of the survey gave students the opportunity to think about their own behaviors in the classroom. Do you pay attention in class? Do you complete your homework? Do you get to class on time? This is just a sampling of the questions students are asked to think about before filling out the sections on classroom management and instruction. It helps students take responsibility for their own learning before they commend or criticize teachers. After developing this tool and piloting it in a small group of students, BSAC felt they had something ready to use across the district.

With the support of union and district leadership, BSAC officially administered the survey in BPS high schools in 2010. We released the tool with a step-by-step implementation guide for schools. In its newsletter, union leadership encouraged teacher participation. Teachers praised the feedback, with many saying they learned new things about their teaching. Students, protected by the anonymity of the survey, also were empowered to say what worked and what did not without fear of backlash. In a teacher survey completed afterward, over 65% of teachers reported finding the tool useful. More than 40% of teachers reported they will implement changes in the classroom based on student feedback.

Refining the Process

Our first year of implementation taught us many valuable lessons and created the space for us to revise the process for future years. Our peers shared challenges with administering the survey. Fortunately, we heard many more success stories. With an overall success of constructive feedback, BSAC felt ready to tackle student feedback in official teacher evaluation. Even more great news came as preliminary findings from the Measures of Effective Teaching project on teacher evaluation said student perception data is one of the most reliable ways to measure teacher effectiveness. With these two pieces of information, BSAC turned to the district to further the work. Thanks to the guidance of Superintendent Carol Johnson, BSAC then approached the state task force created by the Massachusetts Board of Elementary and Secondary Education and charged with developing recommendations on new educator evaluation regulations. We shared our tool with the task force and received positive feedback on the tool's design as well as an affirmation of the importance of student feedback.

To further garner public support and build excitement among youth, BSAC held a rally in May 2011, in front of Boston's city hall under the slogan, "We're the Ones in the Classroom, Ask Us!" More than 250 people attended, including the student representative on the state board of education, Michael D'Ortenzio. He urged BSAC to testify before the board, and many members gladly did. In June 2011, the Massachusetts Board of Elementary and Secondary Education unanimously agreed to adopt new regulations requiring all districts in Massachusetts to include student feedback as a form of evidence in educator evaluations by the 2013–14 school year.

An important part of our fight is to keep the conversations alive. Even with the student feedback component of educator evaluations, we want to make sure teachers can still see our feedback and can still have conversations with us about instruction, classroom management, homework, learning styles, etc. It is ultimately about supporting teachers in the classroom and creating environments where students can achieve academically. Youth voice needs to be at the center of these conversations.

Bibliography

❖

Adey, Philip, and Justin Dillon. *Bad Education: Debunking Myths in Education*. Maidenhead: Open UP, 2012. Print.

Apple, Michael W. *Can Education Change Society?* New York: Routledge, 2013. Print.

Best, Joel, and Eric Best. *The Student Loan Mess: How Good Intentions Created a Trillion-Dollar Problem*. Berkeley: U of California P, 2014. Print.

Chany, Kalman. *Paying for College Without Going Broke*. Random, 2013. Print.

Donaldson, Jonan. *Massively Open: How Massive Open Online Courses Changed the World*. North Charleston: CreateSpace Independent, 2013. Print.

Fulton, Kathleen. *Time for Learning: Top 10 Reasons Why Flipping the Classroom Can Change Education*. Thousand Oaks: Corwin, 2014. Print.

Gliksman, Sam. *iPad in Education for Dummies*. Hoboken: Wiley, 2013. Print.

Kendall, John S. *Understanding Common Core State Standards*. Alexandria: ASCD, 2011. Print.

Krause, Steven D, and Charles Lowe. *Invasion of the MOOCs: The Promises and Perils of Massive Open Online Courses*. Anderson: Parlor, 2014. Print.

Lubienski, Christopher, and Sarah T. Lubienski. *The Public School Advantage: Why Public Schools Outperform Private Schools*. Chicago: U of Chicago P, 2014. Print.

Means, Barbara, Marianne Bakia, and Robert Murphy. *Learning Online: What Research Tells Us About Whether, When and How*. New York: Routledge, 2014. Print.

Myracle, Jared. *Common Core Standards for Parents for Dummies*. Hoboken: Wiley, 2014. Print.

Picciano, Anthony G, Charles Dziuban, and Charles R. Graham. *Blended Learning: Research Perspectives*. Vol. 2. New York: Routledge, 2014. Print.

Rothman, Robert. *Something in Common: The Common Core Standards and the Next Chapter in American Education*. Cambridge: Harvard Educ., 2011. Print.

Selingo, Jeffrey J. *College (un)bound: The Future of Higher Education and What It Means for Students*. Boston: Houghton, 2013. Print.

Selwyn, Neil. *Education in a Digital World: Global Perspectives on Technology and Education*. New York: Routledge, 2013. Print.

Silbert, Linda B, and Alvin J. Silbert. *Why Bad Grades Happen to Good Teachers: Creating Environments Where All Students Learn*. New York: Strong Learning Centers, 2014. Print.

Whitaker, Todd. *What Great Teachers Do Differently: Seventeen Things That Matter Most*. Larchmont: Eye on Educ., 2012. Print.

Websites

❖

Common Core State Standards Initiative

www.corestandards.org

The Common Core is an initiative started in 2012 to standardize United States curriculum and encourage critical thinking and analysis. The website is designed to foster understanding of the initiative and offers a wealth of free content for educators and parents alike. Notable resources and features include an in-depth overview of the development process behind the standards, a state-by-state interactive map of implementation, and an extensive listing of support statements from bipartisan organizations.

Council for American Private Education (CAPE)

www.capenet.org/index.html

The self-described "voice of America's private schools," CAPE is a national coalition that advocates and works for private education in the American education community. The website offers a wealth of literature and reports that stress the differences between private and public education, and also offers numerous related publications and resources.

International Society for Technology in Education (ISTE)

www.iste.org

The nonprofit ISTE is a leading global advocate for the implementation of technology in education. In addition to professional learning resources, white papers and reports, and in-depth overviews of the ISTE standards for students and educational professionals alike, the website offers downloadable toolkits for computational thinking and hosts an online store as well as a resource directory for the EdTech marketplace.

National Coalition for Technology in Education and Training (NCTET)

www.nctet.org

The nonpartisan and nonprofit NCTET works to promote the use of technology in American education and training. Select resources, such as a webinar on education through technology, can be accessed through the organization's website. The website is highlighted by a list of relevant resources such as reports and research documents and links to related national initiatives.

National Education Association (NEA)
www.nea.org

This organization and labor union represents public school teachers and other educational personnel. Self-described as a "professional employee organization," the NEA provides information on relevant issues and actions related to public education through its website and provides a wealth of tools and ideas related to teaching, including lesson plans, classroom management tools, and teaching strategies.

StudentLoanHelp.org
StudentLoanHelp.org

An objective service of the Student Loan Alliance, this website offers nonprofit counseling and educational needs to individuals seeking student debt relief. Visitors can engage trained counselors one-on-one or access the wealth of information available through the website, including overviews of repayment plans and types of financial aid.

Index

❖